SELECTED CHORUS OF PRAISE FOR
INVISIBLE GIRLS

"Until now we have not heard the voices of teen girls quite like this. In this work, the author offers us a glimpse into the worlds of teenaged girls and young women who are abuse survivors. These young women tell their stories of incest, date rape, acquaintance rape, and mentor abuse. The stories deserve to be heard. The truth hurts, but it also heals."

—Canadian Women's Health Network

"Sex trafficking is an epidemic of monumental proportions. *Invisible Girls: Speaking the Truth About Sexual Abuse* helps our culture and society look straight into the experience of sexual abuse through the souls of the girls who have so beautifully articulated their pain and their healing. We have not heard the depth of pain and recovery quite like this before. This book and Dr. Patti's work gives us hope."

—Carol Smolenski, executive director of ECPAT USA

"I love Dr. Patti's message to the world! Sexual-abuse survivors heal and become victorious! In this battle zone field of sexual abuse with pain, hardship, and discomfort, these beautiful goddesses found their freedom and became victorious by walking in their honesty, truth and vulnerability. When we reveal our wounds, we heal and we help others heal. Owning your scars isn't shameful at all; in fact wearing them is very liberating and freeing. That's exactly what *Invisible Girls* did for one of my best friends, it saved her life. *Invisible Girls: Speaking*

D0176531

the Truth About Sexual Abuse is a form of art that makes the unseen visible, it is a tale of the refusal to be broken, the determination to become whole and victorious."

—Madison Jaye, global media personality, spiritual journalist

"These voices of young abuse survivors and Dr. Patti's compassionate insights make this *the* important book for anyone who wants to begin to understand the trauma of sexual abuse and how girls and young women survive and thrive after the crime."

—Scott Berkowitz, president of RAINN

"As a provider to those most vulnerable, I opened *Invisible Girls* and it spoke to me...like it was written just for me, from my perspective. Not only as a feminist, or an advocate, or a health-care provider, but as a soul that needed to find asylum from the toxicities and trauma witnessed daily on those I care for. Sharing this resource with survivors gives strength and resilience to those arriving with feelings of defeat. When I need help understanding the violent world around me, the human need for forgiveness, and capacity for recovery, I pick this book up again...again...and again."

—Cynthia Wathen, Center of Hope Forensics

"*Invisible Girls* is remarkable in featuring first-person accounts by girls who have survived incest, abuse, and rape like you have never heard before. Myths are debunked and survivors and their allies are guided toward a beautiful path of healing."

—Girls Coalition of Greater Boston

"I highly recommend *Invisible Girls* if you are a survivor of sexual violence, or know someone who is. As a lawyer for survivors of sexual violence, this book is a fantastic resource."

—Rachna Goel, Jane Doe Advocacy Center

"I give *Invisible Girls: Speaking the Truth About Sexual Abuse* credit for healing so many of my clients. I have purchased several copies for my staff and survivors as an invaluable resource. The feedback in my community is extraordinary."

—Victims Crimes Assistance Program, Connecticut

"*Invisible Girls* speaks the truth of sexual abuse like no other book has dared. The voices of courageous adolescent girls and young women shed light on the darkest realities of pain so deep and wide that we feel the bottom drop out and find ourselves in the language and imagery of the unconscious. We experience the resilience of those who have lived through the unspeakable. Only by enfolding us in the realities of suffering can we know the rage and the hope necessary for recovery."

—Lyn Mikel-Brown, author of *Girlfighting, Raising Our Voices, Packaging Girlhood, Powered by Girl,* coauthor of *Meeting at the Crossroads*

"I recommend *Invisible Girls* to everyone! This amazing book opened my eyes to the reality of sexual abuse and how girls actually get through it. I understood what girls in the book went through: silently shouting for help, living in households controlled by the feared abuser, being rejected by mothers who tried to keep their daughters from speaking out, and feeling as if they'd never be rid of the shame. But in it all I learned that girls do heal and thrive."

—Natasha Santos, Youth Communications

"This book gives girls who have gone through the unspeakable their voices loud and clear, like we have never heard before. We are forced to listen to these extraordinary voices. *Invisible Girls* shows us the way to recovery."

—Eva Vives, film writer, director of *All About Nina*

"Thanks to Feuereisen's expertise, thoughtful advice, and ability to speak directly to the girls, *Invisible Girls* has created a space for girls to tell their stories and break through the walls of silence and begin to heal. More girls and young women will find the courage to come forward and no longer feel 'invisible' after reading this book."

—Katie Feifer, Voices and Faces Project

"More than advocating one path or set of choices, Feuereisen applauds not just survival; she validates the difficulties of being a young woman today. From a practical perspective, *Invisible Girls* offers a lot of useful information for young survivors. Feuereisen believes that telling one's own story as early as possible will lead to greater healing over a lifetime. She explains the ins and outs of recovering from abuse and puts the tools for healing in her readers' hands. This is a groundbreaking book."

—Britney Shoot, *Rewire*

"Feuereisen addresses myths about female sexuality and abuse, and offers advice on preventing, reporting, and recovering from abuse with personal voices as the strength reminding other victims that they are not alone and that healing is possible. An important book."

—*School Library Journal*

"*Invisible Girls* taught me, whatever your age, you are the right age to be coming out and telling your truth. It's time to let go of all the self-blame that we've carried. After reading *Invisible Girls* I let go of a thirty-year secret."

—Forty-year-old incest survivor

"This amazing book tells us we are not alone, and I can honestly say without *Invisible Girls* I would still be stuck in a hard place mentally and physically."

—Twenty-five-year-old incest survivor

"After my daughter read *Invisible Girls,* she told me about her rape. This book gave her the courage to come forward. She testified in court today holding her copy."

—Teen rape survivor's mother

"I have finished your wonderful book *Invisible Girls*. I never thought I'd hear a story somewhat similar to mine. I am an incest survivor. I cannot tell you how grateful I am to have found this book. I already feel that I am healing just by knowing I am not alone."

—Eighteen-year-old incest survivor

"*Invisible Girls* offers hope, health, release, letting go, and a freeing lightness despite what we have been through. There is understanding of the deep and difficult emotions and aftereffects of abuse, while also knowing that girls who are sexually abused can be healthy, high-functioning, successful, thriving girls and women from all races, religions, and economic classes."

—Twenty-three-year-old incest survivor,

"As a foster mother of two girls who suffered incest, I want you to know that this book has literally saved their lives. We sit at the dinner table reading together. Thank you and thank all the brave girls who told."

—Foster mother of two teen incest survivors

"I read a lot of books, but the book that had the most positive impact on me and changed my life was *Invisible Girls*."

—Sixteen-year-old rape survivor

"*Invisible Girls* literally taught me that my voice matters! *Invisible Girls* said that getting out your trauma any way you can is healing. I did a photo piece on incest which started a whole conversation and openness. Without this book I would still be alone in my dorm room. Thank you, *Invisible Girls*."

—Nineteen-year-old incest survivor

"Simple. *Invisible Girls* saved my life."

—Twenty-year-old incest survivor

DR. PATTI FEUEREISEN

INVISIBLE GIRLS

Speaking the Truth About Sexual Abuse

NEWLY UPDATED AND REVISED

SEAL PRESS

Copyright 2018 by Patti Feuereisen

Hachette Book Group supports the right to free expression and the value of copyright. The purpose of copyright is to encourage writers and artists to produce the creative works that enrich our culture.

The scanning, uploading, and distribution of this book without permission is a theft of the author's intellectual property. If you would like permission to use material from the book (other than for review purposes), please contact permissions@hbgusa.com. Thank you for your support of the author's rights.

Seal Press
Hachette Book Group
1290 Avenue of the Americas, New York, NY 10104
www.sealpress.com

Printed in the United States of America

First Edition: March 2005

Second Edition: September 2009

Third Edition: December 2018

Published by Seal Press, an imprint of Perseus Books, LLC, a subsidiary of Hachette Book Group, Inc. The Seal Press name and logo is a trademark of the Hachette Book Group.

The Hachette Speakers Bureau provides a wide range of authors for speaking events. To find out more, go to www.hachettespeakersbureau.com or call (866) 376-6591.

The publisher is not responsible for websites (or their content) that are not owned by the publisher.

Library of Congress Cataloging-in-Publication Data has been applied for.

ISBN: 978-1-58005-860-5 (paperback), 978-1-58005-859-9 (ebook)

LSC-C

10 9 8 7 6 5 4 3 2 1

To my daughter, Aviva

To my mother, Helene E. Feuereisen, who always loved
me unconditionally, in loving memory

And to all daughters everywhere

WELCOMING PANDORA
My Take on the Ancient Greek Myth

According to Greek myth, Pandora was the first woman, like Eve of Hebrew myth. She is said to have received many, many gifts from the gods—hence her name, which means "all gifted" or "all gifts." Aphrodite gave her beauty; Apollo gave her musical talent and a gift for healing; Hermes gave her a box and told her not to open it. Then he gave her curiosity!

Here she was, holding this beautiful box she had been ordered not to open. A smart and energetic young woman, in defiance of the patriarchy, she opened the box. Out spilled all the great misfortunes of the world, including the pain of all girls and women who had ever been sexually abused.

Others might have feared letting such troubles out of the box, but Pandora knew that when you keep a box closed you also close off hope. She knew that hope lies in opening the box, in revealing the truth, in releasing the trauma. She was not afraid. She knew that girls are healed every time girl's and women's sexual trauma is let out of its box and released into the world. I invite all of you to join me in opening Pandora's box.

CONTENTS

PART FOUR
The Road Back

INTRODUCTION TO THE THIRD EDITION

Healing After Your #MeToo Moment

In January 2018, more than 160 brave, resolute girls and young women made history by testifying against Larry Nassar, who had sexually abused them for years in his role as head doctor for USA Gymnastics. Gold medal–winning Olympic gymnast Ally Riesman concluded her powerful testimony by saying, "There is no map that shows you the pathway of healing realizing that you are a survivor of sexual abuse."

My clients and I wrote this book to be that pathway. If you have experienced sexual abuse, we invite you to find your road map to healing here. The courageous voices who tell their stories in these pages will lead your way. Please join us and blossom, become visible and strong, righteous and vibrant. We know you can. You are important and vital, and you deserve to recover, thrive, flourish, and create a beautiful life filled with love, success, and happiness. Surviving sexual abuse never means you are damaged goods! Sexually abused teen girls and young women are the strongest, most sensitive, most vibrant and resilient people I know.

And I know many. For the past thirty years, I have worked as a psychotherapist with sexual-abuse survivors in individual and group sessions, where I have listened to teen girls and young women talk about their sexual-abuse experiences and helped them on their journeys to heal from their abuse. I am never surprised at the elegance, stamina, resilience, strength, and love that survivors manifest. *Invisible Girls: Speaking the Truth About Sexual Abuse* came from what I learned from my beautiful clients; within these pages, I offer you encouragement to speak your truth and a healing path to overcoming the trauma so that you can thrive.

As our book continues to reach teen girls and young women from all over the world, sharing their stories, telling their sexual-abuse experiences, we continue to be gratified and awestruck at the bravery of women everywhere. Sexual abuse takes place all over the world, and I knew the statistics were staggering: one in four girls is sexually abused before her sixteenth birthday in the United States alone.

In our 2009 edition we expanded the book and added even more information about getting past what was done to you. We also acknowledged the experience of our sisters in the world of prostitution. We explained that prostitution is sex abuse and included those girls' voices with the other sexual-abuse survivors. Finally, we added more resources for everyone.

Now, with the stunning numbers of teen girls, young women, and women of all ages coming out with their #MeToo stories, almost ten years after that second edition of *Invisible Girls* was published, this third edition is here to help a whole new readership, a new group of survivors we haven't reached yet and everyone who cares about them. In this third edition are updated and expanded resources including blogs, the latest statistics, more follow-up with the original girls in the book more voices speaking out in our chapters, as well as new e-mails from girls. Also intensely covered is a very important topic that's not being talked about in today's media coverage: incest. Incest is the most common form of sexual abuse—and the most unreported. We go deep into the topic to explore the wound of incest and how girls get through it and past it. We reach the full circle of healing with an amazing afterword: a letter from an incest survivor, called "How I Found Love."

Following the Trump election, there has been a cultural shift, starting with the Women's March, the pussy hats, and the #TimesUp movement, with women in the film industry funding the legal defense of sex-abuse survivors. The Take Back the Night movement is still going strong, confronting sexual violence on college campuses. With this change in politics, the culture is shifting more than ever. In an open and empowered fight against misogyny, girls and women are going up against politicians, coaches, doctors, and priests. Brave teen girls and women are fighting back by coming forward to reclaim their voices, sharing their sexual-abuse experiences, and, in some cases, confronting their abusers.

Tarana Burke, an activist focused on working with black and brown girls in marginalized communities for the past two decades realized that saying "me too" after a young girl shared her story of sexual abuse could have helped her not feel so alone. Tarana wanted to help survivors release some of the shame and isolation they felt and thus began the hashtag #MeToo more than a decade ago. Then when actress Alyssa Milano told her #MeToo story, the movement went viral, and teen girls and women of all ages are now coming forward by the thousands to speak about their sex-abuse experiences publicly. For many, this is the first time that they are telling anyone their stories. As one girl and one woman after another opens up about surviving sexual violation, sexual intimidation, and sexual abuse, more come forward with their stories, creating a culture in which there is greater safety in numbers. The dam has broken, and girls and women's experiences of sexual abuse are flowing out.

This has been a long time coming. For three decades, teen girls and young women have been reaching out to me privately, one by one, quietly, sharing intimate details about how they had been sexually abused by their fathers, stepfathers, uncles, brothers, coaches, rabbis, teachers, cousins, and dates. I knew it would be many years before these survivors would speak out about sex abuse openly, freely, and publicly. It has taken all these years of teen girls and women telling their truths, of feminists working through the court system to change the laws, of feminist politicians and their allies working for women's rights to make a cultural change that allows girls and women to come forward and reclaim their voices.

Yet, even before this public moment of disclosure, the feedback from readers and the experience of my young clients has been hopeful and righteous and filled with resilience. I receive countless e-mails and letters, the majority from teen girls and young women all over the world telling me how they are embracing their lives because they have a road map to healing: *Invisible Girls: Speaking the Truth About Sexual Abuse.* These girls and women had held their secrets, some for decades, and they are now releasing their pain and moving forward into strength. They tell me of their isolation, and how, through our book, they have a sense of belonging to a strong community of survivors and thrivers.

Take note: you will not hear the term *victim* in this book. The teen girls and young women in this book are not victims, they are survivors. They have surpassed what someone else did to them. They are no one's victim! If you have survived sexual abuse, neither are you!

Now, with the shift that is allowing girls and women to let out the secrets of sexual abuse, we have inspiring examples: from the Olympic gymnasts testifying against their abuser Larry Nassar, resulting in a jail term of up to 175 years, to the outpouring of disclosure that followed actresses in Hollywood calling their abusers by name. Although we know some brave survivors have been telling their stories for years, these were public figures going up against public figures, and this brought the conversation to the forefront. We see that, with support and with more voices joining in to stand up to sexual violators, there may be justice and a change in the culture that enables, normalizes, and even encourages the sexual abuse of girls and women in record numbers. The serial abuser Harvey Weinstein's career has ended; other directors, musicians, athletes, and actors have been outed as abusers. Meanwhile, girls and women in other industries have stepped up as well. Janitorial workers, hospitality staffs, students, models, photographers, and more have called for a change to workplace policies to build in protection against sexual aggression.

Although I have been processing abuse with survivors and helping them to rise above and beyond their abuse with vitality for decades, today these public conversations are changing with the power of disclosure, and we find ourselves at a new beginning, where talking about sexual abuse is more possible.

Credit must be given to the survivors who are speaking out. But there are still survivors of sexual abuse who are struggling to tell someone what happened to them. What about the girls who are still living under the roof of their molesting fathers? What about the girl on a college campus whose boyfriend rapes her, and she is an incest survivor whose experience of incest taught her not to feel worthy of more? And what about the survivors who are still in danger every day and are being triggered over and over again by social media and news coverage? What about all the survivors who have not yet told their stories? Where are they now in their healing? Have they found a path to healing? We are here for you too.

If you are a survivor, remember this: *It is never the survivor's fault.* You never asked to be abused, and you never asked for abuse to continue. *Invisible Girls* can help you to stop blaming yourself and to let go of shame, responsibility, and guilt. Our book has given thousands of teen girls, young women, and women of all ages comfort, guidance, strength, resolve, and healing. Your job as a survivor is to heal yourself and get past the abuse that happened to you, and to live a life filled with love. Your job is to know how precious you are, to know you deserve love and respect. And we can help.

This book is not only filled with heartfelt stories of girls' abuse and healing. You'll also find essential information, options, tools, and a totally updated Resource Center. But, most important, these pages are filled with support, hope, resilience, and love.

One reader, an eighteen-year-old rape survivor, wrote to me:

Dear Dr. Patti,

My name is Ariel and I want to tell you that *Invisible Girls* honored me for what I went through and taught me that I was not alone. Now I want other girls to know they are not alone. *Invisible Girls* is my healing, my friend, my road map. My destinations from here are endless.

We know your destinations are endless too. *Invisible Girls* brings girls out of the shadows into the light of healing and thriving. Invisible girls are becoming visible every day. We know you can too.

With love,
Dr. Patti

PREFACE

It's Never the Survivor's Fault

Invisible Girls taught me that my mother was wrong, that I did not ask for my stepfather to rape me. It is not my fault. Thank you, Dr. Patti, thank you, *Invisible Girls.* I am ready to heal now.

—*a seventeen-year-old from Texas*

I receive e-mails like this every day from teen girls all over the world, girls who found my book and are awakening to the fact that the sexual abuse they have experienced is not their fault—and that they can heal.

Before we published the first edition of *Invisible Girls* in 2005, girls who had survived sexual abuse found me and my psychotherapy work through an underground network, with one girl telling another and then another. What this book has done is expand that network, enabling me to provide a lifeline to girls in every corner of every state and continent. The book has made its way around the world, touching and empowering girls and women from Australia to Indiana, from Kansas City and Seattle and Louisville, to China, Mexico, Italy, and France—even Saudi Arabia. I know because I hear from them every day.

Every day, girls who have found our book reach out to me. They are building networks and making extraordinary connections. Girls and women—and their mothers, sisters, boyfriends, girlfriends—find *Invisible Girls* at their college or neighborhood bookstore or online; they are given copies to read at residential treatment centers and by therapists, teachers, friends, lovers, parents. They've found the book at the school library, from my website, a cousin, pediatrician, rape crisis center, aunt. Our intent was to reach girls in our urban centers, where books are easier to come by, and way beyond, where they are not, and we did it. Every day invisible girls, girls who were scared and alone and thought they were to blame or going crazy are becoming visible. They are finding the help and hope they so deserve, and they are healing—and thriving.

Sometimes their first contact is simply reaching out. A girl wants to know whether what she experienced is really abuse, or she wants to tell someone how guilty she feels for what happened to her. She thinks it must somehow have been her fault. Most of my e-mails are from girls and women who have never told anyone about their abuse. Some of these girls are as young as twelve years old. And some of the women are in their sixties. The e-mail to me is the first telling. She somehow got her hands on the book, and now she wants to tell me what happened. She feels she can trust me. And because I make myself available to my readers, I become a kind of springboard for these girls and their healing. They make that first contact, and their whole world begins to shift and change. Some of the girls who have written to me have kept in contact for years now.

One eighteen-year-old from Minnesota e-mailed me: " 'It is never a survivor's fault.' I have carried these words with me for the past six months until they finally sank in. This saying along with one that I tell myself every morning when I wake up and when someone ridicules me, 'Being the abused one isn't the crime, but not telling is'—I believe this to be very true. I have soaked up every word that is in this book, and I have become a strong survivor!"

Girls and women from all over the world write to say thank you, to say they'd never had the courage to speak about their abuse out loud until they read the book. They write to say I'm "healing." I can't imagine work more rewarding than this. These readers are creating a strong community of healing and strength, and resolution.

Every day invisible girls are finding their way to the book and to their own healing and wholeness. In this edition, we want you to hear their voices. In Chapter 17, "Five Years of E-mails and Letters from Around the World: Girls Become More and More Visible Every Day," you will hear directly from girls and women who contacted me after reading the book. They want you to hear their responses and their stories of healing and how they were changed by reading *Invisible Girls*.

It also became clear to me through my recent work that we needed to add the voices of girls "in the life." Sex trafficking, prostitution, and pornography are forms of sexual abuse, and the voices of these girls and young women are so strong and clear. Chapter 12, "Stop Calling Us *Whores*: Prostitution Is Sexual Abuse," addresses the issues involved in these forms of abuse, especially in light of the ways violence against girls and women has become so much more tolerated and normalized through popular culture. I have the honor of working with girls from GEMS (Girls Educational and Mentoring Services), an organization committed to helping young women ages twelve through twenty-one get out of the commercial sex industry, and in the chapter, you will hear their amazing voices. Girls who have been prostituted feel the same as the invisible girls who have been molested by their fathers, uncles, or brothers. They shared their experiences on a retreat I sponsored through Girlthrive, my nonprofit where girls from upper-middle-class suburbs bonded with girls from marginal urban areas who were prostituted.

Through our index, you can more easily return to particular issues and stories, as well as a few organizations for boys and men to step up and join the fight to end violence against girls and women. When I ask myself what has changed in the world, in the law, in public policy and awareness since the first and second editions were published, the answer is, not enough. But we are fighting the fight and healing is happening with girls and women. The teen girls and young women who reach out to me through *Invisible Girls* and my organization Girlthrive, and all our readers, are living proof that this strength and healing is happening in spite of the misogynistic culture against girls and women.

When we first published *Invisible Girls,* my hope was not only to get girls on their paths to healing but also to participate in some meaningful way in the global movement to stop the abuse of young girls and women. I intended to do my part in changing the culture around sexual abuse and violence against women, by sharing the voices of my brilliant clients and giving guidance throughout. And we have certainly succeeded by giving girls back their hearts and souls. With every girl who finds her voice and stops her abuse or the risk of ever being abused again, we helped her to open up and to love and to trust, and most of all to know she is worthy. My mission was, and is, to reach sexually abused girls directly with the simple message that the abuse they suffered was not their fault and that the very best thing they can do for their healing is to begin to open up about it. And to keep opening up and talking.

Girls are getting the message. They are speaking out, finding their way out of abusive homes, and reclaiming their bodies and moving into healthy, adult relationships. This special book has done what I dreamed it could, and it has been an unbelievably rewarding journey so far.

With this new edition and this new time where conversations about sexual assault and abuse seem possible, we hope to spread our wings even further. As one teen girl from London told me in a recent e-mail:

I read your book and it made me see that I'm not alone, but surrounded by love and compassion. If it wasn't for your book I probably would not be here today doing what I am now. I just wanted to say thank you for writing such a beautiful book. I will never forget the wonderful things it showed me, how to heal and recover from a traumatic event. God bless all the wonderful girls—God bless us all—we are now filled with love and hope. We will never be invisible again!

> With love and thanks from the
> other side of the pond,
> Evelyn

WELCOME, READERS

Thank you for picking up this book. One out of four girls in the United States will be abused by the time she is sixteen. This book is for all of you. Please know that whoever you are, you are not alone!

If you are a survivor, I want to offer you a special welcome. Whether you are already hard at work healing from the trauma of abuse or are just admitting for the first time—perhaps even to yourself—that you were abused, I hope you will find this book an important step in your healing process.

This book is filled with survivors' stories, and they may trigger some intense feelings and painful memories for you. Please know that the message woven throughout is that there is deep healing after sexual abuse. Please feel free to skip around and take the book in the doses you can handle. But I will let you know that I was very careful to go slowly and break it down into sections, similar to the ways that girls disclose their sexual abuse. I want you to always feel safe and supported as you are reading. You might want to keep a journal to record your thoughts, feelings, and memories. If you're not currently in counseling, I hope you will find someone you can trust to share the feelings that come up for you as you read.

If you don't have someone you can talk with, or cannot find your own community, please know that you can always call RAINN (Rape, Abuse, and Incest Network), the national hotline for rape and incest survivors, at (800) 656-HOPE (800-656-4673), or you can write to me personally at our website, www.invisiblegirlsthrive.com, which can serve as a companion to the book and an Internet community of girls and young women.

Invisible Girls opens up sexual abuse to the community and to the culture at large. It offers a porthole into the worlds of teenage girls and young women who are abuse survivors. You have never heard the voices of young survivors in quite this way before, where secret worlds and inner coping mechanisms are revealed. To clinicians and medical professionals, parents, high school and university guidance departments, students of psychology, personnel at rape crisis centers and at adolescent and young adult psychiatric units, high school and college psychology classes, partners of survivors, and relatives of abusers: *Invisible Girls* will lead you to new answers and a deeper understanding of sexual abuse, and it will help you to transform the culture of shame and secrecy that surrounds abuse.

In my thirty years of working with sexual-abuse survivors, I have never stopped being amazed by the ingenuity and brilliance of girls, by their ability to thrive even through horrible experiences. I learn so much from them. I learn how they've coped, how they've found comfort in the world, how they've moved on in their lives and found good, healthy love. These girls are my teachers, and now some of them have come forward to share their journeys with all of you.

The stories, quotes, questions, and poetry included in this book were contributed by some of the hundreds of girls I have worked with over the years. These are girls I know personally. I have worked with some of them for years and followed their success in life. I want you to know them, too, and to grow and learn from their strength, resilience, and experiences. They are all grateful for the opportunity to reach out to you. To ensure their privacy and safety, however, I asked them to choose pseudonyms. With perfect synchronicity, some girls asked whether they could be called by gem names, others flowers, and I realized how perfect that was—that they would be seen in all their brilliance and beauty and radiance: Zinnia, Lily, Coral, Garnet, Topaz, Sage, Ivy, Amber, Jasmine, Iris, Dahlia, Pearl, and Ruby Rose.

In my eyes, each and every one of these girls—and every other sexually abused girl who finds her voice, finds someone to whom she can tell her story—is a heroine. Whether or not you are a survivor, we invite you to join these extraordinary girls in their movement to end the silence, to release the shame and guilt and fear, and to begin the healing of the collective spirit of girls everywhere.

PART ONE

WHAT IS IN PANDORA'S BOX? SEXUAL ABUSE AND HOW IT AFFECTS US

CHAPTER 1

WHO WE ARE AND HOW WE GOT HERE
The Birth of Our Book

> When I was twelve years old my father explained that I was a beautiful young girl and that he had to have me because he was a hungry man. He said that one could not put a plate of spaghetti in front of a hungry man and expect him not to eat it.
>
> —a twenty-two-year-old incest survivor

Incest and all sexual abuse knows no color, class, or nationality. Survivors are of European American, African American, Latin American descent. They are Jewish, Buddhist, Muslim, and Christian. They identify as gay, bisexual, straight, queer, and transsexual. There is only diversity within the experience of sexual abuse, no division of wealth, color, religion, entitlement, or poverty. These teen girls are our neighbors, our classmates, our friends. They are from single-family homes, they are only children, they have six siblings, they struggle in school, they excel in school, they are artists, scholars, athletes, boxers, musicians. They come from upper-, middle-, and working-class backgrounds. These girls are any girl. When you meet these girls, you have no idea they are sexual-abuse survivors. Like you, they are typical girls—girls on the soccer team, the debate team, in the drama club; highly functioning and high-achieving; or academically challenged but striving to do well. These girls are at top prep schools, top public high schools, or struggling urban public high schools; these girls live in rural areas, in urban communities, in marginal communities. These girls are destined for top colleges, the military, or supporting their families, and they are young women already in college and those starting careers. Girls you'd "never think" had been, or were being, abused. I call them invisible girls because they defy any imagined stereotypes. And the fact is, no one can tell from the outside whether you have experienced sexual abuse. There is no stereotype.

Throughout this book, you will hear directly from teen girls and young women who have endured sexual abuse. They will tell their stories of father-daughter, brother-sister, cousin incest; date rape, acquaintance rape, and mentor abuse; and prostitution. All too often, as you'll see, they wonder, "Why me?" or "Why didn't I stop him?" Even today, with all the disclosure of sexual abuse, there is still so much cultural denial, so much personal guilt and shame surrounding the subject of abuse that girls still often feel it is their fault.

When you live in the same house as a predator your sixth sense is alive and kicking at all times. You know he is going to do something that night, even before he considers what is at stake. The fight is only on the surface, a delicate exchange of looks, of using the other bodies around to try and plan your escape. It's futile and you know it. In the Disney story, Bambi had a chance. The chance of running as fast as he could in the open field. That doesn't mean he will make it, but he can run. I didn't know I could, because no one had shown me how to. It would take me a while to learn—after all the harm was done.

—a twenty-two-year-old incest survivor

BOYS WILL BE BOYS

Why didn't you stop him? This is a question that the culture has promoted, "Hey, you should have just stopped him—isn't it your fault?" And it is a question survivors of sexual abuse ask themselves all the time. But there are very good reasons why you didn't stop him. You didn't stop him because you lived under "his" roof, because you depended on him financially, because your abuser wove a web of fear and entrapment around you, because you were confused, because you were young and didn't have good options or a strong support system in place. Or you just moved away from home for the first time, you were insecure, and vulnerable. You were not brought up in a home with good boundaries. You did not believe it was possible, and many times, especially in the case of incest, it is not, until you are out of your home. This book will help you work through these feelings of entrapment and fear to see that sexual abuse is never your fault and that you did nothing to cause your own abuse.

Why didn't you stop him? You didn't stop him because we live in a culture where "boys will be boys"—a culture that, through its fairy tales, movies, and advertising, persistently pushes the sexist belief that young girls are ready for sex when their bodies first develop; a culture that insinuates that these girls "really want" the older men who abuse them; a culture that still questions the survivor's role in the crime, whether it be a young girl raped by her uncle ("Was she being flirtatious?")

or a guy who rapes his date ("Was she leading him on? What was she wearing?").

We live in a culture where a male-dominated government decides the laws about rape and incest, pornography, child and spousal abuse, and abortion—laws that directly impact women's health and happiness. Simply put, we live in a culture that does not honor women and children; where sexuality, especially female sexuality, is a commodity, something that is used to sell products or satisfy male desires; where women, and especially women of color, are depicted on music videos as little more than prostitutes.

In this culture, men still sexually abuse girls at staggering rates. And now with #MeToo the culture is forced to hear this reality with all the girls and women coming forward sharing their stories of sexual abuse publicly, reclaiming their voices.

THE HISTORICAL COVER-UP

The shameful fact is that forced sexual contact without consent—from inappropriate touching to sodomy to rape—has been with us throughout history, and it wasn't even widely acknowledged as a crime in the United States until women in the 1970s began to speak out. As far back as the late nineteenth century, the father of modern psychiatry, Sigmund Freud, made efforts to publicize the trauma of incest. He had become increasingly disturbed as patient after patient—affluent women from conventional families—described sexual abuse at the hands of their fathers, uncles, family friends, or male relatives. At first he took these women at their word and rushed to present his startling findings to his colleagues (some of whom, it is now known, were molesting their own patients and nieces). He was roundly ridiculed and harshly rebuked in the professional community. To redeem himself, he "rethought" the whole issue and decided that these women had only fantasized about the abuse—that their accounts were nothing more than an elaborate wish to be forcibly taken by their fathers, uncles, even their therapists! This is what has come to be known as Freud's "seduction theory," and it set a precedent for disbelieving survivors of sexual abuse for the next hundred years.

THE FEMINIST UNCOVERING

Yet, in the 1970s, women started speaking out about their incest and abuse experiences, and feminist clinicians followed. Freud's theories were challenged and criticized within the medical field. And with the work of pioneering scholars like Judith Lewis Herman and Diana Russell, as well as the publication of Sandra Butler's *Conspiracy of Silence* and Louise Armstrong's personal memoir of incest, *Kiss Daddy Goodnight*, the silence and disbelief around incest and abuse slowly broke open. But it wasn't until the publication of Ellen Bass and Laura Davis's *The Courage to Heal* in 1988 that the issue really took the spotlight. In this book, dozens of women spoke about the ongoing trauma of the sexual abuse they had experienced as children. The book gave women permission to believe in themselves in a most profound way. But, invaluable as all these books were and are, all of them told the story of abuse from an adult's perspective. Now there are more books written about sexual abuse but still most speak from an adult's perspective, while teen girls and young women in their twenties remain the most vulnerable to sexual abuse.

Beginning in the 1990s, adolescent girls started writing their own books. They wrote about love, life, family, sex, drugs, depression, and eating disorders, beginning with Sara Shandler's *Ophelia Speaks*. Then girls who had been sexually abused started publishing zines and writing songs about it. In the early 2000s websites started popping up, including Pandora's Project, with stories of sexual abuse. My website, Girlthrive, has more than fifty personal stories of girls writing to me to share their experiences and get advice. Now, with the popularity of social media—Facebook, Instagram, Snapchat—teen girls and young women began to reveal their stories publicly. The blog project Unbreakable created by college freshman Grace Brown in 2011 showed survivors holding signs with quotes of what their abusers told them. They were proving they were unbreakable. The #MeToo movement began in 2006, yet it was only in 2017, in response to the ways in which our misogynistic culture has been exposed across politics and many high-profile industries, that the movement brought thousands of faces and voices to the Internet sharing their sexual-abuse experiences. In 2017 US gymnasts broke open the largest sex-abuse case in history to reach the courts against their serial abuser.

All this uncovering and reclaiming voices is wonderful, exciting, and necessary. Healing after the disclosure is vital. Through the voices in our book, we hear their stories not only of sexual abuse but also of resilience, in their own words with the kind of internal detail that touches every core of their souls. We also are taken into the worlds of each girl's road to recovery and the inner life of the struggle and the strength. We hear the resolution. *Invisible Girls* takes you to the next step, the step of understanding, relating, and not only reclaiming your voice but literally having the tools to begin to heal in a deep way.

And because the girls in this book are girls I have worked with, some for years, I am here as your guide, your support with intricate knowledge of these wonderful girls. The fact is that teen girls and young women are brilliant and resilient and can heal from sexual abuse. When survivors are given the opportunity to talk about their abuse in a safe environment, to let go of confusing feelings of shame and guilt and self-blame, they have every chance of healing and of realizing wonderful, satisfying lives and relationships as adults.

Talk about it now. If you hold your abuse inside you into your late twenties, thirties, forties, fifties, and beyond, it can deprive you of healthy, loving relationships and self-esteem because you never get the chance to process the shame and the secret. As survivors discover time and again, not telling can mean living in a perpetual state of fear and mistrust and result in an inability to have trusting sexual relationships. Not talking about it and not processing your abuse can mean not feeling safe in the world. And keeping it secret can prevent you from embracing the love and joy that are your birthright.

DON'T WAIT TO TELL...

Liz, a thirty-four-year-old incest survivor, left home at nineteen, marrying the first man who asked her to. That marriage lasted about fifteen years, until he beat her so badly she was hospitalized. During the hospitalization, Liz began having vivid flashbacks of her early childhood sexual abuse and was eventually referred to me. It took her several months to reveal to me that she was a survivor of sexual abuse. She had never told anyone. She was so afraid that revealing her abuse would make her life even worse, yet when she disclosed and worked in therapy she felt enormous relief.

Another client, Shari, a thirty-eight-old social worker who had survived incest throughout her adolescence, had held her secretly tightly, too, and was on her second divorce from an abusive man when she attempted suicide. In our therapy when she was able to face her childhood demons, she began to understand she could be safe.

Amara was referred to me after a hospitalization for clinical depression. She was an attorney. She'd been having nightmares since her stepfather raped her at fourteen, and she finally had a breakdown at age forty-three. Through our work together she was able to "break up" with a family that did not respect her.

Keisha, fifty-two and a high school teacher, was also an incest survivor. She came to see me in the middle of her divorce because her fifteen-year-old daughter had been molested by her husband. Because Keisha never processed her own incest and blocked it out for more than forty years, she ended up marrying an abuser. Her fifteen-year-old daughter made a suicide attempt and the truth came out. Daughter and mother began their healing in our therapy. As her teen daughter began to thrive because her mother believed and supported her, Keisha was still racked with guilt because she was not able to stop the cycle of abuse.

Joanna, an artist, couldn't sleep because of recurring nightmares. She had survived a rape during her freshman year in college and never told anyone. At thirty-six she was still afraid of getting involved in an intimate relationship with a partner. In our uncovering of her fear of intimacy, she faced the rape and realized how many years that experience had informed her relationship choices with unavailable men.

In my private practice I work with women who've suffered through years of migraines, nausea, memory lapses, failed relationships, thoughts of suicide, drug or alcohol abuse—all problems stemming from a history of sexual trauma. Through friendships, college, jobs, and relationships, these women kept their secrets tucked away in a safe place and tried to forget about them. But, as they eventually discovered, forgetting doesn't work. Working with women in their thirties, forties, fifties, and sixties convinced me that I had to do whatever I could to help young survivors heal from their abuse so they wouldn't have to endure years of torment and harmful decisions based on their unresolved sexual-abuse history.

As younger clients, girls in their teens and early twenties, started to come into my practice and talk about their abuse, there was a different quality to their disclosure. There was always hope underneath their pain; their abuse had not had enough years to dig itself into their souls. So back in 1993, when a few of my teenage clients told me they wanted to start a survivors' group, I jumped at the chance. I organized a group that met in my office, and, to reach out to an even larger community of girls, I began running pro bono workshops about sexual abuse at one of the top, most diverse public high schools in Brooklyn, New York. The girls put up posters for the group in the bathrooms, and soon I had a vibrant group of girls that was racially, socially, economically, and ethnically diverse. There were girls that were born in Haiti, Israel, Russia, Jamaica, Iran, China, and the Philippines, and girls also born here in Brooklyn, a melting pot of its own.

One of my most effective techniques for helping girls in these groups and larger workshops to open up is to have them write out their questions and experiences anonymously on index cards and then to read each other's cards aloud. The experience is never short of phenomenal. Hearing other girls' questions and comments unlocks the floodgates of long-held secrets. These were #MeToo moments long before that movement:

"I survived rape last year, but I've never told."

"My cousin molested me when I was six. I never told."

"How can I protect my little sister? I think my father is messing with her the way he did with me."

"My boyfriend forced me to have sex; I said no. Was I raped?"

"My parents are divorced now, but my father abused me. I never told my mom or anyone."

"I am having nightmares about when my cousin molested me. I never told anyone. I am afraid of what will happen."

One girl told another, and then another, and then a kind of underground network of girls from other area high schools and colleges brought more and more girls to my workshops, support groups, and counseling sessions. Pretty soon I was seeing hundreds of survivors. The more they talked, the stronger and more confident they became.

What I witnessed over and over again was that, as these girls found a safe place to talk, they began to speak of their experiences, and, as they spoke of their experiences, they began to heal. One young woman said, "I sealed myself off. I figured if everything looked okay from the outside maybe the inside would eventually change, but it never did, until I admitted what had happened to me and stopped hiding." Another said, "I used to tell myself it never really happened, but when I started talking and I faced it, it became smaller and smaller, and so did my father." And another: "When I began to tell, it was like I had jumped off a freight train and had finally reached my destination."

In situation after situation, what I witnessed convinced me that it is far easier to come to terms with sexual trauma during adolescence and early adulthood than later on in life. It makes sense. We are at our most resilient during this time; we're still growing and changing. If you can talk about trauma while you're still young, still figuring out who you are, it simply can't plant its roots as deep. You see, it's the secrets that really do us the most harm. In all these girls I felt an urgency to get better and a resilience that simply was not present in the women in their thirties, forties, fifties, and sixties who had let their abuse eat away at them for ten, twenty, thirty years or more.

THE BIRTH OF OUR BOOK

Invisible Girls was conceived out of this urgency, out of a deep passion to tell the truth, to uncover the trauma so that girls and women could begin to heal from their sexual abuse. My experiences with these girls made me realize that the sooner these young women acknowledged the abuse and let go of their closely held secrets, the sooner—and more completely—they would heal. It was the girls I worked with who urged me to publish their stories and experiences. They wanted to reach out and create a great circle of girls and young women speaking out, supporting each other, healing. Their passion for revealing the depth and truth was unstoppable.

According to the National Sexual Violence Resource Center, statistics remain difficult to come by. But this is what we know: Most sexual abuse, especially incest, is never reported. As of 2017, ninety-one percent of survivors of rape are female, and half of those survivors are under the age of eighteen. Nine percent of sexual-abuse survivors are male. Ninety-six percent of the perpetrators of abuse are male. Four percent of abusers are female. One in four girls will experience sexual abuse by the time she is sixteen. It is a fact that young women aged sixteen to twenty-four are most vulnerable to sexual violations by intimate partners. These statistics come in spite of persistent underreporting of incest and all other sex crimes. The statistics for sexual abuse of adolescent girls and young women are simply staggering. Girls who have been through the experience deserve to be heard and to hear from one another. I wrote this book to bring you into the deep inner world of the amazing girls who reflect, and take us deep inside, the soul of sexual abuse so that we can understand it. *Invisible Girls* gives voice to the voiceless as it uncovers all the secrets.

I also wrote this book to help girls and young women who have not been abused to become aware of the realities of sexual abuse, to become smarter and safer as they come into their sexuality, and stronger and more resilient in the face of a culture that still defines girls and women by how well we satisfy the needs of men. The wonderful girls and young women who speak in this book share their experiences of ongoing sexual abuse within their families, as well as of one-time abuse by an uncle or cousin or family "friend." You will learn about acquaintance rape, date rape, and stranger rape, and the specific emotions and issues that tend to arise from each situation. For example, in the chapter on incest, one survivor writes a lengthy account of her six years of being raped by her father and how he coerced her and controlled the family. Through her insights, we begin to see and feel what the incest survivor is up against and to learn strategies for surviving this hellish experience. In the chapter on rape, a survivor writes about how she had been unable to trust boys or men, totally unable to connect in a romantic relationship, until she began to speak out. What we learn from all these girls is that help is out there, that healing is possible, and that sexual abuse is never a girl's fault.

An organization called Generation 5 was founded in 1997 with a mission to end the sexual abuse of children within five generations, and it continues its work to reach that goal. This book is a part of that work of stopping sex abuse generation after generation. The more that girls are able to speak out and reach out, the more other girls will be encouraged to do the same. The less taboo the subject becomes, the more possible it will be to make changes—to public awareness, to the law and public policy, to the options available for girls living with abusers or would-be abusers. You may not have been able to stop the abuse that happened to you, but you can start getting your life back together now and reach out to other girls. Together, eventually, we will make it impossible for men to get away with taking out their own rage or anger or fear or despair on women and girls through sexual violence. If you are no longer being abused, this book will offer you perspective and healing. If you are currently living at home and being molested by a relative, it will provide you with critical emotional support and resources—even if you are not able to get away immediately, this book will help you to open up and find your support. And if you are just beginning to remember abuse that happened when you were younger, this book will help you find the strength and the right people to talk to so that you can start to heal.

We know that many teen girls who are abused end up taking detours in their lives—getting into drugs, sex, self-harm, or eating disorders. They often feel that the abuse is their destiny, the map of their lives. But I work with these girls, and I can tell you that every girl can heal from sexual abuse. My hope is that by shedding some light on the problem I can help you turn away from some of the darker choices other abused girls have made.

THERE IS HELP

If you are looking for urgent or ongoing support, please turn to the Resource Center at the back of this book for help. There you will find hotline numbers, websites, blogs, podcasts, and counseling centers across the country. Included in the recourse center is my website, www.invisiblegirlsthrive.com, where additional resources, a Q&A, and letters from young women can be found.

Together, we will be like artists building a beautiful mosaic: All the tiles we need to rebuild your soul, with its many nuances and imperfections and exquisite, colorful complexities, are here. We just need to put them in their right places.

INTO THE LIGHT

Girls and women are brilliant at surviving and at doing very deep psychological work to heal their own trauma. Whether through counseling, poetry, songwriting, art, or writing stories, or whether through telling a friend, a therapist, a parent, a school counselor, or a volunteer at an abuse hotline, the most important thing you can do is simply tell someone, because telling is the beginning of healing.

The girls whose stories fill this book all did heroic work overcoming shame and guilt and the tremendous burden of secrecy. It all began with telling someone. All they needed was a safe place and the permission to let out their secret. As I see it, my role and the role of this book is to provide that safe environment for other abuse survivors, as well as to enlighten those who have not been through the experience but who care about these girls—parents, loved ones, counselors, or educators. If you are not a survivor, you will witness just how resilient the human spirit really is. If you are a survivor, you will be able to take comfort in the fact that you are not alone. And if you have just begun to process your experience, this book is here to help you make your way through the dark maze of feelings you have been holding inside. Together we will find the light. As one eighteen-year-old wrote:

Out of all the piles of dirt, garbage, and shit we have been handed, we can grow a patch daisies.

CHAPTER 2

ASK DR. PATTI

Answers to Girls' Questions About Sexual Abuse

Over the years, girls have asked me hundreds of questions about the many confusing feelings, statistics, and terms that surround sexual abuse. I'm sure you have some questions, too, so I thought it would be helpful to share some of the questions, comments, and concerns I encounter most frequently—and my responses—to help clear up some of the most common misunderstandings surrounding sexual abuse and point you toward the chapters that might be most helpful to you.

Dear Dr. Patti,
I keep hearing that sexual abuse is really widespread. I have never been sexually abused and I don't have any friends who have been. Is it possible that the statistics are wrong?

Signed,
Wondering

Dear Wondering,
Sadly, it's possible that you do know someone who has been or is being abused, but you just don't know it. Because of the stigma and the shame surrounding sexual abuse, many girls have trouble telling anyone about it, and that means that, if anything, the statistics you've heard are probably too low, not

too high. The latest information I have (from a 2017 National Sexual Violence Resource Center report) is that one out of four American girls will experience some sort of sexual abuse by age sixteen—everything from a single incident where someone touched a girl's breasts without her permission to a ten-year experience of being raped nearly every day by a relative. These statistics apply across all economic and ethnic lines; again, 96 percent of abusers are men.

Dear Dr. Patti,
When I was ten years old, my uncle put his hand under my shirt and touched my chest. I got him to stop. He also rubbed up against me and tried to hold me to him. He lived far away and I never saw him again. I never told anyone. Was I sexually abused? What exactly is sexual abuse?

Signed,
Concerned

Dear Concerned,
First, let me say that I'm very glad you do not have to deal with this uncle anymore. I'm sad to say that what you experienced was abuse. Even one inappropriate, unwanted touch is abuse. Generally, any unwanted sexual encounter constitutes abuse. The reason it's important to acknowledge that it was abuse is that otherwise it can eat away at you or make you feel ongoing conflicts about yourself and your sexuality. It's important to know that it was abuse so you are clear that it was not your fault.

There is non-touching sexual abuse and touching sexual abuse. Here's a list of some of the more common forms of both:

Touching Sexual Abuse:
- Having any of your private parts touched
- Being fondled
- Being penetrated genitally through sodomy or intercourse
- Being asked to sit on the lap of an adult and having the adult rub their genitals against you
- Having an adult rub against you or touch you in any way that makes you uncomfortable and refusing to stop
- Having to watch an adult masturbate
- Forced to perform or receive oral sex

Non-Touching Sexual Abuse:
- Being asked to view pornographic materials
- Having pictures taken of you in sexual poses
- Being spoken to with sexual intonation (i.e., "you look like a slut," "you must be screwing around," "look at your breasts; they look really firm")
- Being repeatedly walked in on in the bathroom or your bedroom
- Having an adult repeatedly leave the bathroom door open when they are inside
- Being asked by an adult if they can check out your breasts and genitals
- Being forced into conversations about sex

Dear Dr. Patti,

My uncle molested me and several of my cousins for years until one day my cousin (his daughter) couldn't take it anymore and told her mom. There was this big court case and he actually went to jail for a short time because I told and then five other cousins came forward, too. All of us had been molested by him before we were even teenagers. When he was arrested he said "he just couldn't help himself." What is a pedophile and what makes someone a pedophile or a child molester?

Signed,
Confused and Hurt

Dear Confused and Hurt,

First of all, there is no consensus on what makes a child molester. There are a variety of opinions as to why. What we do know is that these are men who seek out children. Some are homosexuals and seek out only boys. In our book we are looking specifically at men who sexually abuse girls. Many men who abuse children were abused in some way when they were younger. People who work with pedophiles tell us that these men may have felt they could not express themselves, that they felt they had no power except their power over someone much smaller. Sexual abuse is about sexual gratification, but it is also very much about power and manipulation. What we do know is that statistics tell us that 96 percent of sexual abuse is perpetrated by men.

Pedophilia is described as a condition of having deep sexual urges for children, but many, many pedophiles have sexual relations with adults, too. A father or uncle who abuses a daughter may still be having sex with his wife, for example.

In her book *Sleeping with a Stranger,* Patricia Wiklund describes sexual molesters as men who feel repressed and inadequate. They are morally and sexually indiscriminate. They have no conscience. I often find that molesters want us to feel sorry for them. That certainly seems to have been the case with your uncle when he whined that he couldn't help himself. What you need to remember is that it is never the survivor's fault. All the blame is with the abuser.

Dear Dr. Patti,

I moved here from Trinidad when I was five years old. Many of my relatives still live in Trinidad and often come to visit in the summertime. The summer when I was nine years old, one of my visiting cousins started molesting me. He was sixteen when it started and each summer he would do more stuff to me. He was always very nice to me and I kind of liked the attention, but then he would make me touch his genitals and masturbate him. I was very confused. In a way it excited me, but it also scared me and made me feel weird.

He never penetrated me, but he performed oral sex on me and he made me perform oral sex on him. The oral sex made me gag and sometimes I even vomited after. He was a very loved family member and I never told anyone. It stopped the summer I turned fourteen; my cousin was in college by then and had stopped coming to the States. I am now nineteen and having a hard time sexually. I find myself turned off by sex and scared. Is this normal? Was I sexually abused? Was it incest? Is something wrong with me because it felt good to me sometimes?

Signed,
Confused and Scared

Dear Confused and Scared,

Yes, you were most definitely abused, and, yes, it was incest. Any sexual contact between family members (or any adult figure you consider a family member) is incest. Your cousin knew better than to molest a nine-year-old girl. Girls who are being abused often get really confused when their bodies respond positively, but our bodies are stimulated by touch and the fact that you liked this cousin would probably only add to that.

There is absolutely nothing wrong with you! As you will learn throughout the book, our bodies sometimes respond to touch and genital stimulation. It does not mean that you wanted sex when you were nine.

I don't know all the details of your family, but I'm assuming you didn't feel safe telling a parent. I understand. Often girls are afraid that if they tell a parent they will be blamed. Many girls also tell me that they are afraid of sex after any form of sexual abuse. They don't know whom or what to trust. Remember, it's okay to just explore romance at your age. Most girls go on to have good, healthy sexual relationships after abuse, but it can take some time.

You do not have to have sex with someone you are dating. You are in charge and you can set the pace. If you do start dating, you can tell the guy you want to go very slowly.

If you have a trusted friend or adult you can speak to about what happened with your cousin, I encourage you to do so. You may also want to call the RAINN hotline or try some counseling. The more you talk about it, the better you'll feel (see Chapter 8 for more about sexual abuse by brothers, uncles, cousins, and stepfathers).

Dear Dr. Patti,
I am seventeen years old and go to high school in suburban Chicago. I have been dating my boyfriend for the past five months. I am a virgin and want to stay that way for now, but we

just began to have oral sex. I did not like going down on him very much, but I agreed to do it a couple of times. Last week we were at his house and we both were drinking. I think he was a bit drunk and while I was giving him head I started gagging. I stopped and he was very upset and begged me to "finish what I started." I said no and he pushed my head down forcefully. I felt like I couldn't breathe. He forced me to make him ejaculate. I was shocked. I never knew he was like that. I felt so vulnerable at the time; it was horrible. I felt like I was a toy and he could do anything he wanted with me.

I thought he loved me. I guess I was wrong. I hate loving somebody who doesn't really love me back. I could not seem to get him out of my mind and I chalked it up to his being drunk. Even though he did this to me and he did not apologize, I went out with him again. The next time we were alone he did the same thing, but this time I tried to fight and pull my mouth off his penis. He pushed my head so hard I could not move or breathe. He would not let go of my head and shoulders to the point where I started gagging and actually vomited. I felt a mixture of disgust and embarrassment. He threw me off of him in disgust. We broke up after this last incident and I feel really gross about what happened. Did I get sexually abused? Is this date rape even though he did not force intercourse on me?

Signed,
Nauseous and Disappointed

Dear Nauseous and Disappointed,
First of all, let me say how sorry I am about what happened with this boyfriend. Many girls talk about feeling nauseous performing oral sex on guys. There is a lot of pressure out there

these days for girls to perform oral sex. No girl needs to agree to this if she does not want to. I should add that if you do not use a condom during oral sex, you are susceptible to sexually transmitted diseases. You should probably see a doctor to be sure you're okay.

Even though he did not penetrate you, I and many other psychologists would define forced oral sex as rape, in your case date rape. Not all guys you date, of course, will do this.

Date rape, by the way, refers to any time you are forced to have sex with someone you are with on a date or ended up with at a given time by choice. Acquaintance rape is when you are raped by someone you know only slightly but were with voluntarily. According to an extensive study by the Pennsylvania Coalition Against Rape in 2002, ninety percent of both date and acquaintance rape involves alcohol (see Chapter 10).

Dear Dr. Patti,
I am in college and one of my professors has made some comments to me and some of my friends that have made us kind of uncomfortable. He said we are pretty. He seems to stare at us. He told me not to worry about my grade because I am so attractive. Are we being sexually abused or sexually harassed? What's the difference?

Signed,
College Blues

Dear College Blues,
Although *sexual harassment* is the generally accepted legal term it can still feel like abuse and violation. For example, if you are walking down the hallway in school or on the street

and some man or boy calls out something like, "Hey babe, you look sexy! Nice ass! Let's screw!" or "Can I have some!" it may not result in a physical assault, but it can certainly feel scary, especially if you are alone, and it can even bring up some of the same bad feelings that you'd have in an ongoing abusive relationship. I would suggest that you and your friends keep a record of these comments and then go to the dean and file a complaint. His comments could turn into abuse, and in any case he has no right to make you feel uncomfortable.

There is a very fine line between sexual harassment and sexual abuse. You may read many different definitions of these two terms. Usually abuse involves some sort of physical violation, but it is more complicated than that. If I have a client who tells me that during her entire adolescence her father never touched her but he looked at her in a sexual way all the time, walked around naked in the house, left out pornographic materials, and called her a slut when she went out with her boyfriend, I would have to say she was sexually abused. Thus, abuse really does encompass those situations where sexual statements are so constant that they create a climate of abuse.

Sexual abuse refers to being violated sexually. If the perpetrator never touches you but you feel totally violated by his words and looks and lack of boundaries, you may have the same feelings as a girl who has been violated through touch, so there's not always that much difference in the end. Quite often, too, verbal sexual violation accompanies physical violation (see Chapter 11).

Dear Dr. Patti,
Is sexual abuse happening more now than in earlier times, or are we just hearing about it more, and is there any ethnic group that is more abused than another?

Signed,
Millennial

Dear Millennial,
It is only in the past few decades that people have been able to compile any reliable statistics on sexual abuse, because before that the whole subject was so taboo that very few people ever reported or talked about it. However, over the past ten years or so researchers have consistently found that one out of four girls in the United States will experience some form of sexual abuse—from invasive sexual touching to rape—by the time she is sixteen. Psychiatrist Alice Miller wrote extensively about the abuse of all children, particularly girls, going back to the nineteenth century, and recent work has suggested that Freud's "seduction theory" was a cover-up for the rampant sexual abuse of young girls (see the Introduction). Unfortunately, we have no reason to think that sexual abuse hasn't been happening for centuries.

That is the whole point: sexual abuse is so often invisible, and you never know who is being abused. A girl or young women from any ethnic or racial group is at risk.

Dear Dr. Patti,
I feel trapped in a catch-22. Obviously, if it were not for my father I would not be here. But to be genetically connected to a monster like him—he raped me for most of

my childhood—scares me so much. I am afraid that I will end up hurting children, too. I am very protective around kids, but the truth is I am afraid to babysit because I think I will do something weird. Is pedophilia genetic? I can't even imagine ever hurting anyone, especially a child, but am I destined somehow to be like him?

Signed,
Trapped by My Genetics

Dear Trapped by My Genetics,
No, no, and no! You do not have any genetic predisposition for child molestation. I can assure you that there are almost no reported cases of female sexual-abuse survivors ever molesting anyone. You do not have any genes that will turn you into a pedophile. I would suggest that you take on some babysitting to prove to yourself that you will be fine with kids. I trust you. Please trust yourself. If you are very nervous about this, you can think about the way you are with children. If anything, I have found incest survivors to be particularly protective of small children.

Dear Dr. Patti,
I saw this movie once where a woman suddenly remembered her father molesting her when she was a girl, but, when she had her court case, they said she made it up. They called it "false memory syndrome." Do girls make up sexual abuse? What exactly is false memory syndrome, and when did this all come about?

Signed,
Confused

Dear Confused,

False memory syndrome, as you suggest, refers to stories that are supposedly "made up" by suggestible patients under hypnosis. The "syndrome" was named in 1992 by clinicians at the University of Pennsylvania and Johns Hopkins University in response to charges and lawsuits having to do with allegations of childhood sexual abuse ten, twenty, fifty years after it had happened. They claimed that memories can too easily get distorted over time, and that there simply wasn't good evidence to support the stories of thousands of women who were coming forward with memories of past sexual abuse. In all cases of sexual abuse, evidence is difficult to gather, unless a woman or girl actually has a semen sample from inside her own vagina. Let me say this: Children don't usually lie, and I have never met a girl or a woman who has made up a sexual-abuse experience. On the contrary, girls are hesitant to disclose sexual abuse. Statistics show that incest is the least-reported sex-abuse crime. Sometimes, if abuse happened before a baby knew how to talk, the memory will be stored in the form of feelings called precognition, and it can be trickier to reconstruct what happened, but that isn't the same as a lie. (It is interesting to note that the False Memory Syndrome Foundation was created by two parents, Pamela and Peter Freyd, who were charged with sexual abuse by their own daughter Jennifer Freyd, who with the support of her grandparents confronted her father for sexually abusing her during her adolescence. Shortly after those accusations, the Freyds came out with the false memory syndrome theory.)

Of course, there are exceptions to every rule, and there have undoubtedly been some cases where a child or young woman was misled by an incompetent therapist into believing she was abused. But the evidence suggests that this is very, very rare. The vast majority of girls know the difference between reality and fantasy well.

Dear Dr. Patti,
When I went to see a therapist about my abuse, she wanted me to go under hypnosis. I was really frightened. She had me close my eyes and asked me to do what she told me. I couldn't relax because my father always had me close my eyes before he would molest me. Then she wanted me to do EMDR [eye movement desensitization and reprogramming, another therapeutic technique], and that scared me, too. I have never been back to a therapist since. Is hypnosis really necessary for therapy?
Signed,
Eyes Wide Open

Dear Eyes Wide Open,
Some people claim that long-repressed memories are best recovered under hypnosis, and professionals do undergo very specific training to become hypnotherapists. However, it is not proven as a "cure" for repressed memories, and in the wrong hands it can certainly be misleading and harmful. For hypnosis to work, the person being hypnotized must trust the hypnotherapist enough to give up control to her, which makes it a complicated and controversial technique for sexual-abuse survivors.

Proponents of hypnosis claim that it can open up and clarify memories that were otherwise vague. Opponents claim that thoughts and memories can be "planted" by suggestion. Many sex-abuse survivors have told me how frightening it is to undergo hypnosis and give over trust to someone else. In any case, hypnosis is generally not recommended for adolescents because their memories are usually pretty sharp.

EMDR is another therapeutic technique that is based on the idea that hidden memories can be uncovered. It was developed in the late 1980s on the theory that because disturbing memories are stored in the brain, they can be "replaced" by new memories that are uncovered by thinking about the disturbing event while also focusing on something pleasing. In other words, the memories can be reconfigured. Some claim great results with EMDR, and it has the added benefit of working with your eyes open.

Both hypnosis and EMDR are best used in conjunction with psychotherapy. In my experience, longer-term psychotherapy is the most curative, because you have time to establish trust with the therapist, which is so important when trying to heal from something as traumatic as sexual abuse.

Dear Dr. Patti,
A few days ago, I reported my father to the police for sexually abusing me. My whole family has now broken up. I haven't eaten in two days and I cannot get out of bed. I am lonely, miserable, and on top of it I feel guilty. My mother says I am seriously depressed and is threatening to make me go to a psych hospital.

Signed,
Despondent

Dear Despondent,
What you did takes great courage, and the feelings you are having are not only normal but very, very healthy. You are

finally allowing yourself to feel the feelings you had to repress to protect yourself at the time of the abuse so you could get through it. You are allowing your body to break down under the weight of what happened. Please tell your mother not to be afraid of these feelings, and encourage her to get counseling so she can understand what to expect during this time. In fact, in most States, in cases of incest the courts will mandate therapy for both the child and mother. The father may receive treatment as well as punishment often resulting in jail time.

Depression lasts at least a few weeks and involves too much or too little sleep, loss of appetite or overeating, disinterest in your usual activities, and feelings of hopelessness. If you continue to sleep all the time and feel miserable, you may be headed toward a depression, and by all means I urge you to get some professional help (with a counselor or therapist or guidance counselor) to clarify and get a handle on your feelings. But, for now, you and your mother should understand that it's healthy and normal to feel scared and depressed after reporting sexual abuse. You might try to find a support group for you and your mom. Also, show your mom this book. Try to reassure her that you are all right and you need *her* right now, not a psych hospital.

As far as guilt goes, if your father abused you, you have nothing to feel guilty about. He is the one who is guilty. (For more about incest see Chapters 7 and 8.)

Dear Dr. Patti,

I have reported my father for incest. I am sixteen now and he molested me from the age of twelve. He was given eight months in prison and then ordered to go to therapy for two years. My mother wants our family back together again, and my father says with treatment he won't touch me again. I am scared and want to go and live with my very supportive aunt. My mother says I can. Should I? Do you think my father is "cured"? Are child molesters ever "cured"?

Signed,
Wanting Out

Dear Wanting Out,
First of all, I agree with you. I think you should move in with your aunt.

This is really a two-part question, and first I will address the moving-out part. There are different schools of thought about this. Some therapists believe that it is often best to keep families together and that after treatment most abusers can work things out with their families. I belong to the opposite school. I believe that if a father or stepfather molests his daughter, the mother must make it her first priority to protect and support her daughter and should never take him back. This is an unforgivable abuse. The daughter is not the guilty party and should not be made to live with a man who abused her. I think that therapy may be necessary for mother and daughter, but I believe that both should be encouraged to keep away from the molester. Your mother pushing you to support your father's re-entry into the family will make you feel violated all over again. This result is often why girls don't tell. Yes live with your supportive aunt. I think you should do it and not put yourself further in emotional or physical harm's way.

My colleague Dr. Kay Jackson has worked with all types of sex offenders, including pedophiles, for thirty years. Although she has seen few families actually come back together with some success, she warns that cases like this are extremely rare, and she cautions you to understand that pedophilia is not "curable" per se. She says that it lasts forever but that some men can learn to control it. It has been her experience that only through severe punishment (i.e., jail time) and intensive therapy can some men rehabilitate. But you shouldn't have to be a guinea pig. Your only responsibility is to care for yourself (see Chapters 3 and 6).

Dear Dr. Patti,
I have seen movies where women have multiple personalities. In the movies they are usually incest survivors. Is this just in the movies? I am an incest survivor, and sometimes I feel like I change my personality a lot. I can be pretty moody. My friend tells me I may have multiple personality disorder. Do all incest and sex-abuse survivors have it?

Signed,
More Than One Me?

Dear More Than One Me,
No, not all incest survivors develop multiple personality disorder. MPD is a clinical diagnosis defined as a "splitting" of a personality into two or more separate personalities to protect a person from various memories. A person with MPD actually creates a second personality (or more), with its own complete (or near-complete) identity. Incest survivors who are suffering deeply will often develop another persona as a survival strategy—to withstand the abuse. Also, as you will see in later chapters, girls who are experiencing sexual abuse often

develop elaborate fantasy worlds, but this shouldn't be confused with MPD. As a matter of fact, I see these fantasy worlds
as very healing for girls. Girls have an amazing ability to protect themselves and survive the unspeakable (see Chapter 6).

Dear Dr. Patti,
I am an incest survivor. The problem I have is that I am so
unaware of my body. When I fall, I don't feel pain. When my
friends hug me, I barely feel their hugs, and, even worse, when
my boyfriend kisses me, I don't feel any excitement. I want to
feel connected to my body, but when I was molested I went
numb; I felt as if I was floating out of my body. Will I ever have
feelings again?

Signed,
Uncomfortably Numb

Dear Uncomfortably Numb,
The sensation of floating you describe is often reported by incest survivors. The clinical term for it is *dissociation,* which is
defined as removing oneself from a situation as a way to avoid
the physical contact. You floated out of your body and became
numb to protect yourself. You floated away to live through
the abuse.

It will take time, but you will be able to feel again. As time
goes on and you are away from the perpetrator of your abuse,
you will begin to trust again. It may begin in nonsexual ways,
with friends hugging you. You might want to make an effort to
give a close friend a hug and try to be aware of how you feel.
The fact that you are letting your boyfriend get close is a good
sign. Some girls say that, when they tell their boyfriends about

their abuse, it helps them to physically feel again. If you would be comfortable doing that, you might want to broach the subject and see how it goes (see Chapter 6).

Dear Dr. Patti,
After 9/11, after so many school shootings, after returning from the army, I heard a lot about posttraumatic stress disorder. Is this disorder something that happens with sexual abuse, too?
Signed,
Stressed

Dear Stressed,
Yes, posttraumatic stress disorder, or PTSD, is a commonly accepted diagnosis for individuals who have experienced sexual abuse, the trauma of war, or serious tragedy. It is often the case that people are able to survive trauma only by becoming numb to their feelings about the trauma. For example, during a war soldiers can't allow themselves to feel their feelings of terror, or they would probably fall apart. In very much the same way, a sexual-abuse survivor (particularly one who is repeatedly abused) cannot afford to stop and feel the terror and trauma, or she could not withstand the abuse.

After the trauma, the survivor may be haunted with recurrent and intrusive memories of the trauma; recurrent dreams of the trauma; fear that the trauma will recur because of a stimulation in the environment, like a sensation from sight, sound, touch, or smell (also referred to as a "trigger"); trouble sleeping, even insomnia or hyper-sleep (too much sleep); depression; panic attacks; or trouble concentrating. These are all symptoms of PTSD. If you think you may be suffering from

PTSD, please speak with a trusted adult and then find a professional to speak with about your symptoms (see Chapter 6).

Dear Dr. Patti,
I think my cousin may be getting abused by her dad. She denies it, but she's suddenly been very depressed and doesn't want to go out. She says her dad wants her home most of the time, which seems pretty strange to me. Meanwhile, her dad's been acting really weird and possessive around her. He's always had a creepy vibe around girls anyway. How can I tell if he's abusing her?
                                        Signed,
                                        Concerned Cousin

Dear Concerned Cousin,
While none of the following traits in and of themselves is "evidence" of abuse, there are some common survivor's traits to look out for. Some could be in combination or isolated. But remember, girls are expert at hiding sexual abuse out of fear and knowing there may not be a way out at that moment in time:

- Low self-esteem
- Promiscuity
- Fear of sex
- Fear of intimacy
- Large blocks of memory loss
- Nightmares
- Anxiety attacks
- Mistrusting men
- Poor relationship with mother
- Perfectionism

- Repulsion at certain "triggers," that is, a gesture, a touch, a smell, a voice, or anything that might bring up memories of the molestation
- Poor body image

If you really think your cousin is being abused, find someone you can trust to talk with—perhaps your mother or an older sister or a counselor. You can also call the RAINN hotline at 1-800-656-HOPE (4673) and get some advice. If you can locate a counseling center nearby (RAINN can help), you could ask your cousin if she is being abused and then let her know that you are willing to go with her to counseling if she wishes. We address all the above survivor traits throughout the book.

Dear Dr. Patti,

I am eighteen years old and a senior in high school. I was born here but my parents were born in Russia. They have brought over many family members through the years. My uncle, who came here about five years ago, started molesting me when I was fourteen. I basically put up with it, but when he started bothering my younger sister I decided I had to do something. So I told my mother. Then I went to school and told my school counselor. The police came and arrested my uncle.

My mother threw me out of the house and won't let me come back until I go to the police and tell them that I lied. I am so scared. I'm about to graduate from high school. What should I do? Was I wrong to tell?

Signed,
Made to Lie

Dear Made to Lie,

First of all, telling is almost always frightening. Sometimes it may not feel as if telling is the right thing to do, even when it is, because it is so scary. For girls from cultures that view girls as less important than boys, or cultures where the mother is less powerful than the father, deciding not to tell her family might be the thing a girl can do to take care of herself. Until she can leave that household.

Please go back to your school counselor and ask for help. Find a trusted friend to stay with. The fact that you broke open the abuse may have saved your sister (in many incest situations, a girl doesn't tell until a younger sibling or cousin is being threatened, too; see Chapters 3, 4, and 8). If you have no one to turn to, please see our Resource Center for guidance.

Dear Dr. Patti,

My uncle molested me five years ago. When I told my counselor at school recently, he told me that he had to report it because he didn't want the "statute of limitations" to run out. He explained that as a professional he was what is called a mandated reporter, someone who has to report abuse if he or she knows someone is in present danger. He was also worried, he said, because my uncle has two daughters under the age of fifteen.

It turned out that my uncle was arrested and my mother and father were really grateful to me for telling, but I'm really confused about the laws about reporting and everything. Can you explain?

Signed,
Confused About the Law

Dear Confused About the Law,

First let me say bravo! It took courage to tell your school counselor about your uncle. He was right in explaining to you that he is a mandated reporter. Dealing with reporting and the courts can be very confusing, and it's true that the laws vary from state to state. But there is always someone in the police department who works with "victim's" services. The term *statute of limitations* refers to a time limit on when a person can be prosecuted for crimes he or she allegedly committed. Please see Chapters 7, 9, 13, and our Resource Center for more information.

Dear Dr. Patti,

I'm in college and a few weeks ago my friend came over to my house crying. She had just been raped by her boyfriend, who was visiting from out of town. I didn't know what to do for her. She told me she just wanted to take a long shower to wash off all she was feeling. She took a shower and then I made her some hot chocolate and she went home. A couple of weeks later she asked me to come with her to the police to report the rape. The police told us we had no evidence and it would be really difficult to prosecute. My friend is despondent. When should a rape be reported?

Signed,
Trying to Be a Good Friend

Dear Trying to Be a Good Friend,

Your friend is lucky to have you in her life. You did the best you could for her. Unfortunately, what the police told you is true. It's almost impossible to prosecute a rape case without physical evidence, and as soon as your friend showered she effectively destroyed what evidence there was.

It's very important to first go to a hospital and do what's called a "rape kit." During this medical exam, a specialized nurse takes a tissue and fluid sample from the vagina; checks for injury, STDs (sexually transmitted diseases), and pregnancy; and administers RU-486 (Mifepristone, known as RU-486, is a medication typically used in combination with misoprostol, to bring about an abortion) to prevent pregnancy, where possible. The police will also come to the hospital to make a report. Please see Chapter 11 for more about what to do following a date rape, as well as the Resource Center.

Dear Dr. Patti,
I am a lesbian and I was at a club with some friends. I was dancing all night with this girl I was attracted to. After we left the club we went to her apartment. We had both been drinking and we started fooling around. I only wanted to kiss and she wanted more. She became violent and pulled off my shirt and pants and forced her fingers inside my vagina. I tried to push her off but could not. I finally got away. Was I date-raped?
Signed,
Female Raped?

Dear Female Raped,
I'm so sorry this happened to you. Yes, you were date-raped. It may not be considered rape by law, but it is just as emotionally damaging. Whether it's done by a boy/man or a girl/woman, whether it's "just" oral sex or full-on penetration, whenever force is used, it's rape. We shed more light in Chapter 11.

Dear Dr. Patti,

A female friend and I explored each other's bodies when we were about six years old. We played doctor and touched each other all over. We didn't hurt each other or anything, just explored. I don't feel really weird about it, but I am wondering if we sexually abused each other. I really like guys and don't think I'm gay, but why did we do this that one time?

Signed,
Child's Play

Dear Child's Play,

Sounds like you and your friend were indulging in normal curiosity. If you had been hurt by each other, felt coerced, did it multiple times, or felt a real drive to touch your friend's genitals and have your genitals touched; or if a same-age playmate, cousin, or sibling tried to force a toy or finger into your vagina or anus, that could certainly qualify as abuse. But many children explore once or twice, and that's perfectly healthy.

Children usually know, intuitively, the qualitative difference between exploratory fun play that includes some touching and being violated.

Dear Dr. Patti,

This feels like a stupid question, but it is something that haunts me. I was sexually abused by my father from the ages of nine through thirteen, until he died. Now I am eighteen and I am in love for the first time. When my boyfriend and I made love, I told him I was a virgin. I am not ready to speak about my abuse, and,

I feel like a virgin even though my father penetrated me. Could I still be considered a virgin?

Signed,
Hoping

Dear Hoping,
I consider you a virgin. I have spoken to hundreds of girls who feel exactly the way you do. They were penetrated by their molesters, and they would never have lost their virginity to them by choice. Giving yourself sexually to your boyfriend is the first time you chose to do it. Others may disagree, but, in my opinion, you are a virgin.

Dear Dr. Patti,
How can families let sexual abuse happen? Don't parents want to protect their children?

Signed,
Perplexed

Dear Perplexed,
Now there's a question that deserves a whole chapter. Read on…

CHAPTER 3

CROSSING OVER

Girlhood to Womanhood

One minute I'm up, the next I'm down
One minute I'm here, the next I'm there
My feelings seem real, but then they don't
At times things make sense, but then again they don't
One minute I'm happy, the next I'm sad
Where will I be? Where can I be?
Will you love me if I want your love?
Will you love me even if at first I turn away?

The teenage girl who wrote this poem was describing all the normal ups and downs of adolescence. Most sexual abuse takes place during this very vulnerable time in a girl's life—between the ages of around eleven and fifteen. This is the time of your first period, your first budding sexual feelings. Your body is undergoing extraordinary changes. Perhaps this is when you have your first crush, and maybe you grow six inches. And you are vulnerable to abuse because you are in such a major transition and don't yet know how to handle your developing body, all these new expectations of how you should look and act and be, not to mention your own burgeoning sexual feelings. All sexual abuse is about being pushed beyond your own natural boundaries, but at twelve or thirteen or fifteen, girls usually don't even know what their own boundaries are. It's all so confusing.

In this chapter, we'll get into the psyche of the young teenage girl. We'll look at the cultural, physical, emotional, sexual, and psychological changes and pressures on adolescent girls, so that when we hear from the sex-abuse survivors later in this book, and when you look at your own life, you will have a full perspective on all that goes on during this time of great change.

Until around nine or ten years of age, many girls are still supportive of one another. They still communicate openly with each other about their feelings and struggles. They still trust their gut instincts. They go for the ball in soccer with a vengeance; they smack the tennis ball and don't worry if their skirt flies up. They know whom they like and whom they dislike and are not afraid to go after things they want.

But as their bodies start to develop, things change. As their breasts grow, it becomes more and more difficult to run fast. It's more challenging to swim when they have their period. It becomes harder for them to choose what they "want." Gender roles, hormonal changes, and cultural expectations all collide as girls try to figure out how to fit in. Because of the male-dominated culture they live in, they begin to distrust their instincts; they begin to doubt themselves and give a lot of weight to what their peer group thinks.

Girls look to their friends for guidance and social footing. At the same time, adolescent girls may start to feel intense competition with one another as they jockey for social position, and they can become downright cruel as they compete in a male-dominated culture. There is confusion and deep waves of emotion. Sometimes friendships with other girls are their lifeline, and yet sometimes that lifeline gets lost. That kind of competitiveness just doesn't happen among younger girls. It can begin during a girl's teen years.

It's hard being an adolescent girl. And add any other stresses—divorcing parents, the death of a close friend or relative, moving and starting a new school, breaking out with acne—and you can end up feeling very helpless and alone, and much more vulnerable to social pressures.

Adolescent girls are desperate to fit in, but they also realize that there's more at stake than ever. Because of social pressure to act and look a particular way (i.e., demure and sexy), many girls find it more difficult to speak their minds. Depending on their cultural background and peer group, they may start to edit themselves in an effort to fit in.

In her research, psychologist Lyn Mikel Brown found that girls like some of you, girls from middle-class and affluent homes, have a much more difficult time expressing their anger than girls of lower income and less privilege. These girls are raised to be good, compliant, and successful. Some girls have to overcome many years of conditioning to find their power and their voices. When girls and young women embrace feminism, they find support from each other in all aspects of their lives. But even so it can be complicated for girls to find their power along with all the insecurities that accompany being an adolescent girl. With increased social media exposure, things can go both ways for girls. There are more young feminist groups forming online, but there is also an uptick in online bullying and also sexualizing girls by posting photos without their permission. As of 2018, although the laws vary from state to state, "sexting" photos is a crime, and promoting sexually explicit photos of a minor can actually result in jail time—a teenager who takes a naked picture of herself and sends it to another teen has committed a crime with legal consequences. So you really need to be mindful of being pressured—even by your boyfriend—to send any photos that are sexual. Make sure you protect yourself because *you* could be the one in legal trouble!

With all this going on, it's also around this time that girls start to require greater independence from their parents. They'll start to push their parents away, even though they still need them—sometimes desperately. That push-pull is all part of the transition from girlhood to womanhood, from childhood to adulthood.

Adolescent girls begin to suffer, often acutely if not consciously, from the effects of sexism and male domination, all of which may have seemed irrelevant when they were younger. They can sense that their options in the world are shrinking. People are now more interested in how they look and how they interact socially than in their achievements. They know that they are being increasingly defined by their sex appeal, even if they don't feel sexy at all and often don't know how to handle all the sexual attention.

Consider how all females are socialized to take on blame and responsibility for everything that happens at the interpersonal level. Girls who have been molested are no different. You often feel tremendous guilt and shame; you often feel it's somehow your fault. Let us say it again: It never is.

And our culture is pushing girls earlier and earlier to be "sexy." This is reinforced constantly by music videos in a male-dominated industry, which has an impact on boys' attitudes and role in reinforcing the sexualizing of girls. Music videos sexualize girls at younger and younger ages.

Let's begin in the late '90s with Britney Spears: in one of her videos, "Baby One More Time," Britney was made up to look like a young schoolgirl as she strutted around in her little school uniform. Cut to ten years later in 2010 and Miley Cyrus at just eighteen years old in her video "Can't Be Tamed" with strong lyrics like "don't change me, I wanna fly, I wanna drive, I wanna be, I wanna go, I wanna be a part of something I don't know." But of course the video is all about sex, and Miley is the sex object of everyone in the video. This is a business like so many others run by men. The "Lolita" story gives us perfect evidence of the disparity between what a young girl may be feeling and how her actions are interpreted by older men. I'll never forget hearing a radio interview with Adrian Lyne, the director of the 1998 remake of the film *Lolita*, in which he talked about the fifteen-year-old girl he chose for the title role. Apparently, she was chewing gum when she came in for her screen test, and when it was time for her to perform she took the gum from her mouth and stuck it to her leg so she could read the script. We can guess that she simply meant to save her gum for later. Well, that's not what this sixtysomething man saw. He said it was one of the most "sensuous" gestures he had ever seen and that he knew instantly that she would get the part. This is the way teen girls are seen in our sexist culture—as a handy package of "innocent" and "seducer" rolled into one.

No wonder girls can begin to distrust their instincts and act in counterintuitive ways. Girls may know what they are feeling, but they also feel an intense pressure, from inside and out, to go against their feelings and conform to societal pressures and messages. They're usually dealing with intense school pressure, they're busy negotiating greater independence from their parents, and at the same time they are being bombarded with advertisements and articles and imagery that are constantly telling them how to be sexier. Advertisers, TV sitcoms, magazines, music videos, overexposure through social media—the whole world is telling them it's great to become a woman, it's great to be sexy and attractive, and it's great to have sex.

One of my clients who was an incest survivor wrote at twenty:

> No one saw all the pain and suffering locked inside me when I was thirteen, no one took me aside and told me I would be all right. I wish I could go back and look at that girl. Because I think I would tell her to stop giving herself away, to keep some part of her soul for her own, to tell the truth, everywhere and always. To stay out of the myths and conspiracies and the "protection" of the family. I would hold her and tell her to live for herself, and to get the hell away from the crazy people.

All this said, as difficult as adolescence can be, it can also be a time of wonderment. Many girls fall in love for the first time before they are eighteen, and many girls have loving, beautiful relationships with boyfriends or girlfriends. And, even if you are an abuse survivor or you come from a family with lots of troubles, you too can find this comfort and love once you leave your abuse behind you.

CHAPTER 4

TROUBLED FAMILIES
Daughters Betrayed

That incest survivor who wanted to go back and hold the thirteen-year-old girl who had been so damaged knew, at twenty, that her family was crazy to allow the abuse and not protect her. That's how sexual abuse happens. Innocent children need guidance and protection and don't receive it. In some fundamental way, all sexual abuse, with the exception of stranger rape, is about families failing their children. Girls would rather blame themselves, would rather hold their abuse inside, than go to their parents when they know that their parents would not believe them, would blame them, would fall apart if they knew. This is failure on a massive scale.

In the coming chapters, you will be meeting many girls whose parents failed them. Amber, whom you will meet in Chapter 10, had parents who may have loved her but were "old world" and not emotionally equipped to help her with the unhealthy sexual relationship she'd developed at camp with an older boy. Coral, in Chapter 7, suffered incest at the hands of her biological father for six years because she knew her mother, who turned out to also be an incest survivor, would not protect her. Sage's parents (Chapter 8) were too preoccupied to notice that anything was wrong. And on it goes. None of these girls had the kind of family support that makes a girl feel protected and cared for, loved and cherished.

It doesn't matter what kind of family you live in—one parent, two parent, grandparent, foster, or adoptive: when the adults you count on to protect you aren't there for you, you are more vulnerable to being abused both inside and outside the four walls of home.

Of course, it's dangerous to make too many sweeping generalizations about families where abuse occurs. There are well-meaning families who are just blocked from their own troubles. This can include a history with, for example, addiction, which can blind family members, as we hear in Chapter 14 with Emily's mother. The point is simply this: if you were sexually abused and could not go to your family for support, you deserve to realize that your family failed you fundamentally. Your parents did not provide a safe atmosphere of support and protection for their children, which is a parent's first responsibility. It was not your fault. You were abused because no one was there to protect you or teach you the necessary skills to be safe.

Of course, some families do give abused girls the support they need, but those girls are not the invisible ones with the deep scars, because they knew they had no support from their families. If you were abused, even randomly by a stranger, and did not feel safe enough to run to your parents for protection, if you feel in any way that your parents would blame you for the abuse, would fail to stand up for you, would not confront your abuser, it is important for you to understand that the problem lies in your family, not in you. You'll see this clearly when you read the other girls' stories.

INCEST FAMILIES

I was such a little girl then and I knew it felt bad and I
knew it hurt, but my daddy said it was the right thing to
do, our little secret. He said it would upset my mommy
to know. My mom never asked why my daddy always
needed to give me a bath, so I never told her. I would just
sit there in the tub, numb, and listen to her footsteps as
she walked by the closed door.

—*a seventeen-year-old incest survivor*

I believe that incest families are unhealthy and unsupportive families if only because they don't protect their daughters.
Men don't get away with incest when a strong, able, in-tune
mother is present. They just don't. Incest continues when girls
know they wouldn't be safe telling. They know their mothers can't or won't protect them. I have spoken to hundreds of
girls who tell me they would rather be molested by their fathers
and stepfathers than face the possible blame and rejection of
their mothers. Of course, sometimes these girls don't have a
mother alive, or with them. But in the great majority of cases
the mother is present and simply can't cope with the reality of
the abuse. There are exceptions when the mother is loving but
has a history so deep and damaged that she cannot tune in. We
meet some of these mothers in Chapters 14 and 17. These are
mothers who fiercely love their daughters yet were blind to the
incest taking place.

Many of our mothers were themselves sexually abused, either as children or as adults or both. Although the beginnings
of an open dialogue about sex abuse and incest is starting to

take place, sex abuse was not even talked about before the late 1990s. Did you know that until 1970s the only way to prove rape in a court of law was for a woman's testimony to be corroborated by other evidence such as a witness? This law was derived from the seventeenth century! Again, feminist attorneys worked to change the laws and now we have rape kits (more in Chapter 11). The point is, even if your great-grandmothers, grandmothers, or mothers suffered incest, there was no conversation about it and the laws did not protect them.

Thus, historically, women learned to put up with whatever men dished out. They felt they had to, and they've passed along that passivity and fear to their daughters. Since they were not able to heal from their own trauma, they often carry their damaged self-esteem, their addiction, or their mental illness into their roles as mothers. But you have a chance to do things differently.

One of my clients tells a remarkable story. When she finally told her mother and grandmother that her great-grandfather had molested her when she was a little girl, her grandmother said, "He molested me, too." And her mother said, "Me, too." But when my client tried to dig a little deeper, both women clammed up. Here were three generations of abuse survivors, and still they couldn't quite face up to the truth. You can break the cycle.

EMOTIONALLY UNSUPPORTIVE FAMILIES

It's not just in incest families that families let their daughters down. I've worked with many girls whose families ignored their pleas for help after an experience of sexual abuse. I've had girls tell me of parents who blamed them after they spoke of being pushed too far by their boyfriends, called them sluts and whores, and accused them of "asking for it." In Chapter 8, "Too Close for Comfort," Sage talks about getting thrown out of the house at eighteen because she was "too much trouble." Often these girls are in a real bind, too. They might want to go on to college, but they're often on their own financially. Some are caught in the financial trap of being claimed as dependents on their parents' taxes—and thus unable to get financial aid—even though their parents are no longer supporting them.

Another way parents let their daughters down is by having no clear boundaries—not just emotional boundaries but also physical ones. I consider certain actions that might not be incest per se to be incestuous. For example, I have heard many stories from girls whose fathers walked around naked or never shut the door when they were getting dressed or made suggestive comments to their daughters about their breasts or "asses." Often, when these girls spoke up to protest their father's behavior, their families accused them of being prudish or repressed, and the girls developed real insecurities about their own rights to boundaries. Their families made them feel that something was wrong with them for being uncomfortable or being modest around their fathers.

Fathers don't have to rape their daughters or do anything secretive or behind closed doors to effectively violate and silence their daughters. Girls know when their feelings will not be respected or when it's not safe to set their own terms within the family. Girls left voiceless like this are at much greater risk of being abused.

When we are small children, we depend on our parents for everything. Without them, we would be unprotected. Without them we would be unclothed, unfed, uncared for. We begin in the world needing our parents for survival, and as life goes on they are the ones we should be able to turn to for comfort and guidance.

But our families sometimes either do not guide us at all or give us poor guidance. I've worked with many girls whose parents simply couldn't cope, where the kids had to take on the role of adults, with no one to protect them, as well as girls from families where kids have no voice at all; families where the parents are too busy, too wrapped up in their own lives to notice; and families where girls are made to feel ashamed of their sexuality. The list goes on.

The fact that so many families betray their daughters is just another symptom of the way our culture perpetuates male domination. For all the gains women have made, girls still struggle to make their voices heard, to have power. And girls whose parents can't take proper care of them are left to float without a life preserver. They are made to fend for themselves to navigate their sexuality and emotions; they are more or less set up to be mistreated because they have not been taught how valuable they are as human beings.

During adolescence, girls are just beginning to seek full expression of themselves, and if that expression is blocked, girls tend to go either inward into depression or outward to unhealthy behaviors. This is why I believe so strongly that, for girls who have been sexually abused, now is the time to talk about what happened to you, to express the emotions surrounding your sexual abuse, to expel all the difficult feelings about the abuse and begin to heal. You are still young enough to get rid of the emotional baggage of sexual abuse that might otherwise haunt you into adulthood. You are young enough to become whole, to become visible, to heal. Believe me, once you start to realize that you have the right to voice what happened to you—when you stop feeling it was too big or too small, and you just accept that it is safe and healthy to disclose your sexual abuse to a trusted friend or adult—you will feel as if a cloud has stopped following you around. You will feel lighter and stronger. I promise.

In a perfect world, of course, there would be no sexual abuse. Men and boys simply wouldn't cross the line, and, if they ever tried, girls wouldn't be afraid to fight back or speak up. They would be able to count on support, and they'd know that they would be believed. With all the voices now driving the #MeToo movement, with girls speaking out in huge numbers, with the heightened social media exposure, be aware there is pushback. Pushback by friends and acquaintances on the Internet, pushback by the talking heads in media. You may get ten positive comments on your feed, but that one comment that puts you down or disbelieves you can really hurt. Make sure to protect yourself; call in your posse if you feel vulnerable disclosing. Because this isn't a perfect world, of course you'll need to find the people who will advocate for you and protect you and cherish you. Friends, aunts, cousins, teachers, counselors—these are the people who can be your anchor in the world when your immediate family fails you.

As you read the stories in the following chapters, remember that you are here now because you are strong and capable and a survivor. Your family may not have been there to help you, but you did what it took to get through the experience of your abuse, and now you are ready to heal. You are ready to find and face your truth. You are ready to become visible.

CHAPTER 5

FINDING YOUR TRUTH

Facing the Emotional Aftershocks and the Beginning of Healing

All at once the ghosts come back...
Slip-sliding at a pace unlike any other...

—*a twenty-two-year-old incest survivor*

Kathleen Hanna, of the punk feminist band Le Tigre, is open about being a sex-abuse survivor. She cautions girls to be careful about whom they disclose their abuse to. Hanna acknowledges that one thing a lot of abuse survivors have in common is that they were not taught how to have good boundaries, and it's easy to wind up telling someone who isn't really all that safe. I think she's right. You want to be cautious about whom you tell. However, she also describes girls telling as the links in the chain that will make the world a better place for everyone. I agree here, too.

The more girls speak out and tell their stories, the more healing there will be and the harder it will be for the culture to keep sexual abuse so invisible.

We are in the beginnings now of a social media blitz with girls and women telling their stories of sexual abuse publicly. But if you decide to speak out on social media, there may come the backlash and the pushback. When you tell a trusted friend or relative in confidence, you get to choose when you talk about it again. And maybe you get a hug and some very thoughtful eye contact. Maybe you open up and end up chatting for hours; maybe you go out for ice cream. These are very tangible responses to hold onto. The point is you choose who and how to tell. With social media, you don't get to choose when you want to talk or deal with it, and you also don't necessarily get to choose who reads your story. You could be bombarded with tweets, Instagram, Facebook comments about your experience. Remember, take care of yourself during this time, protect yourself.

Disclosing your story on social media also means you can set social media boundaries. This is part of your healing. You can say, "I am healing and growing, and I do not want to discuss my experience any more on social media." "Part of being a survivor who is strong is setting boundaries, I do not want any more discussion of my sex abuse." "I am dealing with this privately now, please respect that." "Part of my healing is asking for privacy now and respecting that I will let you know when I want comments." You are not obligated to discuss anything further. Let your public disclosure be a healing experience, not a source of pressure to respond when you are not comfortable.

We are here to guide you through finding the strength to share your sexual-abuse story with a trusted person. We are also here for after you have talked about your sexual abuse. The basic premise of this book is that the best way to heal from sexual abuse is to talk about it, and that the best time to talk is now, while you are still young. Adolescence through your midtwenties can be the time when you are most able to change and grow. This is a time of tremendous transformation, and you can heal the scars of your abuse the more you talk about it—now. Sexual abuse leaves wounds, but wounds heal, and if you can get to them while you're young, they won't have time to grow deep roots and cause you lifelong suffering.

If you wait until you are in your late thirties, forties, or fifties, the years you are developing your career and building a family, problems stemming from childhood sexual abuse will almost always have grown those deep roots and be harder to deal with. Sexual abuse can rob women of their self-worth and self-esteem, and such untended wounds put women at greater risk of date rape and abusive marriages. That's one of the reasons it's so important to speak out now and start healing.

FINDING OUTLETS FOR YOUR FEELINGS

When I run the track at school, I am in a zone—a zone where there is no abuse and no rape.

—a seventeen-year-old rape survivor

Often, before we can talk about the traumas that have happened to us, we have to find outlets for our feelings. Whether you realize it or not, you probably already have a number of such outlets. Maybe those long runs at the track are helping you get out your anger. Maybe singing those blues songs have been giving you a channel to release some deep pain. Maybe sketching strong women with full bodies in drawing studio has been making your body feel healed. Perhaps working with clay and banging it on the table to get out the air bubbles, you are releasing some deep-seated anger. It could be that Zumba or Soul Cycle class or boxing lesson that leaves you exhausted that is working through some lost energy. That's part of the genius of the body and mind. We are often self-healing without even realizing it.

Girls find many different ways of expressing their feelings about their sexual abuse. Some girls find writing to be the best way to get it out. I know an eighteen-year-old who filled three journals with drawings and writings about her incest. She said that every time she wrote or drew some of her feelings, she felt herself letting go of pieces of the pain. In our Resource Center, we have listed some zines, blogs, and websites where young incest survivors share their artwork and writing.

Whatever helps you get the feelings out—kickboxing, drawing, jogging, dancing, writing poetry—do it. I've heard girls describe how running gives them a visceral feeling of letting go of some of the tension in their rigid bodies. They are literally letting go of the inner shame and pain with every stride. Girls who dance several times a week talk about dancing the pain out of their bodies and souls.

Digging Deep

Drumming is my mantra. I bang out all my anger.
—a nineteen-year-old rape survivor

All of the above assumes, of course, that you have access to your feelings. Sometimes, especially if you are still living at home, it can be too dangerous to let yourself feel. You may still be living with your incestuous father or still go to school with the boys who gang-raped you or attend the church where the priest abused you. Often, when girls are living under the same roof as their abuser, they need to suppress their pain. It's a survival mechanism you may need until you move out. But once you are ready to acknowledge that you were sexually violated, the healing can begin.

Triggers

It feels like I try to calm the anger that erupts inside like a volcano, as my mind blows like a hurricane.

—*a nineteen-year-old incest survivor*

Some girls find that memories of their abuse experience come back with certain smells or sounds, when they hear a certain song, or when they are touched in a certain way. These are called "triggers." One of my clients was molested in the bathtub and was triggered to a memory of the molestation anytime she tried to take a bath. Another client could not stand having her lover whisper to her during intimacy. Her brother used to whisper and cover her mouth when he abused her.

All kinds of experiences can act as triggers—whether you like it or not or expect it or not. It can happen when you're watching a movie or reading a book and you find yourself identifying with a character who was abused. Or it might happen when you hear a story on social media, or when another girl starts telling you what happened to her and you suddenly realize, "Yes, that happened to me, too. What my brother/uncle/father/family friend did to me was rape. It was incest; it was sexual violation!" "That was not a date gone bad, that was date rape!"

Other girls talk about seasonal triggers. One of my clients recounted how her father would molest her under the changing leaves of a tree in her backyard. When the leaves would change and the brisk wind would brush against her face, she used to remember and feel ill. Another client remembers being gang-raped in the heat of summer. There are certain smells that come up in humidity that would bring her right back to the scene in her mind.

Triggers are not controllable. But, by recognizing what they are and when and why they occur, you can consciously re-map your emotions. The girl who felt ill in the fall decided to take long hikes through the woods and mountains with dear friends. It took a while, but she reclaimed the fall and now it is her favorite season. My client who was molested in the bath, for instance, made the choice to take back the experience of bathing. She bought herself bath oils and candles and plays soft, sweet music so she can relax into the soothing waters. It didn't work all at once, of course, but now she really enjoys a hot bath and no longer associates it with her abuse. The girl who was gang-raped in the summer has taken to jogging and has learned to embrace the heat. These girls refused to let their abusers have power.

The fact is, your abuser tried to map your life for you. But he does not own you, and you have the freedom and the power to overcome and transcend these kinds of associations. You deserve to be happy, to be free of any feelings of shame or guilt or fear. You have the right to a completely satisfying sexual life. You are a righteous young woman. If you can get in touch with these feelings and consciously change the awful associations, you can re-map your life.

The feelings may not come all at once. That's perfectly normal. If you feel detached from your feelings as you begin to tell your story, so be it. Don't let anyone tell you that you have to connect with these feelings. You will do so when you are ready.

Sometimes connecting your heart and your mind would bring more pain than you could bear.

Eventually, feelings will begin to surface—usually some combination of fear, shame, and guilt. Let's look at these feelings squarely and see if we can begin to break their grip on you.

Fear

> No one knows how far I've been pushed, and how I hate the skeleton my flesh is walking around with. I carry my fear like a rock in my heart.
>
> —a twenty-year-old rape survivor

Not surprisingly, fear is the most common response to sexual abuse—fear of what's happening, fear that someone will find out, fear of not knowing when your abuser will attack again, fear that the abuse will never end, fear that you'll be harmed if you tell, fear that you're damaged for life. You may even be afraid that abuse is your destiny. Incest, stranger rape, date rape, acquaintance rape, abuse by clergy/coach/mentor—any kind of sexual abuse carries the weight of fear along with it.

Abusers are usually really good at instilling fear. Maybe your cousin told you you're only worth being molested. Maybe your dad put such fear into you that you're afraid if you disclose the abuse, everyone in the family will suffer. Maybe he told you that your mother knows and has asked not to talk about it, or that your mother will blame you, or that it will break up the family.

Abusers set just such traps. The truth is, your abuser does not care if he hurts you. If he cared, he wouldn't abuse you. All he cares about is his fulfillment, his control, his needs. In the case of incest, you may feel love from him at times, and there may be moments when he is actually loving toward you, but his love is self-serving and the trap he lays is often so tightly sealed that you feel there is no way out.

The first step toward overcoming the fear is to recognize that your abuser is responsible not only for the abuse but for the fear that accompanies it. He put it there, not you. Talking about your fear with a therapist or a friend can help you see that the fear was instilled in you and give you some distance from it.

When the abuse is over and your abuser is out of your life, keep reassuring yourself that he hurt you and he is gone, and that no one else will ever hurt you again in that way. You can try making a list of everything that gives you strength in the world. And remember that it's still all right to be afraid sometimes. Very often I find myself telling girls that it's fine to check under the bed before they go to sleep; it is fine to sleep with a stuffed animal or their pet; it is fine to check the locks on the door. If that's what you need to do to convince yourself that no one can get in, that no one can hurt you, do it. It's perfectly natural to feel fear. Talk about it, define it, label it, and you will work through it.

Guilt

God didn't love me. It didn't matter if I prayed before I climbed into my little bed with the Power Rangers sticker or not. I had already spent enough time thinking it was my fault, that if I'd done something, just been cleverer, I could have stopped him.

—a nineteen-year-old incest survivor

Another emotion surrounding sexual abuse is guilt. If you are a survivor of incest, you might feel guilty for not having told anyone, and yet you cannot imagine having told. You might wonder why you didn't stop it. You might feel guilty about it. If you were date-raped while drunk or stoned, you might feel totally responsible for what happened.

In fact, the guilt can be pretty overwhelming, especially if you got any pleasure from the experience. Some girls' bodies can't help but respond to physical stimulation. That's just the way they're wired, and it's perfectly normal. But then they'll feel racked with guilt and wonder, How could I have enjoyed this? What kind of horrible person am I? Try to remember that *you* did not enjoy the abuse, *your body* responded.

Other girls feel something, but it's not pleasure; it's sheer pain and terror. And still others will go numb, removing themselves from their bodies so they don't have to feel anything at all. I even know gynecologists who have reported seeing girls with bruised vaginas who had no memory of forced sex and no pain.

It's like having an ice cube put down your back. At first you feel the cold, but if more ice cubes are put down your back, you might become immune to the cold—after a while you might not feel it at all—but you still know the ice cubes are cold. Many incest survivors talk about being physically numb. Even some girls who have contracted herpes or STDs that cause physical discomfort say they are practically numb in the genital area.

Just remember: Whether you feel pleasure or pain or nothing at all, you didn't do this to yourself. It was done to you, usually in a thoroughly calculated way, and there is absolutely nothing to be guilty or ashamed of. Sexual abuse is never a survivor's fault. Never. Even in cases of date rape, if you lost your voice, couldn't say "no," but resisted, the blame rests with your abuser, not with you.

Shame

The shame covers me sometimes. I sit in the cold and refuse to close the window. I'll go out without a decent coat in the middle of winter. I'll sit somewhere shivering and not even consider just getting a sweater. I feel like I deserve this cold, this discomfort.

—a twenty-two-year-old incest survivor

All survivors of incest at some point also feel shame. Other types of abuse cause girls to feel shame as well, but shame is embodied in the very nature of incest. Shame differs from guilt in subtle ways. Shame is not only connected with the act itself; it's the secretiveness of it all that causes shame. After all, if it weren't something to be ashamed of, it wouldn't be such a big secret, right?

Shame usually brings on a kind of quiet numbing; it can seem to reach to the core of who you are, and you might even begin to believe that it defines you. You're sure that people can tell that your father or stepfather or brother is molesting you. You carry around that shame and eventually begin to believe that the shame exists because of you, because you're keeping this awful secret. You might try not to think about it, but it starts coming out in your dreams. You might walk around thinking that people would judge you, shun you, blame you if they knew.

Although incest is not the only sexual abuse that carries shame, the shame of incest is one of the most difficult emotions to overcome. Time and again it holds back girls from telling. But believe me about this: once you tell a trusted friend, relative, counselor, or therapist, the shame does begin to lift.

If you are a survivor of incest, please understand that your father didn't start molesting you because of anything you said or did. He did it because he is a sick person with a totally warped idea of right and wrong. He tried to pull you into his demented reality. He undoubtedly planned how to get into a sexual situation with you. It was not your fault. You had no choice. This goes for all other types of sexual abuse, too.

As you begin to face your abuse, you may feel despondent, or angry and depressed, afraid of intimacy, but you don't need to feel bad or ashamed. Your father/brother/uncle/acquaintance is the one who is sick and set a trap for you. When you begin to shed some of the shame, you begin to shed some of your sense of responsibility, and vice versa, and that's vital for healing.

There is shame in all abuse. But the shame belongs to the act, not to you. It's so important to remember that someone committed an act of violence against you and you could not stop it. It can be difficult to see this in relation to yourself. But think about other girls who are molested. Isn't it easy to see that it wasn't their fault? Wouldn't you tell them not to be ashamed? Do the same for yourself.

OTHER AFTERSHOCKS: SEX AFTER ABUSE

My lover says, "It's awfully crowded in here." That's because I carry my father with me.

—a twenty-year-old incest survivor

Many sexually abused girls go on to have very complicated feelings about sex. Some girls report being promiscuous because this is their drive, to keep having meaningless sex because that's all they feel they are good for. They feel worthless, and so they go off with guy after guy and let themselves be used for sex and feel virtually nothing. But in fact these girls are trying to gain power through these sexual liaisons. They are trying to overcome the feeling of powerlessness instilled by the sex abuse and "prove" that they can choose whom they have sex with.

Some girls get really freaked out if they have violent sexual fantasies. They can't believe they get turned on by fantasies of violence and feel a lot of shame about them. Or they fear that the only way they'll be able to get turned on is through being violently dominated. Just talking about this and admitting it, even on a hotline, can be really helpful. You are not alone. Many people who have been tortured have such fantasies. *You are not alone.* As long as you are open to looking at them and talking about them, they will pass. You will begin to understand that you are not a freak and that you are simply responding to what's been done to you. Eventually, you will be relieved of the shame by getting more control over your fantasy life.

Many girls talk about being afraid to be touched, being afraid that if they are touched in the same way their abuser touched them, they might freak out. Some girls are afraid of physical intimacy. For some, severe pain accompanies any sexual intimacy. Others report feeling nothing when they are touched because they spent so long escaping their bodies during the abuse.

If any of this is happening to you, give yourself time. You can and will have healthy, loving, affectionate, intimate, and sexual relationships after abuse.

Once you are in a relationship with a sensitive lover who understands (and if he or she doesn't, he or she is probably not the person for you!), refer them to a book by Laura Davis, *Allies in Healing: When the Person You Love Was Sexually Abused as a Child*. As the subtitle suggests, it has some wonderful insights for partners of girls and women who were sexually abused.

Let's get one thing clear right now: You are not damaged goods. You are entitled to a fine, satisfying sexual life—with someone who respects your boundaries. The act of sex, when accompanied by love and desire and deep attraction and connection, is the opposite of rape, sex abuse, and incest. So consider your first sexual love affair your first. Don't worry and don't be afraid if in the beginning you have triggers and déjà vu. It's okay to take it slow and be honest with your partner, who respects you, about what you're feeling and how much touch and what kind of touch you are comfortable with. Those feelings will be replaced eventually with healthy sexual and sensual pleasures. Just give yourself time.

LET GO

I sealed myself off from my emotions, locked them in a Ziploc bag, and put them in the freezer. Now I am ready to defrost that frozen bag.

—*a twenty-year-old survivor of date rape*

However you choose to face and reveal your abuse—through your poetry or art or dancing or track, whether you've told one friend or many, told your parents or not—don't worry about how it's coming out. And don't worry if some days you want to talk about it a lot and other days you don't want to talk about it at all. It's all okay. These are your feelings, and you get to determine what to do with them. You may feel embarrassed after telling people, or you may feel an incredible burden lifted right away. The bottom line is, by telling your story, you are letting go of the shame and the guilt that have been keeping you conflicted and full of self-doubt. You are building new road maps, undergoing a kind of metamorphosis, and taking back what the abuser tried to steal but never could. There is so much power in the simple act of speaking out.

Whatever your age, you are the right age to come out and tell your truth. Find someone to tell—and tell, tell, tell until your lungs ache. Tell until you can't tell anymore. It won't take away what happened to you, but it will re-map your life and take away the power from the abuse and the abuser. Read on— and remember, you are strong and resilient, beautiful, and righteous. And you are not alone.

PART TWO

BEFORE WE OPEN THE BOX

CHAPTER 6

GIRLS' GENIUS

How Girls Get Through the Actual Abuse Experience
(Zinnia's Story, Lily's Story)

While my father was molesting me I would look at the wallpaper with all the little fairies. I would pretend they were
my friends and that they were sprinkling fairy dust on me. I
made up names for all the fairies and I was the queen fairy
and I could protect every little girl in my world.

—a seventeen-year-old incest survivor

When I was being molested I would picture myself swimming and then diving into beautiful blue water. There was
coral and beautiful shells, I could breathe underwater and
all the little fishes were swimming with me protecting me.
I had magical powers, and the water was cleaning me over
and over again. The water was making me pure.

—a twenty-year-old incest survivor

If you are not a sexual-abuse survivor, you may be wondering
how on earth girls get through such experiences, but if you are
a survivor, you probably understand all too well. You too have
lived through the unbearable and gotten up the next day and
dragged yourself to school, sat through classes as if nothing

had happened, played on the soccer team, debated on the debate team, created art or music or poetry. Somehow survivors learn how to live with their abuse. They have to—it's the only way they can function.

One of my clients recounted an amazing dream she had several years after the abuse had stopped, in which she was her younger self in her childhood bed. In the dream her father came to her as usual, got on top of her, and started to have sex with her. As he started raping her, a part of her—what she called her "transparent self"—got up out of the bed to watch "the girl" and her father. Then she saw all these healing little angels surrounding the girl on the bed. They lifted the father off her and made him disappear, and then the hovering girl descended back onto the bed and melted into her own body.

This dream depicts what so many young women experience, whether consciously or unconsciously: leaving their bodies to survive their abuse. Clinically, this is called "dissociation," and many inexperienced clinicians working with sex-abuse survivors think of this leaving of the body, this floating, as a psychological problem. Clinically, dissociation can be thought of as a negative, as a way to not be grounded in reality. But who wants to feel and be grounded in reality while being sexually abused? You'll learn in this chapter, not only is it not a problem, or something negative, it is a lifeline, a brilliant strategy for trauma survival. Don't let anyone try to tell you otherwise!

Some girls leave their bodies or create fantasy worlds; others focus all their mental energy on something in the room or outside the window as a way of walling themselves off from what's happening to their bodies. Girls have been known to count, catalog, sing silently, memorize flowers, design elaborate gardens, create a piece of art, choreograph a dance, memorize complex mathematical problems, write lyrics, design a room, renovate a building, swim with dolphins, surf the waves, create poetry, do their homework, memorize a movie, take a plane ride, build a cabinet, become a superhero, learn a language, project themselves into a painting on the wall, grow wings and fly—all ways of separating their minds from the situation.

In the coming pages, you will be hearing from Lily, who recounts envisioning herself as a heroine rescuing trapped children. Garnet will describe repeatedly singing the childhood song "Miss Mary Mac" in her head. Other girls will talk about focusing on the color of the wallpaper, the nuances of the light coming in through the window, the sounds of the birds outside. One of my clients even counted the flowers on her wallpaper until she reached the number 643. One girl talked about disappearing into a painting of a boat and sailing away. I spoke to one girl who recounted memorizing the lyrics to an Italian opera. One of my clients even used a different name at work so she wouldn't have to identify with the soiled name her abuser-father called her.

The point is that often the only way to get through traumas like these is to not feel. And that's exactly what these fantasy worlds allow: they give girls a place to go so they don't have to be present in their violated bodies.

In 1992 Judith Herman, one of the major contributors to the field of understanding sexual abuse, published a book called *Trauma and Recovery*. In this groundbreaking book, Herman compares the violence of being a war prisoner to the violence of being a sexual-abuse survivor. She brilliantly brings out the similarities between being politically terrorized and being sexually terrorized. She shows us that both types of survivors suffer through overwhelming feelings of guilt and shame, often with nowhere to go and no one to talk to about it. And so they turn inward. By 2018 it is common knowledge that soldiers commonly suffer from posttraumatic stress disorder, as do sex-abuse survivors. Soldiers in confinement have been known to survive by making obsessive lists or by counting. Girls do these same things while they are being abused. Their minds and spirits will invent fantastically creative ways to survive torture.

Herman talks about how the Vietnam War Memorial, by acknowledging the reality of all the death, suffering, and trauma, gave vets a kind of container for their pain. It gave their suffering credibility. Our book is meant to be that memorial for sexual-abuse survivors—that proof of pain, that acknowledgment that you are still alive inside and out after your perpetrator tried to kill your spirit and rob you of your rights.

That doesn't mean it's easy to talk about your fantasy world. Girls know it can sound "a little crazy" to divulge the details of their fantasies. But I have found in my work with girls that over time, as they become more comfortable talking about the abuse itself, they will reveal some strategy they used to get through it. If they ask me whether I think they're crazy, I always reassure them that the worlds they created are a measure of their extraordinary resourcefulness and that I admire their skill at surviving. The fact is, a girl's ability to go elsewhere during her sexual abuse, to create a safe, inviolable place for herself, only means that she won't allow her abuser to kill off her spirit. However much he may violate her, this is one thing he cannot steal.

Often, a therapist will not fully understand these strategies. I have had several clients come to me only after having worked with a therapist who wanted to help them "resolve" their fantasy "problem." But these girls knew intuitively that there was nothing at all wrong with their fantasizing and that it was, in fact, what had enabled them to get through the abuse. Their fantasies are like a baby's security blanket, accessible when they need them for comfort or to get through a transition, but not a substitute for reality.

Of course, some girls simply can't disappear into fantasies during molestation. If your father or molester keeps talking and talking or instructs you to do certain things, you have to stay present to be safe; you can't escape. For example, the uncle of one of my Asian clients used to make her go through a ritual of bowing down at his feet and reciting a statement that she worshipped and adored him and wanted to have his baby as soon as she came of age. During the molestation, he also forced her to repeat these things. She was fourteen at that time. Another client talked about her father forcing her to comment on his body and male prowess continuously during the molestation. Another girl told of her father forcing her to say how much she "wanted daddy." Although often girls don't have the option of taking themselves away, stopping their abuse, they still manage to leave their bodies most of the time they are being abused.

And girls who do have options use them. In this chapter, Zinnia and Lily will tell you about the amazing fantasy worlds they constructed to survive their rapes and molestation. If you have any doubts about their sanity or your own, read on. These are remarkable, strong, courageous, and perfectly sane girls who used their minds to survive the unspeakable.

ZINNIA

Zinnia is one of those girls whose experience was so brutal you may wonder how she survived it. It's hard to believe that a girl could be trapped with an abuser for ten years with no one to help her. Zinnia suffered this long-term incest at the hands of her stepfather. Her mentally ill mother knew about the abuse and didn't stop it. In her story, Zinnia takes us inside the elaborate fantasy world she created to escape from her stepfather time after time.

Zinnia came to me through the underground network of girls who bring their friends in for help. She had been working with kids at a camp when she broke down. She had seen a little boy try to put his hands down a little girl's pants and freaked out. She actually fainted. When she came to, she told her supervisor she felt ill and needed to go home. That night she called a friend who she knew had gotten some therapy and told her she was an incest survivor and was having flashbacks. She asked her friend to take her to her next therapy session.

I met Zinnia when she was twenty-three. A beautiful Mexican woman, she was tall and strong and articulate beyond her years. But, when she began to talk about her abuse, her voice became very, very small. She said she was sorry to burden me with her story and explained that she'd thought it was all behind her. After all, the abuse had stopped four years earlier and she had pressed charges already and had seen a court-appointed counselor for five sessions. She felt ashamed that she had more work to do.

I assured her that there was nothing to be ashamed of, and we began our therapy and the opening of the depth of Zinnia's long-held secrets.

Zinnia told me that her mother is a schizophrenic, her stepfather an alcoholic, and she an only child. Zinnia's biological father abandoned the family soon after Zinnia's birth, and Zinnia was just six when her mother married a man who had already served a jail sentence for child molestation. He waited two years before starting to molest Zinnia. He then continued to molest her until she was eighteen.

The family lived in an old trailer in a dirt-poor area of the Texas foothills. Her mother was on welfare, and her stepfather never worked. Zinnia often went without food. When she entered school and spoke only Spanish, she was put into special education.

But she proved the school wrong and went on to become a perfect student. That was Zinnia's MO. During those many years in which she was being molested, to the world Zinnia showed only a perfect girl: a perfect student, a perfect friend, a perfect daughter. She did exactly as she was told, and she took care of her sick mother as well as she could. She excelled in school and received several scholarships to top universities. She was the compliant girl at home, at school, and everywhere.

Until she went to college, that is. During her freshman year she tried to kill herself with an overdose of pills. Luckily, her roommate found her in time, and in the hospital Zinnia told social services about her home life. Her stepfather was arrested and arraigned, and her mother put into psychiatric treatment. Zinnia's roommate had a friend who was my client—that's how Zinnia came to me.

Zinnia has been in therapy with me for the past four years, and it has been a real roller-coaster ride. Because she finds it so difficult to trust anyone, it was a full year before Zinnia opened up to me and had any faith that the therapy could help her.

When she started therapy, she had never been in a relationship, and she was terrified to let anyone get to know her, including me. Now, at twenty-seven, she is in a doctoral program in social work on a full scholarship at Columbia University. She has slowly begun to date and has developed new friendships. She is passionate about her work and wants to help socially disadvantaged children. I believe Zinnia will reach and save many children. I also believe that her story and depth of honesty will help incest survivors come out on the other side, knowing they are not alone.

ZINNIA'S STORY

Building Houses, Building Dreams

All through my childhood, I was the one in charge of things. At least, that was the illusion I liked to maintain. I had control. Of course, I knew this control was only available to me as long as I didn't shake things up, as long as I played my role. This role included being quiet about the rapes I suffered for ten long years at the hands of my drunk, old, disgusting stepfather. The first time he attacked me, he must have been at least seventy already. I was alone in the trailer with him. I was around eight. He approached me, pinned me down on the dirty couch, and put his fingers inside my vagina, forcing his dirty, drunk mouth on mine. When he was done with me, he pushed me aside.

When my mother came home that night, she found me huddled in a corner, shaking and crying. I told her what had happened. I pleaded with her to help me, but she just stared back at me blankly and said, "Look, he helps us with money. Just try not to put up so much of a fight." I knew my mother was crazy, but I had no idea she'd make me put up with this. She heard voices that weren't talking and saw people who weren't there, but she was all I had. So I began my retreat.

I ignored the smell of cat pee everywhere, the dirty dishes always filling the sink, the overgrown lawn, the empty cupboards, but I couldn't ignore my stepfather. I remember the gun closet, repository of the switch and the rifles. These were the weapons my stepfather threatened to hurt me with if I told the authorities about him. Tell the authorities? That was the last thing I wanted. I just wanted to be as walled off as possible from everyone. I couldn't imagine that anyone would ever take care of me.

I retreated deeply into books and school. I would stay after school whenever possible and read until the building closed at 6 P.M. I joined the Girl Scouts, then 4-H club. As I got older, I was on the swim team, the debate team, the cheerleading squad, school government—anything to keep me away from home.

I tried everything I could think of to stay away from my stepfather, but he managed to corner me and would mess with me whenever he could get his hands on me. But when I hit adolescence, I began to fight back. I started keeping a knife under my pillow, so that if he came to me in the middle of the night in a drunken stupor, I could pull it on him and threaten him. Sometimes that worked, and he'd leave me alone. But it wasn't always that easy. A lot of times he would just sneak up behind me and pull me to him in situations where I could not get away. Even though he was an old man by then, he was still very strong because he had been a construction worker.

Trying to get help from my mother was completely hopeless. By this time she was hearing voices almost all the time and could barely bathe herself. I knew that my mother had no right to demand my complicity—she was the adult, the parent—and yet it was crystal clear that she was incapable of protecting me.

My mother told me that I could handle the molestations because I was an "old soul." She said I was a soul who had lived many lives in many places, endured many things, and would continue on. I almost felt as if people would be able to see it when they looked at me, all that pain, all that time, all those centuries of living and dying locked behind my child's eyes.

But no one seemed to notice.

And all the while I was sleeping at night with a knife under my pillow, scared to death that that disgusting old man would rape me again, I kept winning academic and sports awards at school. Talk about a split reality.

Starting when I was really young, I had these secret little worlds that I would escape to. I would imagine myself as different people with complex personalities. I saw myself as a warrior, protected by the wind and the sky.

Even when I was little and curled up under the covers and would hear him come in and smell the cigarettes and beer on his breath and in his dirty, smelly clothes, and know what was coming next, I would retreat to my little world of cleanness and perfection and keep myself safe.

I would pretend to be asleep—he didn't care—and would invent a new fantasy world each time. By the time he finished with me, I could fall asleep peacefully because I was no longer a scared little girl in a rundown trailer; I was a princess on an island, a warrior queen, a waif turned into a strong beauty. I was in control.

I would transport myself to beautiful places. I had a friend who lived in a beautiful house and when I'd go over there, I would pore over the magazines and catalogs I found lying around in the living room. That's why my fantasy houses were always so beautiful. They would have sparkling clean floors and windows, beautiful curtains swaying in the breeze, fresh flowers, clean rugs.

Sometimes I would imagine myself in a garden full of lilacs, honeysuckle, mimosas, peonies, orchids, roses, magnolias. I'd never actually seen magnolias, but I loved the word and would roll it around in my mind. I imagined how magnolias looked and smelled. What I thought about didn't matter. As long as it kept my brain engaged.

I would also transport myself to the places I read about in books, changing them if I didn't like certain parts, adding extra bits to keep my mind engaged. I loved reading about horses, and I liked to imagine myself on an island with no one else around, no cars or streets or stores or schools, just a big house full of white things, and open windows and horses outside on the grass. Or I would be in a cozy cabin in the woods having to fend for myself. Of course, I had built the cabin myself. I'd have Herculean powers, and I would be able to chop down trees too. I'd pick wild strawberries and catch fish in a stream for food. I made up fairylands and mythical landscapes.

When my brain ran out of fantasy material, or just refused to go that far away, I would picture words in my head: L-I-L-A-C B-U-S-H-E-S. Then I'd count the letters and spaces in the words and picture them being slammed out by a typewriter's keys. Any time I had an empty moment that could be filled with something painful, I would take words, phrases from television ads, and entire sentences, and count, count, count, count.

After I would hear his footsteps leave my room, I would keep counting until I fell asleep. Even now, at twenty-seven, I can retreat to some better, safer place in my mind if I need to. And sometimes my fantasy has me going back to that scared little girl huddled in the night and putting my arms around her and holding her and telling her she'll be all right.

My fantasy worlds saved me, there is no doubt in my mind. I was the angel keeping myself alive.

MY THOUGHTS

It is clear that Zinnia kept herself alive spiritually and physically by using her brain and her imagination. When she moved out and went off to college, everything fell apart—and everything came together. She suddenly had clarity about the abuse. It took moving away and being on her own for that to happen. That's when she could afford to feel. And, once she was no longer on autopilot, once she didn't have to keep it all together just to make it through the day, she realized how truly horrendous her experience had been. And that is when and why she made a suicide attempt.

This is so common—that girls have some sort of breakdown or shatter emotionally after they leave the abusive home. While they're still living under the same roof with their abuser, they simply can't afford to fully feel or to process what's happening. But after they leave and can let down their guard, they fall apart.

This is also often the time when girls come to see me, when they are out of imminent danger and can begin to process their abuse.

LILY

When I met Lily, she was eighteen, living on her own, and working full time. Lily is a beautiful Afro-Trinidadian woman from a culture where being gay was not readily accepted. She said she was in love with her partner, a young woman of twenty. They had a good sexual connection that was not at all threatening to Lily, but she was not able to be intimate with her partner emotionally and wanted to get to the bottom of this problem. She was in a loving, supportive relationship, but she was terrified. Lily survived abuse from the age of seven through fifteen at the hands of her biological uncle and cousin.

Lily talked about being certain that she was gay but still going out to bars and cruising guys. She wanted closeness in her relationship, but she kept pulling away. Lily had never shared with anyone that she was molested throughout her childhood and young adolescence. She guarded her secret fiercely, until one day she broke down and confided in a good friend. This good friend happened to be one of my clients, so she brought Lily in to see me.

During the years of abuse, Lily often inhabited an elaborate fantasy world with very specific details. She could spend hours upon hours in this world. In Lily's world she was the most wonderful, interesting, diversified superhero you could ever imagine. In the "real" world, of course, she was a frightened little girl with no power. When I met Lily, she knew that her fantasy world had saved her, but she also knew it was time to join the "real" world.

I have worked with Lily for two years now. She still retreats to her fantasy world when she needs to, and she has done some amazing healing, too. She is a member in good standing of our world, and our world is better for having young women like Lily in it.

LILY'S STORY

A Superhero Beyond Superheroes

Ever since I can remember, I have loved my imagination. As a child I loved to spend hours alone in my room, where I could escape into my own little world of dolls and books and colors and safety. I would make little dollhouses out of shoeboxes and streets out of colored paper.

I remember the first time I was molested. I was about ten years old and was alone in my room working on one of my creations. My teenage cousin came in to say good night before he went home for the evening. He came over to me and kissed me, and then he put his hand down my shirt and squeezed and grinned at me. It felt weird, but I liked this cousin and I just let it go.

My mom was working two jobs. My parents had divorced when I was two, and I don't really remember my father. He left the country and went back to Trinidad, where we were all from. There were always relatives in and out of our house, and lots of different people were left in charge of my care. This particular male cousin used to have me sit on his lap while we watched TV. At some point he started putting his hands down my shirt and pants. I would try to wiggle away, but he would tell me that this is what cousins did. He told me it was my fault he was doing it and that my mother would only get mad if I told her.

I'm not sure why I didn't tell my mom—probably because I didn't see her much. She was usually sleeping when I left for school and gone when I returned home. I also believed she would blame me. My mother was also a really devout Christian and always said that sex was dirty and I'd better stay away from it. At the same time, she was very subservient to the priests and to any man, my uncle being one of them. So, whenever relatives were looking after me, I would just try to spend as much time as possible alone in my room.

When I was around twelve, my cousin's dad, my uncle, forced oral sex on me. That began the abuse I suffered at the hands of my uncle and cousin.

My uncle would instruct my cousin to do things to me while he watched, then my uncle took his turn all the while making it clear that I had no options. They told me that they would tell my mother that I was coming onto them, that I was wearing sexy clothes when my mother was out of the house. They also threatened violence against me if I did not comply, and they would send me back to Trinidad. I was terrified. My uncle and cousin went right on abusing me until I was fifteen and had the physical strength and the guts to get them to stop. I snapped, I started beating up my uncle, and I was stronger than I knew, stronger than they knew. Until then, their threats that I would be sent back to Trinidad were enough to keep me silent. But I felt like a used rag doll, and I was also feeling suicidal, so I felt that I had to stop them. Turns out that when I did, they actually left me alone.

During the abuse I created a world where I was strong and brave and could fight off anyone. I made up different names for myself. Sometimes I was Truth, sometimes I was Victory, but I always killed the bad guys.

In this world of mine, I did all sorts of things that a real person couldn't possibly do. In my fantasy world people liked and respected me for my character, not my looks. I was skinny, not too tall, attractive but not beautiful. I was attractive in a way that people wouldn't necessarily notice at first, but I would become more beautiful as they got to know me.

In "real life," I was serious, well behaved, and quiet—but a strong kind of quiet. The fantasy me could be really funny, the kind of funny that everyone loves to be around. I had a very sharp tongue. I was also very mysterious. I loved that there were many things about me that people didn't know. For example, in my fantasies I was this amazing singer. I could sing opera, blues, and jazz. I could sing like Bessie Smith and Billie Holiday and Aretha Franklin. I knew everything there was to know about music. People would come to me from all over the world with questions about music, and I would gladly give them the answers.

I could also fight very well. I was an expert boxer, and I had the highest belt in the martial arts. I knew how to use a gun and had incredible aim. I think I got this from cowboy movies such as *Rio Bravo,* which I loved. I had a great love for animals, and I could communicate with them. I could speak dog language, kitty language, bird language, monkey language. I knew what these animals needed from me. And naturally that was almost always to save them from some cruel human who wanted to hurt them in some way. Of course, I always succeeded.

In my world, I could predict the weather. I knew what people were thinking before they did. I was all powerful. I was able to take care of myself and anyone else who needed my help.

I also created this school in my mind, and that's where most of the fantasies took place. I worked in the school and ran it behind the scenes. There were other teachers and students, all of whom had names and personalities. There were classrooms and assemblies in the auditorium and everything. Whenever a child needed help, if they were hurt or hungry, they were sent to me. I helped them, I brought them back to health; I entertained them and made them happy.

As I got older, the stories I made up became more elaborate; my powers grew. Sometimes I would be called away from the school because I would be needed somewhere in the world. If there were cornfields on fire in Mexico, I would be called there. I would fly off and put out the fires. I would put up tents for the people who were displaced and arrange for airplanes to drop food and water. I would rebuild their fire-ravaged towns and cities. And then I would go on to my next adventure. People were always thanking me and telling me how much they loved me and appreciated me. That really made me feel good inside.

I would get ideas from places I had seen on TV or that I had been to. For instance, the school had a large wooden spiral staircase with ornate carvings of cherubs, just like the one I had seen at a mansion we once visited on a field trip. The wood was maple and smelled like the outdoors. The floors were shiny marble with hairline designs of deep black. I could imagine the sound of the children's footsteps on the marble. There were paintings on the ceiling. The paintings were like Michelangelo's, and were of beautiful, muscular bodies.

Sometimes I would memorize the bone structure of one of the figures in the paintings on the ceiling. Sometimes I would imagine how some of the people in my world walked or ran. I would imagine them running in slow motion. I would see the hair on their heads move with the breeze, I would picture the minute details of their expressions.

I lived in this fantasy world much of the time, though I could always bring myself back to "reality" if I had to. When I graduated from high school and moved out and began to support myself, I was able to be in the "real" world more and more. But even now when I have bad memories of my cousin or uncle, I find myself becoming Victory swooping down and catching a falling baby in midair, bringing her to safety. I know my fantasy world saved me, and it also made me strong enough in "real" life.

MY THOUGHTS

Like so many girls, Lily and Zinnia both figured out ways to stay whole while their molesters were raping them. They know that their fantasy worlds saved them. They see their characters as their saviors. They know that they saved themselves, perhaps not in body but in spirit.

Because Lily could not save herself from her cousin or her uncle, she saved hundreds of children and villages. Because she could not have a voice during her rapes, she imagined herself singing as well as any blues singer. Because she could not get away, she could fly and scoop up falling children. I learned through Lily that all girls are superheroes during and after their molestations. You are the superhero—saving yourself. And you deserve credit for getting through however you can.

Because Zinnia lived in a dirty, rundown trailer, she was able to build a beautiful home in the woods that was clean and fresh and beautiful. You see, that's what girls do. They find places to go to, worlds to discover, plants to count, lyrics to memorize, mathematical problems to solve, people to save, because they are resourceful and resilient and courageous.

Don't let anyone ever tell you that you were crazy for leaving your body. Just know that you were taking care of yourself. Don't let anyone tell you this is denial. It is survival. When we're so unsafe, we have to create our own safety. Lily told me that sometimes at night she can't sleep and the memories come back. When that happens, she just puts on her superhero cloak and saves a hurting child, and soon she is asleep and dreaming sweet dreams.

PART THREE

OPENING PANDORA'S BOX: GIRLS TELL THEIR STORIES

CHAPTER 7

THE DEEPEST WOUND

Father-Daughter Incest
(Coral's Story, Garnet's Story)

The little girl in me died
the moment he forced himself inside.

—*an eighteen-year-old survivor of incest*

As Coral spoke, her eyes were dead, her voice was monotone. It was as if she were telling me of some far-off experience that she had watched from the sidelines rather than the experience of being sexually molested by her father from the time she was twelve until she turned eighteen. Twenty-two years old, Coral sat in my office and told me about the time when she was fifteen and her father brought her into his office library before dinner, opened his pants, and pushed her head to him. After he climaxed and wiped himself off, Coral washed her face, and they went around the block to their home and sat down to dinner with Coral's mother. What was so chilling was not just that her father was abusing her but that the abuse was so thoroughly integrated into Coral's family life.

Coral is one of the many courageous young women who have come to my private practice through an underground network of sexual-abuse survivors. What Coral experienced—for a period of six years—was incest.

WHAT IS INCEST?

What, exactly, is incest? Incest is forced sexual contact with a family member. As with all sexual abuse, incest is a sexualized relationship between two people where one has the power to coerce and the other does not. Some incestuous behavior involves touch, some does not; it can be a one-time experience or go on for many years. Being forced to engage in unwanted genital touching or fondling, being made to look at a relative's private parts or to show yours, being asked to pose nude for photos, or being penetrated—all these acts violate the boundary between adult and child, or child and child.

Father, stepfather, brother, stepbrother, uncle, cousin, foster father, even a mother—all can be perpetrators of incest. Even a sexual experience with a close family friend can have some of the same effects as incest. Whenever someone you trust as "family" violates you in this way, it's incest. Zinnia and Lily both found ways to mentally escape their incest. You will read many examples of girls mentally escaping incest through dissociation.

One sixteen-year-old incest survivor described her experience like this: "I see him walk toward me and try to think of an escape, but there is no safe place and now it is too late. As he reaches out for me I simply fall to the floor, which is no longer strong enough to hold me up."

If you are an incest survivor, maybe you've had that feeling that you were about to fall through the floor and that your world couldn't hold you up, either. That's what happens when someone you're told to trust or depend on violates you sexually.

While incest may not be as violent as other sexual violations, like stranger rape or date rape, of all forms of abuse it usually creates the deepest wound. Of course, it can involve force, but often it is something that happens over time and involves a lot of seduction, manipulation, bribery, and lies. Fathers, especially, will often take their time convincing their daughters that the incest is their destiny. They will manipulate their daughters into believing that they don't have a choice. This "destiny" line is just one of many myths that surround incest. Let's take a look at some of the others.

MYTHS AND TRUTHS ABOUT INCEST

MYTH: "I need you to have sex with me because your mother won't." One popular myth is that men demand sex from their daughters because they are not "getting any" from their wives. Some men even go so far as to say that "your mother would want you to do this because she wants me to be fulfilled, and she's too ill [busy, etc.] to meet my sexual needs."

TRUTH: In fact, the clinical information we have is that men who molest their daughters usually continue to have sex with their wives.[1] It goes without saying, of course, that regardless of whether they are "getting any" from their wives, they have no right to abuse their daughters!

MYTH: "It's my job to teach you how to be a good lover." Some girls are told that it's their father's job to teach them how to be a good lover. Their fathers tell them that they need to teach their daughters everything about sex.

TRUTH: Not only is it NOT the father's job to teach his daughter to be a good lover, but, in a healthy father-daughter relationship, a father will be very hesitant and a bit uncomfortable to go into any discussion of his adolescent daughter's sexual relationships. There are usually appropriate boundaries around these issues.

MYTH: Girls seduce their fathers, or "You're so tempting [in those shorts, that dress], I have to have sex with you!"
TRUTH: Not only do girls not seduce their fathers, but they need their fathers to see them as their "little girls." This helps a girl develop trust in family boundaries, and thus in the world. When her father does not sexualize her, she feels more secure and less objectified. The last thing a girl desires is to seduce her father. This is a frightening distortion.

MYTH: Young girls are very attracted to older men—their fathers, uncles, teachers, you name it! This myth is constantly being fed to us by Hollywood. Many films continue to show teen girls falling in love with men in their forties and older. Helped by the publication of Vladimir Nabokov's *Lolita* in 1955 (which, by the way, has been made into a movie not just once but twice!), in which a pubescent girl seduces her pathetically unlovable mother's boarder (substitute father figure) with her naive sexuality, we have held on to the myth that girls are often desperately attracted to older men.
TRUTH: There's a big difference between things like acknowledging your budding curves and feeling the first blush of sexual feelings and preying on older men. And men should be mature enough to realize it! The myth that a child wants sex with

her father or a father figure is, simply put, a lie perpetuated through film and literature and a general cultural sexualization of children. But, because girls really want to trust and believe the adults in their lives, it's easy for men to take advantage of their vulnerability.

The book *Reading Lolita in Tehran* by Azar Nafisi compares the forcible sexualization of the character Lolita to the complete subjugation of Iranian women to men. It couldn't be clearer that incest is a form of patriarchal control.

CORAL

Coral came to see me when she was in her early twenties. She was ten years old when her father started being sexually inappropriate with her, eleven when he started molesting her, and eighteen when the molesting stopped because she got out of the house.

From the beginning, her father told her that she needed him and that it was obvious from the way she dressed and looked that she really wanted him to sexually arouse her. When Coral started developing, he actually said that having her under the same roof was "like putting a plate of spaghetti in front of a hungry man. Of course he'll want to eat it!"

About three years ago, Coral and her boyfriend got my name through a friend of a friend in my underground network of incest survivors. Before he had my name, he looked online and found a therapist. He called and told the therapist that his girlfriend just revealed her years of incest and she was in a panic state. The therapist said they could have an appointment in two weeks. He then asked around and found me. When they called me a few days after their first phone call to a therapist, Coral had already revealed the incest to her mother, who was now coming from Europe to see her. I said come in today. They did.

Coral's boyfriend accompanied her to her first session. She was tormented by her past and afraid that she would never get over her incest. She explained that her boyfriend was the first person she'd ever told. The second was her mother, and the third was me.

In that first session, I learned that Coral was twenty-two and had just graduated from Juilliard with a degree in music. She told me that she had written a composition that had just won several awards. She was having trouble enjoying anything these days, though, she said, because she felt tormented about her father. Her father now had AIDS, and she was terrified that she had it, too, even though she had tested negative.

As she sat in my office picking at her fingernails and looking down at the floor, Coral rattled off her anxieties: "I'm having nightmares and these awful headaches. I pick my nails and skin and grind my teeth when I sleep. I wake up in cold sweats, I'm afraid to deal with my mother, who is coming next week. She is totally dependent and a mess. I can't stand anyone touching me. I'm jumpy about everything. I cry at the drop of a hat."

Even before she confessed to feeling like a basket case, I explained to her that whatever had happened was not her fault. I had to repeat it at least five times. At first Coral sat frozen, then she finally broke down and sobbed.

Those words opened up the floodgates for Coral, who had blamed herself for years. Now, three years after Coral first heard those words—"It's not your fault"—she wants every girl who has survived incest to know it's not your fault, either.

CORAL'S STORY

Cats in the Courtyard

My father took away my adolescence. It started in Greece, when I was ten, but the first time he raped me was after we moved to Holland, when I was twelve. From the ages of twelve to eighteen, I was abused by my father sexually on a regular basis. I was forced to perform oral sex, to receive it, and to have intercourse with him whenever he demanded it.

My father is a multilingual professor of literature. His teaching had us traveling around the world. He is egocentric and has a major persecution complex, but he has cultivated a public image of being very intelligent and wise and calm. He always had some strange theory, but he was a professor and writer so people just accepted that he was a bit eccentric. There was this aura around him, like he was a Zen monk or something.

At home he could not keep up the persona. At home he was less guarded and felt entitled to be moody, controlling, and belligerent. He basically ruled our house. His thoughts were the right thoughts, and my mother and I had to attend to his every mood and desire. He was very forceful in expressing his opinions—so much so that you felt that if you did not agree with him, something in you was inferior. He told us which classical music was superior, which literature to read, and things like that, and there was simply no discussion. What he said ruled.

My mother was a seamstress and costume designer, and she also managed my father's finances and bookkeeping. She catered to his very whim. She took care of the house, cooked our meals, woke me up in the morning, and put me to bed. I remember feeling totally dependent on my mother and getting a lot of love from her, and I remember her love as fun love. Unlike my father, she was never smothering, telling me what I could and could not do, and I remember she played games with me. But honestly those memories are from when I was a very little girl.

I have a lot of blank spots in my memories of my childhood. From what I have pieced together with the help of therapy, I know that when I was a child my father never played with me, though he could be playful. He'd joke with me at times, and he always encouraged me to read. But the truth is, I was on my own a lot as a child. I can remember one summer when I was about six years old and my parents tied the house key to a string and put it around my neck. I was to entertain myself during the day as I wandered around the town and return home by evening.

It has taken me years of therapy to realize that my mother was very afraid of life. What she thought she'd found in my father was a support system; with him she did not have to think on her own. It's pretty clear to me that my father mattered more to my mother than I did. She would rush around to get dinner on the table for him every night, even though he said she didn't have to cook if she didn't want to. She knew that if dinner was not on the table when he expected it, he would go on and on about how hungry he was and how he was a better cook anyway and all that. I learned early on that what he said was not always what he meant. He may have said we did not have to do certain things, but there was never really any choice.

I watched this very closely and learned that the rule of our house was not to upset Daddy. He had an explosive temper, and at times he would throw fits, screaming and breaking things. My father was a master at manipulating reality. As long as we did what he wanted us to do, the household would run smoothly, and my mother would be calm.

When I was very young, my father would leave for months at a time to teach at another university for a semester in other countries, and my mother and I would bond. I would sleep in the big bed with her, which was a huge treat. When I climbed into her bed, I felt very safe and cozy. We would play and eat when we wanted to, travel where and when we wanted to, and just relax. I remember feeling safe those times.

These were also the years in which my parents let me spend summers at my paternal grandmother's. I remember those summers as fun and playful. My grandmother lived in the countryside, and I played with my young cousins and all the animals. As I got older I stopped spending summers there. I don't know why.

At some point my mother started being the one who traveled a lot. She would leave for a day and sometimes a week at a time to make costumes for a play. I don't actually remember sleeping in the big bed with my father (this is one of my memory gaps), but I think it was assumed that when Mother traveled I would sleep with "Daddy," just as I did with her when he was away.

When I was ten years old, my father started holding me just a little too long when he would hug me. I don't have any clear memory of being sexualized at ten, but things definitely got uncomfortable. I know he used to have me sit on his lap a lot. The first time he abused me sexually I was eleven. At least that's the first time I remember clearly. We were still living in Greece. I remember staring out the window at the garden downstairs when he came up behind me and touched my breasts under my shirt. I was wearing white summer pants and a little red top that I really loved. It had little bows on the side. I was wearing little white shoes with black dots. I even remember the underwear I was wearing. I was just starting to develop breasts, and I felt really good in my pretty outfit.

I loved all animals, and I loved watching the cats in the courtyard as they played. As I stared at the cats, my father French-kissed me. My legs started shaking. I was supposed to go to a piano lesson, but he took me to his bed and performed oral sex on me. I remember shaking all over and just focusing on the thought, "Soon I will be at my piano lesson." I don't remember exactly what he said to me, but I know he was telling me that what he was doing would feel really good. I don't think I said anything.

I was shaking the whole way to the piano lesson, and when I got there I couldn't play the music, I was shaking so much. I don't think he did anything else for a while after that, though he may have tried to initiate something at other times that year because I do remember his complaining that I was always going off with my mother and did not give him much chance to be alone with me.

He raped me for the first time when I was twelve. We were living in Holland by then; we had just moved. My memories of it are like a sped-up film. He started to kiss me, and I fought with him, and I told him I did not like this and that I was a virgin and wanted to remain one. But he kept insisting that this was what I needed to do. He got angry. He screamed, "Enough of this!" and then stood up and pushed me and said, "Get naked and get in bed, now." I went into the bathroom and stayed there, then I got into my pajamas and got into my bed. He came and got me and put me in his bed, then climbed in, too. I was wearing my underwear and socks and three T-shirts under my pajamas; he was naked. I kept turning away from him and rolling onto my side.

I don't remember how one thing led to another, but at some point he took off my clothes, put a condom on, and began raping me. I was screaming and he covered my mouth. At that point I was present (I hadn't taught myself to leave my body yet), and I was in excruciating pain. Afterward he teased me and laughed at me and asked me why I was making such a fuss.

We hadn't been in Holland long, and I was having a hard enough time as it was. I did not speak English or Dutch. I had no family there, no friends; my mother was traveling a lot to build her career as a costume designer. I had no protection or resources. My father could be so persuasive. He said that having sex with me was the natural way of things, and he cited all these examples of animals in the animal kingdom who are initiated into sex by their fathers. He babbled on about rituals and coming of age. He said that in the Jewish religion there is a ceremony called a Bat Mitzvah to celebrate the transition from child to woman and that he wanted to initiate me into womanhood by having sex with me.

Thus began my father's invasion of my body and my soul. Any chance he got, he had intercourse with me, and/or forced oral sex. Because my life at home was a living hell, I built an elaborate other world, a fantasy world, and I had easy access to it. This world had elaborate characters with complicated story lines, in most of which I was a heroine saving abused orphans. In this other world, I was always strong and invincible. My memories of that world are so strong. My imagination and that fantasy world gave me deep comfort. I could be back in that world at any moment. It seems I was always in that world when I was at home.

When I asked him why he was doing this to me, he said, "That's like putting a plate of spaghetti in front of a hungry man and asking him why he wants to eat it."

It took me a long time to realize how much that line affected me. It must have been my fault; after all, I was the spaghetti. It must have been my fault I started to develop and was getting more attention from males.

He also said one thing that really got to me. He said that mothers know; they just do not discuss it with their daughters. He convinced me that my mother knew and was fine with it. When my mother would leave for her trips and say, "Take care of Daddy," I began to assume that this was some kind of secret code and she really did know what was happening. Everything felt really crazy and unsafe. In my spare time I would try to keep busy. I taught myself to speak English because I always had a dream to live in New York City. I practiced my music, I stayed after school.

And then I found some friends—the kids you might call rejects—and I embraced punk culture. I related to the angry ideas groups like the Sex Pistols were expressing through their music. I was always fighting with teachers, always getting into trouble. But then I'd go home and have to deal with my father's sexual demands, and there I'd be, this passive little girl, all my strength had disappeared, just waiting for it to end.

The one time I refused to comply, my mother was away on a five-day trip. I think I was fourteen at the time. I screamed, "No! I will not! Keep away from me!" and ran to my room and locked the door. There was a way to lock my door with a key from the outside, and my father actually locked me in my room and told me I had to stay in there without food or water until I came to my senses. I stayed in my room for at least a day and a half, until I felt faint and had to eat or drink something. Then I gave in and asked him to let me out.

Before I could even eat or shower, he raped me. After that experience of being locked in my room, I figured it would be easier to just let it happen, and then it would be over with and I could get on with things. I learned to leave my body and go somewhere else during the rapes. I would count or sing a song in my head or do my homework, and I'd go numb. My body would not respond or get pleasure.

I kept hoping each time would be the last time for a while. From what I can piece together, I was doing a pretty good job of protecting my psyche from what was going on; I was kind of splitting off the incest from my feeling life. I went out with my mother whenever I could, my friends, and kept as busy outside the home as I could and tried never to be alone with my father.

Sometimes my father would talk to me during the rapes. Sometimes his voice was like a buzz in the background; other times I remember him saying that he was a really good lover, and how lucky I was to have him as a lover. But I was always numb. Sometimes he would not say anything, and sometimes he would tell me that I didn't have to do it if I didn't want to. But the one time I asked not to, he became cold and angry, started screaming at me and really scaring me, and when my mother came home he made up some lies about bad behavior on my part and gave us all a really hard time. It was clear to me that I was better off just doing what he demanded. The few times he did not force me, he took it out on my mother and on me, becoming even more controlling, demanding, and angry.

When I was sixteen he encouraged me to have a boyfriend, and I actually did. His name was James. We were not sexual, except for kissing. My father encouraged me to talk about James. I gave him minimal information, but he always pushed. One evening after raping me, my father said, "Go out with James, have fun." Unbeknownst to me, my father had given me this huge hickey, and when I met up with James, of course he noticed it right away. He asked where I got it, but I wouldn't say. So he broke up with me. My father always had ways of trapping me like that.

What makes me so angry now is that I realize how much he knew and how much I did not know, and how much he took from me while he had absolutely no regard for me as a human being. That is the ultimate affront to the human spirit.

I used to think that my mother was not to blame. After all, I never told her about the abuse. But a memory that came back to me during therapy changed my view of her.

When I was about fourteen, my father needed a photo of himself for a literary magazine cover and decided to have me stand naked in front of him. He would be dressed all in black, his eyes closed. He had my mother take the picture. You could not make out my face, but my body was clearly visible. The idea was that the professor can resist the temptation of the naked woman. Through my therapy I realized that my mother was really a coconspirator.

My therapy has helped me to realize that I had no options during my childhood and adolescence and that the incest was not my fault. I now understand that my mother was weak and would not protect me. She did not want to see what was right in front of her eyes. Also, there was no modesty allowed in my home. My parents walked around naked and expected me to do so as well. I was ridiculed by both of them if I expressed a desire to behave modestly. I did anyway. There was not even a door on the bathroom. When I was twelve years old and wanted a bathing suit top, my mother teased me and said that I was to continue to go top-less at the beaches. My mother was exploiting me at the pleasure of my father.

Coming to New York for college when I was eighteen, I felt like an immigrant from the beginning of the twentieth century, when everyone came here from war-torn or poverty-stricken places. I was out of my own private war zone at last. The first couple of years were especially difficult for me. I spent a lot of time numb or floating and would spout my father's belief systems about art, music, and politics. His influence was huge and inescapable.

Even though I've been free of my parents for several years now, I still heard my father's voice inside my head controlling me at times for the first years that I left home. As the years move on, his voice is quieter and quieter. My therapist assures me that someday it will be so faint I will barely hear it. And after that I will not hear it at all.

Getting some perspective has helped me to begin to forgive myself. I still feel depressed at times. During my adolescence I developed severe headaches and frequent nausea, which I con-tinue to suffer from. Some days I feel worthless. But I realize now that as a child and adolescent I did my best to keep myself alive. My mother was passive and frightened of the world. My father defined her every move. He molded her and tried to mold me, too. But with me he did not succeed.

It's taken a while, but I have begun to see things through my own eyes. I have started to hear my own voice. Three years ago, I changed my name so I would no longer have to share a name with my father. I will never go back to Holland, and I will never go back to what my life was. I have choices and freedoms, and I accept my incest as something that happened to me. But it no longer defines who I am.

At the time I was being molested, I thought I was the only one. My father controlled everything in our house, and he always said that what was happening to me was natural and that I should accommodate him. Even though I have to look back sometimes, I am moving forward. And even though it's painful for me to face my mother's complacency, doing so has helped me understand that it wasn't my fault. If I could have read something at the time about sex abuse, if people had talked openly about it, I could have been saved so many years of guilt and shame and secrecy. Each time I talk about my incest, I get rid of some of that shame and guilt. Each person I share with, no matter what their response, takes another piece of the pain away. If my story has reached you, I am forever grateful.

Last week I had a remarkable dream. I was in the forest. Suddenly my father appeared. As I looked at him I had fire coming out of my eyes, rays of fire, and as I looked at him I was burning him with my eyes, and he became smaller and smaller and smaller, until he was as small as an ant and I stepped on him.

MY THOUGHTS

Even after Coral moved out of her house, her father still had power over her. For two years after her move to New York, she still did work for him, keeping up with lectures and submitting reviews to literary and academic magazines based in New York City.

It wasn't until he sent her a pornographic version of "Cinderella" that she snapped. She had literally blocked out the abuse since she had this boyfriend, but seeing his pornographic re-writing of Cinderella, the incest all came back to her. She called him to say she would not represent the story and said, "I think you know why!" Then she started sobbing and cried over and over again into the phone, "Why did you hurt me? Why did you hurt me?" Of course, he did not answer. They hung up.

A few minutes later Coral's mother called her, demanding to know why Coral would not help her father. It was then that she told her mother about the incest, and she urged her mother to get out of the house. Her mother was unhappy in the marriage since Coral had moved out. Her father had become more and more moody and full of rage, and she was looking for a way out. Coral gave her that way out, and she left her husband. That was three years ago, and Coral has not spoken to her father since. She confronted him that day on the phone and then decided to cut him out of her life.

Through therapy, Coral began to understand how both she and her mother were controlled by her father. She began to see her mother's silent complicity regarding the incest and now understands her true place and function in the family. She was the sacrificial lamb, her father's sexual object. And she served an important function for her mother, too, serving her father's every need when her mother wasn't there to do so, or even when she was. (It's important to note that throughout the years of incest her father never stopped having sex with his wife or with prostitutes, from whom he contracted AIDS.)

After Coral disclosed her sexual abuse to her mother, her mother admitted that the marriage had disintegrated, and that her father was having sex with young prostitutes on a regular basis. It was then that her mother told her that her father had AIDS. She even admitted that she had continued having sex with her husband knowing he had AIDS.

Coral's mother had grown up in a household without a father and with an emotionally abusive mother. Coral's mother never had insight into her own home situation or sought any sort of counseling. At twenty, she married the first man who asked her, simply to get out of her mother's house.

When Coral asked her mother what she would have done if she had told her about the incest as a child, she replied, "I really don't know. I can't say for sure that I would have left him, but now the marriage is really bad so I am ready to leave."

Coral's mother claims to love her, and I believe that she does—as much as she can love anyone. But this love has many limitations. She was never really capable of parenting Coral. Coral was left on her own from a very young age, and her mother was completely complicit in the incest. She did nothing to protect her daughter. She left Coral alone with her father for weeks at a time, even when Coral begged her not to travel without her. Never once did she tell Coral that she had choices.

Coral has described many incidents in which her mother failed to prevent her father from exercising his many forms of control and abuse. There was the time Coral describes in her own words above, when she was around twelve and she was trying on bathing suits. Her mother called her father in to see the suits, and he just laughed and said, "She will be topless on the beach!" So her mother took the tops away from Coral.

Holidays were never celebrated in Coral's home. Once, when friends brought over a birthday cake for Coral, her father ridiculed her and her mother for participating in such a ridiculous ritual. Coral's mother told her she could not have a birthday cake again.

And then there was Coral's high school graduation. She wanted very much to attend, but her father forbade it and her mother backed him up. Coral could not receive her degree unless she attended, so in the end she did. Of course, she was one of the only graduates there without a family member in attendance.

Through Coral's story, we come to understand how a girl who is strong and directed can nonetheless become the prey of a very strong and very sick man. Coral's insights help us understand how a girl stays in the incestuous relationship. Coral did not know she had a choice. She lived in a world where her father's word was the law. She coped by learning to numb her body so that she could barely feel the rapes. She intuitively knew that if she told her mother, nothing may have changed, and she endured the rapes rather than risk her mother not coming to her rescue.

The special place Coral could go in her mind during the rapes, with its song lyrics and lists and homework, saved her. Numbing her body and being totally disconnected from it helped her live through the parallel reality of being forced to be her father's "lover" (as he called her) for six years. Also, because she spent so many summers in her early years at her paternal grandmother's home with her cousins, she had a sense of being loved. Sometimes having just one person reach out with love can pull a girl through her trauma. Girls find all sorts of ways to survive incest. Some leave their bodies, others catalog plants in their head, some even develop a totally separate personality during the molestation. These are all survival strategies.

Coral is still with the same boyfriend. They now live together. They have been together for five years, and for the first time in her life Coral is able to enjoy sexual intimacy as a normal part of a romantic relationship, as an expression of love. Trusting her boyfriend and standing up for herself in the relationship are still big issues for her, and because she never learned to trust there is some tension. Coral struggled for a while to identify her pure artistic, intellectual, and musical sensibility and to weed out her father's influence. But, as we learned earlier from other girls reclaiming their joy in life, she has reclaimed her love of music and not only composes but also teaches music to children and teenagers. She is kind and warm and makes any child comfortable and safe at the piano. She has reclaimed those terrified moments at her piano lesson over and over and over again. She has a sense of her agency in every aspect of her life now. She hopes that her truth has touched you in some way that will help you to triumph too.

As a girl, when she wasn't being molested, Coral hung out with her friends and got into music and art. Garnet, another incest survivor, got into some pretty destructive behaviors after the molestation ended. She started smoking a lot of pot and cutting her arms, and she isolated herself from her friends. Garnet thought that all this would help her forget about her father molesting her, and it almost did—until he began to molest her sister.

GARNET

Garnet came to see me when she was nineteen. She was having trouble sleeping because she was afraid that her father, who had molested her over a time many years earlier, was now molesting her younger sister. The experience of her own molestation was also coming back to haunt her.

She had spent some of her young teen years cutting herself, and her parents and teachers never noticed. By the age of sixteen, she had a pretty serious drug and drinking problem. She'd been in a few bad relationships, had had bouts of serious depression, and always felt the shadow of her father's abuse. By the time I met Garnet, she had begun to settle down. She was teaching two art classes to young children and was going to college. She was working hard in her courses and at the teaching, which she really liked. But when she began to suspect that her father was abusing her younger sister and confronted him, he denied it. He denied molesting her sister, and he denied molesting Garnet. He told her that she was imagining things and that she needed help.

She came to therapy to try to get some sense of what to do for her sister. Why didn't she go to her mother? Because she didn't trust her mother and was afraid that she would permanently reject her. In fact, by the time she wrote this story, she had told her mother and confronted her father, and they had both betrayed her.

GARNET'S STORY

My Worry Spot

I was brought up on the Upper West Side of Manhattan. From the outside, my family looked oh-so-respectable. My mom is a high school guidance counselor, and my dad is a lawyer. We are Jewish, and when I was a kid we went to temple every Friday night. We looked like the perfect family—close and connected. But, behind closed doors, we barely spoke.

There are two kids in my family. I'm the oldest. My little sister is seven years younger than I am. Right before my adolescence, when my sister was a little kid, my dad started molesting me, and this went on for years. During adolescence, I got really depressed and started cutting myself. No one knew why—and they didn't even really seem to care. The few times my mom clued in to my depression, she just sort of brushed it off and said stuff like, "Oh, whatever it is you're going through, it will pass. Teens always get stressed out." You see, for a couple of years my dad and I had been acting as if nothing sexual had ever happened between us. I thought I could just forget about it and move on.

My dad first molested me when I was around nine. I remember the first time it happened. We were watching wrestling on TV. My dad and I were sitting on this big easy chair. The fireplace jutted out of the wall, and there was a space between the fireplace and the wall. We moved the chair closer to the TV into that little niche in the wall.

My father put his hand around the top of my jeans. I thought, "This is weird." Then he started to touch me. He groped around inside my underpants. I pushed his hand away and he put my hand under his butt and sat on it. I pretended nothing was happening and that I was just watching the wrestling. You see, my dad had always paid a lot of attention to me. He would take me hiking, he helped me with my homework, stuff like that. My mom was pretty checked out and never gave me much attention or showed much affection. My father was silent. He was putting his fingers in and around my vagina, and it really hurt. I do remember that, feeling the physical pain and then just watching the wrestling. (Needless to say, to this day I cannot watch wrestling. I have to go to the bathroom and vomit if I see it for more than a moment when the channels are changing.)

It's hard for me to explain how I just let him do this to me. Sure, it is crazy to have your dad put his hands into your under-wear, and I even surprised myself by not doing anything, but there was this odd combination of trust and fear and shame and terror that I did not want to deal with, so I actually pretended it wasn't happening.

After that incident, my father was all nice to me again. For about two weeks everything was normal, and I tried to pretend it had never happened. Then one night my father came into my bedroom. I had a very high bunk bed, and he asked me to come down. I said no, I was tired, and he started climbing up the ladder. I'd tried to kid myself that I had forgotten all about the other inci-dent, but obviously I had not. I got this creepy feeling all over and gave the ladder a shove. He fell onto his back. When he stood up again, he said with a sick grin, "What's the matter, Garnet? Daddy just wants to kiss you good night."

I was so scared. He told me that I was Daddy's princess and that he would never hurt me. He asked me to please make him happy. Then he climbed into my bed and started to fondle me. He told me that this was the right thing and that it was time that I learned about men. He said that he would teach me what I needed to know. This felt really weird for about a minute, and then I blocked out the feeling and began to recite childhood hand-clapping games in my head ("Miss Mary Mac Mac Mac, all dressed in black black black, with silver buttons buttons but-tons, all down her back back back, she asked her mother mother mother, for fifty cents cents cents, to see the elephants elephants

elephants, jump over the fence fence fence, they jumped so high high high, they reached the sky sky sky, and they never came back back back, till the fourth of July -ly -ly...Miss Mary Mac Mac Mac"). And then he was gone. I pulled up my panties and fell asleep.

My mother was involved in a lot of educational committees at the school she worked in, and many evenings my father stayed home and took care of me and my baby sister. Those were the nights I ended up in my father's bed. It's so strange. I don't even know how I got in there. It was like I was in a fog. He'd laugh this sick laugh and call out for me, and the next thing I knew my wrists were being tied to the bedposts of my parents' bed with this ugly pale purple scarf. It was one of those cheap ones from a ninety-nine-cent store. (I know that scarf is still in the house.) He always put a pillow over my head, too. He didn't want to see me or me to see him.

I remember the first time he tied me up. All of a sudden his mouth was there. I remember thinking, this feels weird, but I just pretended water had gotten down there. I was just going into puberty. What the hell did I know? At first, I thought, I'll be okay, I'll be okay, but then I realized how totally gross this was, and I was desperate to focus on something else. Of course, it was always really hard to focus on anything with that pillow over my face; it was easier when my face wasn't covered. I would try to pretend that I was floating in a fog, seeing beautiful colors.

He molested me in other parts of the house, too, and in the car; and he almost always kept my back to him. That made it easier for me, too. I could focus out the window of the car or at the TV.

One time we were in his room and he had me tied up with the purple scarf and the pillow in front of my face when I felt something heavy drop on my chest. It felt slimy and hard, and heavy, and I was like, oh my God, and I started squirming around until the pillow came off my face. That was when I saw my father's erect penis on my chest. It was huge and hideous. A drop of his semen had fallen onto this one little spot on my chest. I freaked out and started screaming, but he didn't stop. He just put the pillow back over my face and continued molesting me.

After that night, I started scrubbing that spot obsessively to try to clean myself. Sometimes I'd scrub it until I bled. I would have to put Band-Aids on it. Even now the spot seems permanently bruised and red. Whenever I am really nervous or scared about anything, I still rub that little spot on my chest. I call it my worry spot.

I tried to talk to my mom while all this was going on. I'd plead with her to take me to her meetings at night. But she said she counted on me to help my dad take care of my sister. When I told her that "Daddy tells me to keep secrets" and asked if I could tell her, she said, "If they are secrets then you'd better not. You know you're Daddy's princess."

I felt so isolated. I mean, my mom was nice to me and all; in fact, she was just nice enough to me for me to think she loved me. She didn't yell at me much, we went to temple together, she made my lunch for school. But I never felt my mom was ever really listening to me, and I learned early on that the way to be accepted in my family was not to rock the boat. I was a good, compliant child. I always wanted to be closer to her, but I was afraid that if I tried I would get turned away.

From the ages of ten to fourteen, the molestation continued. I was a good girl and did my schoolwork, played with my friends, and loved my cats. I remember the comfort of my cats and loving to snuggle with them and talk to them. No matter what, they always accepted me. I tried to have a good time in between the molestations.

Then, when I turned fourteen, something strange happened. My dad lost interest in me. My breasts had started to develop and I got my period, and suddenly he stopped coming around. That year felt like a vacation, but there was always the fear that he might start up with me again. I became very anxious and depressed, and I started smoking cigarettes, then pot. My mom wasn't tuned in, and I began to really go downhill in school.

When I was fifteen, I finally confronted my father. I told him that I was messed up and that I needed to talk about the sexual abuse, and he said, "Abuse? By whom?" I was shocked. I said, "By you!" And he said, "Oh Garnet, do not even think about destroying this family. Everyone knows what a vivid imagination you have. Who do you think they'll believe? You or me? Plus, I know all about the pot you've been smoking. I can report you." He actually threatened to turn me in!

That was when I started cutting my arms. When I'd cut, I was the one in control. I think it was like, if I hurt myself first, no one else can hurt me. The problem was there was no feeling, no pain—only blood. But seeing the blood felt oddly comforting. It was tangible proof that I was alive, and I guess I needed to know that.

It's so weird about my mom. Here she was, Mrs. Big in the community. She had lots of friends and was always helping girls at her high school deal with abortions and family problems and stuff.

She even stood up to my father on certain issues. For example, she maintained her Democratic political beliefs, and my father is a hard-core Republican. But nothing I did ever got my mother's attention. She always seemed oblivious to what was going on with me and my dad. She didn't even notice when I started cutting my arms.

I've always wondered how she could have not known about my dad. I told her many times that I didn't want to be alone with him, and I remember always wishing she would figure it out or walk in when my dad had me tied up. But she never did. My mom likes things status quo. If everything looks okay, then it is okay. I tried to bring up the abuse with her a few times, but somehow I knew she would choose my dad. Not that they got along great or anything, but she certainly wouldn't have wanted that mess on her hands. I just tried to bury the memories by getting stoned a lot and hanging out with my friends. I went from an A student to a C or D student. Even though it's been a few years since my father stopped molesting me, I certainly didn't feel good about myself. I would escape any way I could. When I was stoned I would fool around with boys; it didn't matter what they did to me. Things had become pretty unbearable at home. But, every year that my father didn't molest me, I began to feel a little bit better. Eventually, toward the end of high school, I realized that I would have to improve in school in order to get into college and out of their house, so I started focusing on academics and joined the drama crew at school. I stopped drinking and drugging and cutting, but I still hated being around my parents and was having bad dreams. At least I was able to push down the memories more effectively. When I graduated high school, my parents wouldn't pay for an out-of-state college, so I enrolled in school in another borough of New York City and moved in with one of my girlfriends and her family.

After I moved out, I kept in touch with my little sister, who was ten when I left. One day I went to my parents' house to pick up something. They weren't expecting me or anything, I just showed up. When I got to the top of the stairs I could see into my sister's bedroom. I could see my dad's back and my sister struggling to pull up her pants and put on her shirt. My father bolted out of her room and headed for the bathroom. I freaked out. I was shaking all over. I grabbed my sister and said, "What just happened with Daddy?" She pulled away from me and said, "Nothing! Why are you acting so weird?" Her eyes were kind of dead, like she was in a trance or something.

It had been four or five years since he'd touched me, but all the pain just came roaring back. I saw myself as a little girl, and I couldn't stop shaking. When my father came out of the bathroom, he very matter-of-factly said, "Hey Garnet, what's up?" That's when I became determined to stop him.

I found Dr. Patti through a friend, and I started therapy because I had to save my sister and someone told me she worked with abuse survivors. Dr. Patti told me that we would have to call child welfare to report the abuse of my sister, but first we could call my mother in for a session and try to all call from the session. I was so scared. More than anything, I wanted to bust this open and have my mother finally deal with it. So we called my mother in, and my therapist helped me tell her what had happened to me and what I was sure was going on with my sister. Initially my mother actually believed me. That really surprised me. She held my hand and cried. She even revealed to me that she had been molested by an uncle when she was a little girl. I told her about the sick purple scarf my dad had used with me, and she admitted that he had tied her up with that scarf, too. She cried and she held me. I couldn't even remember the last time my mom had held me like that. She said first we will go home and confront your father, then we will call Children's Services.

When my mother went home and confronted my father, of course he flatly—and I mean flatly—denied everything. He said that I had a vivid imagination. He said that he believed that I believed it, but that of course it was not true. He started going on about my drug use and how sometimes drugs can increase the imagination. That's when my world really came tumbling down. My mother called me and told me what my dad had told her, and she ended the conversation with "Garnet, I believe that you believe this, but it cannot be true. Why would your dad lie?" I tried to give her details to convince her, but she ended up taking my dad's side.

I called Children's Services and reported the abuse anonymously. Then where was I? I had opened up the can of worms that my father had warned me not to. I continued to live at my friend's house, but I never told her anything about my family problems. I started going to Dr. Patti's sexual-abuse survivors' group, and I felt a lot of support from the other girls. It was the first time I realized you could never tell from appearances who had been abused. The girls in the group were beautiful girls. They were smart and nice and cool. It made me think, "Wow, I wonder who else I know has gone through something like me?"

Meanwhile my father was interviewed by Child Welfare Services and of course he portrayed me as a drug user and troubled adolescent. I was no longer allowed to go home, and my mother wouldn't even let me take my favorite cat. The Child Welfare

Services investigators decided against prosecuting my father. They said there was no physical proof, and that, because my sister didn't back up my accusations, they couldn't proceed. They described my father as decent and a good parent. Ha.

My father actually had the nerve to call me a few times to say I should drop everything. Then he called me on my birthday and said that I would always be his love. He said that he and I know it is all true but that he will never admit it, so I should just tell everyone it's a lie. Then he started calling me three times a week and pleading with me to say that I had made it all up. He said not to worry and that he would forgive me. His calls only made me angrier. I told him that if he kept calling me, he would have to talk to my lawyer. The calls stopped, but candy was delivered to my door on Valentine's Day with a card saying I should give up the lie and that he still loves me.

Until I spoke about my abuse, I had this strange fear inside me, that somehow he still had power over me because I was keeping his secret. But now my father has no power over me. I'm an adult, and no one can force me to do anything I don't want to do. Now, with the support of my therapist, the group, and a few close friends, I am beginning to reclaim my life. I am working part time and have taken out student loans for school. My parents don't financially support me anymore, and I wouldn't want them to. I still have bad dreams, I still freak out sometimes when I am touched in a certain way, and I still get depressed at times, but I do feel better. I don't feel the need to escape with smoking pot, I don't want to cut myself, I am basically learning to live with myself and have stopped blaming myself for all that has happened. I feel like this incredible weight has been lifted from me—the weight of my father's psyche, the weight of his body, the weight of his secret.

I am taking back my childhood bit by bit. It feels for the first time in my life like I am free. My worry spot is a reminder, but I can rub my worry spot and know that no one will violate me ever again, so I still rub it when I'm feeling freaked out. But now I tell my body that we will be all right.

MY THOUGHTS

Garnet was incredibly brave and loving of her sister. She took a lot of risks. She may not have been able to disclose her own abuse while it was happening, but, as many girls do, she told to protect her sister. By reporting her abuse, she took the risk of breaking up her family. She knew that her family might turn on her and deny the abuse, but she felt that, no matter what the immediate outcome, her little sister would know, somewhere inside, however deep, that Garnet had tried to protect her.

In the short run, her worst fears came true. Her father played out his threat and her sister lied, and she lost her family. She still struggles with this loss. She lost contact with her sister, who ran away from home at the age of fifteen. Eight years after Garnet reported the abuse, Garnet's sister called her. Through her sobs, she told Garnet what she already knew—that their father had been molesting her and that was why she ran away. Her sister admitted she was prostituting and a drug addict. She called Garnet to thank her for trying to help and promised that she would be in touch.

Garnet still holds out the hope that one day her sister, who is now eighteen, will show up on her doorstep.

Meanwhile, Garnet will always have her worry spot, to remind her of her pain—and her triumph.

LIFE AFTER INCEST

I've worked with so many girls who thought they could never be whole again because they were incest survivors, and I've seen so many come through this horrible ordeal, as Coral and Garnet both did. Garnet and Coral are doing really well now. You can read about their lives in Chapter 16, "Flowers Bloom." The beginning of getting through incest is simply knowing it was not your fault—not one bit of it. You are not alone. Wounds do heal. If you were the survivor of incest, you may always feel the remnants of a scar, but you will not always feel the tremendous ache of a gaping wound. Incest survivors do get beyond their incest to lead happy, wonderful lives. They can have healthy, intimate sexual relationships. As you have seen in Coral's and Garnet's stories, and will see throughout this book, there is a strength in the human spirit that cannot be crushed, even in the face of the most violating abuse.

THERE ARE WAYS OUT

If you are still living at home, there are things you can do to protect yourself. You may not be ready to face the consequences that might result from telling your mother, but, no matter how young you are and how dependent you are on your parents for housing and support, there are many other things you can do.

First of all, I want you to realize that through each positive decision you have made in your life—finding friendships that are deep and strong, joining the debate team, playing the guitar, taking up acting, playing soccer, picking up this book—you made the choice to live your life, and please remember it is your life. With each positive step you take, you are healing some of the pain your molester inflicted on you. One young woman once told me, "My father thought he had me, he thought I was his, but I was only lost. Now I am myself and he cannot touch me."

Second, incest is against the law. In some cases I do recommend that you report it. This is not to say that reporting holds no risks. The authorities will check out your situation, and it is usually your word against your perpetrator's. If you live with the perpetrator, he may be removed from the home—or you may be. The truth is that sometimes reporting can cause more problems for a young girl under the age of eighteen. She may be sent to foster care, she may be in the middle of college applications, finding her way out. And mostly she may know that if she reports it, her mother could reject her. If you cannot get out of your situation....In the meantime:

- Try to find someone you can trust and start talking about it. Tell a trusted teacher or principal in your school. Although they are mandated reporters, they can help you figure out where you can live if your mother throws you out.
- Find a family member or friend to take you in. Or a trusted friend whose parents you trust and who will believe you.

If you think that no one will believe you or protect you from your abuser, I do not suggest you run away. I recommend you look into teen centers in your area. Go to one of them, and talk to the social workers there. You can say it is about your friend.

But you can get information on where you could possibly find safe housing in case your family rejects you.

If you cannot leave your home, if you are too scared, if the abuse has stopped for a long time and you believe it won't happen again and you are graduating high school soon, then make sure to stay away from your home as much as possible.

- Stay away from your father (or perpetrator) as much as you can.
- If you see any weakness in your perpetrator, you can try to threaten him with a call to the police.
- If you are pretty sure he won't physically harm you, if he does *not* have a gun or another weapon, try to tell him no. Believe it or not, this sometimes works; more often, of course, it doesn't.
- Sleep over at friends' houses. If you are not ready to tell details until you move out of your home, find a trusted friend and try to stay at her home. I have known girls who've lived at a friend's home during their senior year of high school. Sometimes the abuser will not want to stir the pot and have information come out by pushing you to come home.
- Find some way to support yourself financially.
- Do as well as you can in school so that you have a good chance of earning a scholarship for college or vocational training. Or if those options are not available to you, try to live with a friend while you join the workforce. Once you are eighteen years old, try everything you can to get away from your molester.

Even if none of these suggestions work for you, please know that what you are feeling—whatever it may be—is normal, and that one day you will be able to get away. For now, you can go to our Resource Center to find lots of websites, supportive services, and other resources to help you cope.

When someone forces you into an incest relationship, he forcibly tries to take something precious from you. Just remember, he can't take it forever, and he will never ever own it. Your body, your spirit, and your heart are yours and only yours, and if you start to process your sexual abuse now, you will get them back forever.

CHAPTER 8

TOO CLOSE FOR COMFORT

Other Incest—Brothers, Cousins, Uncles, Stepfathers (Topaz's Story, Sage's Story)

heart jumping
body shivering
fingers clutching
zippers unzipping
sanity escaping
good-bye little girl...

—a sixteen-year-old sibling-abuse survivor

Of course, incest doesn't happen only between fathers and daughters. Many girls are sexually molested by their brothers, uncles, and cousins. The wound may be different and the betrayal perhaps not as deep as when a father or stepfather is the abuser, but abuse within families is always traumatic, no matter who perpetrates it.

BROTHER-SISTER INCEST

Brother-sister incest is one of the most complicated of all forms of sexual abuse. The statistics on it come primarily from the foster-care system. In fact, Mary Walker has observed over her forty years as a specialist on the foster-care system that as many as 90 percent of kids in foster care report having been sexually abused. We have better data on these kids not only because they are in the system but because if they are permanently adopted, their new parents will usually seek services—such as social work or therapy. When a foster child displays unusual behavior, such as overt masturbation or fear of being touched, the prior abuse is uncovered. But it is impossible for us to know how widespread either biological or stepsibling incest is, since what goes on in private families often stays private unless someone comes forward to report it. And, given the shame and secrecy that surrounds incest, that just doesn't happen too often.

What we do know is that brothers (and sometimes sisters) do sometimes sexually abuse their (usually) younger siblings and that many of you reading this book will have had this experience. This chapter is for you. (While foster-care abuse is obviously a very important issue, this book is focused on invisible girls, girls whose stories aren't being told, so we'll be examining biological and stepsibling abuse.)

First, let's define terms. *Sibling sexual abuse* means any inappropriate touching or other sexual behavior between siblings. Being fondled, having your private parts touched or being forced to touch someone else's, being made to watch someone masturbate, being penetrated, being asked to view pornographic materials, being repeatedly walked in on in the bathroom or bedroom—these are all forms of sexual abuse. Any child over six can be an abuser; the abused can be as young as two or three.

Sometimes sibling abuse goes on for years. In his book *Sibling Abuse*, Vernon Wiehe devotes a short chapter to sexual abuse—short, in part, because reliable information is so hard to come by. As Wiehe points out, it is far easier to track emotional and physical abuse between siblings than it is to track sexual abuse. Sexual abuse between siblings is usually kept hidden either because there's so much shame or because there's confusion about what it is and why it is allowed to go on.

Just as with father-daughter incest, in families where there is sibling incest, there is always some problem with weak parenting. Girls will often say they didn't have the necessary closeness with a parent to tell them what was happening. You may occasionally hear about a single incident where a brother tried to molest his sister but got caught and punished. Sure, that happens—but it's rare. One of my clients told me of her mother walking in the room while her brother was molesting her. His pants were open, and he was holding his sister's hand on his penis. Her mother looked in, saw them on her bed, and then shut the door. Later that evening she blamed her daughter and told her that she was bad and dirty for "doing stuff" with her brother. She was nine years old and her brother was sixteen. Often, there's a long pattern of sibling sexual abuse within the home, and the parents are either oblivious or dismissive. And girls are left feeling totally trapped and confused.

Many teen girls feel tremendous guilt and shame about "letting" their brothers "get away with it"; younger girls will tend to have more fears. In all cases, it is safe to say that the parents weren't present in some important way. Again, it is never the survivors fault!

TOPAZ

I met Topaz when she was sixteen. It was her aunt who brought us together. I was speaking about incest and sex abuse at a local high school when one of the social workers approached me to tell me about her niece. She began to sob as she spoke of the guilt she felt about not protecting her niece from her nephew. "Why couldn't I see it?" she choked out, tears streaming down her face. She went on to explain that her niece had just been released from a two-month hospitalization for a suicide attempt by overdose. During her stay, she revealed that she had been sexually abused by her older brother for four years.

As I would later discover in sessions with Topaz, the abuse began when she was ten. She and her brother lived alone with their mother in an affluent New York suburb. Their mother worked long hours in Manhattan and was rarely around. They were Italian American. Both children attended private school and were good students, although John, Topaz's brother, had started getting into trouble for cutting classes in junior high. When he hit high school, he started drinking and staying out late. Most of the time he seemed to be seething inside.

Topaz, by contrast, was sweet and outgoing. She was in the Model UN at school, was very social, and had many girlfriends. Topaz was the type of girl you could count on. She could keep her friends' secrets, she could always be relied on for school projects, and she came through for friends, teachers, and family.

One day after school, when she was fifteen, Topaz came home and swallowed what remained of a bottle of Tylenol. As she began to fall asleep, she realized she did not want to die. She managed to get to the phone to call her best friend and tell her what she had done. Her best friend and her best friend's mom raced over and took Topaz to the emergency room. The hospital contacted Topaz's mom, and she showed up at the hospital within the hour. That's when Pandora's box burst open.

TOPAZ'S STORY

My Aunt Saved My Life

I am sixteen years old and have been in therapy (with Patti) for about a year. For a while I could keep everything together, at least on the outside, but then I crashed. I think that crash saved my life. Pretty ironic that it took an overdose to save me.

My brother and I live in a very affluent area of Westchester County, New York. Our parents got divorced when we were very young. We barely ever saw our dad when we were young, and now we never see him. He moved to London and has a new family. Our mom is something of a workaholic. She is an investment banker and keeps very long hours. My brother and I have always had au pairs or nannies taking care of us.

When my brother got to be a teenager, we all agreed that we could be on our own for the most part and no longer needed live-in help. So from then on—I was ten and he was about thirteen—we would only have babysitters from the time we got home from school until our mother came home at around 8 P.M. That's when things started to get weird with my brother. My mother's room is on the ground floor, and ours are upstairs. Once we would go up to bed, she would go into her home office, also on the ground floor, and do more work. She had no idea what was going on.

My brother and I were very different. I always wanted to be perfect. I wanted to do really well in school, never make waves with my friends, and keep my mom happy. My brother and I never really talked about anything deep, but we did hang out a lot and played soccer together and also talked about music. He was usually pissed off about something or at someone, but he was pretty nice to me. I think that's what was so confusing about the whole thing.

Now a bit about my mom. She has always been super-ambitious, but when she met my father she decided to stop working and have kids. When my brother was little, she spent a lot of time with him, and then I was born when my brother was three. My mom continued to stay home with us until I turned three and my brother was six. That's when my father announced that he was moving out with his secretary. Because I was such a little kid, I really don't know much more about it than that. All I know is that my mother started working again and my world changed. I realize now that my mother became much more emotionally remote when my father left; she wasn't there for me even when she was home. I think it really wasn't her work so much as her depression.

I was really lonely and leaned on my brother for "kid" companionship. We had our babysitters and they were nice, but I still felt lonely. My mother would work long hours and then come home and read or do more work-related projects, but she didn't really talk to us or spend any time with us. I was craving love and attention and affection at that time.

Once I got a little older and started doing really well in middle school, she started paying some attention to me. She liked to help me with my schoolwork and projects and would tell me how proud she was of my good grades. Even though we didn't talk about a lot of personal things or really connect, that was the only time I can remember my mother focusing on me. It wasn't predictable or anything, but I did enjoy it. Until high school, I was still very much a pleaser.

My brother was much more daring and independent. He always did well in school, but he wouldn't give my mom the time of day, especially as he got to be a teenager. He was always off either with his friends or playing soccer.

By the time I was a teenager, I started realizing how much my mom was not there for me, and I started to reject her. I was really pissed off. She did not fight it, and the three of us kind of led parallel lives. Except at night. That is when my brother and I would have sexual contact.

It all started when I was about ten. One day my brother, who was thirteen at the time, brought me over to the neighbor's to play soccer. Our neighbor was a very "cool" seventeen-year-old. His parents were never around, and, as it turns out, he and my brother were hooking up, but I didn't know it at the time. They told me to come inside for some cookies, and then they both asked me to watch them play a game. Up to that point, I was having a great time. Well, it turned out that the game was that the neighbor would jerk off my brother and then my brother would jerk him off. I froze—I was shocked and scared. I didn't know what to do. I sat there and ate my cookies and looked down, and didn't say a word. I avoided the neighbor after that.

That night when I was in bed, my brother snuck into my room. He said, "Hey, what Josh and I did is really fun. I want to teach you how to do it, too." I told him I didn't want to and that it kind of grossed me out. He said okay and left.

Then, about a week later, my mom and brother had a huge fight. He came into my room crying, and I felt really bad for him. He told me he felt really unloved and asked if he could just sleep in my bed with me. I said okay. I was a little nervous, but nothing happened. He actually did this a number of times over the next few months, just come in and sleep in my bed. My mom didn't seem to notice.

My brother really seemed sad and would tell me that I was the only one who really loved him. But he never touched me or anything. He also stopped hanging out with our neighbor. And I started liking the warmth of another body in my bed with me.

After about six months of this, things changed. One night I was dozing off, and I felt my brother begin to rub up against me. I did not know what was going on, but I just pretended to be asleep. He started doing more and more stuff to me, and I just kept pretending to be asleep. He put my hands on his genitals, and then he touched me. I knew it was wrong, but I didn't have anyone to talk to. My brother and I never talked about it, and I never told.

The weird thing is, it would go on for a few weeks and then not for months, and then it would start up again. When I was about twelve, I hit puberty and got my period. This may sound really strange, but that's when I started to like how it felt when my brother touched me. We never had intercourse or anything, but we would touch each other in very sexual ways and my body would feel really good. This was probably the most confusing time in my life. As much as my body was reacting, in my mind I knew it was gross, it was wrong, and yet I didn't stop it. I started to have irritable bowel syndrome, where I couldn't go to the bathroom for days on end. Now I realize it was because I was holding in so many of my feelings, but at the time it just felt awful.

The stuff with my brother continued on and off for the next two years. Then one day it just stopped. My brother got serious with a girlfriend, and he never came to me again. After a few months of my brother not approaching me, I actually started to relax a little, and my stomach problems were less intense.

When I was fifteen he went off to college. That's when I started thinking about the incest a lot. I feared that what I had done was disgusting and wrong and that somehow everyone knew I had liked it. I felt terribly ashamed, but I really missed my brother. So I kept really busy. Honestly, I don't know how my mother couldn't have noticed that something was wrong.

I did try to have boyfriends. Of course, most of them just wanted to hook up, without any relationship, but after what had happened with my brother, that felt natural to me. I just kept finding new boys to hook up with, and I started to get a strange reputation in my school. I was seen as this really nice girl and good student and not really a slut, but a girl who would not say no to guys.

Of course, no one knew how totally depressed I was. One day I couldn't take it anymore and decided I wanted all my feelings to end, so I took a bottle of Tylenol. But once I started to feel drowsy, I got scared and called my best friend, whose mom I also really trusted. Thank goodness they were home. They took me to the hospital, and my stomach was pumped. I was so tired from coming off the Tylenol that I didn't have the energy to lie, and when my best friend asked me why I had done it, I could not stop crying. I told her all about my brother sexually abusing me. I just spilled everything out.

My mother, my aunt, and my best friend's mom were also all in the room, and everyone freaked out.

As soon as I told, I regretted it. I shut down and refused to talk about it anymore. But my mother made me see a counselor. I didn't want to talk about it and I didn't trust the counselor, and things just got worse. I was so depressed that I stopped focusing on school and just slept a lot. Then I was hospitalized. They put me in a ward with other adolescents who had problems—eating disorders, depression, sexual abuse—and I began to talk with other kids about what had happened.

The family therapist made my brother come to a session where I had to tell him how upset I was with him for doing what he'd done. It was in that session that my brother broke down and admitted that the neighbor had sexually abused him starting when he was about ten and the boy was thirteen. By the time my brother was twelve, it had become habitual. He said his abusing me was his way out and away from the neighbor. It really confused me seeing my brother break down like that. I was finally angry and it felt good, but, when my brother started crying, I actually felt sorry for him, and that put me in a strange place.

When I finally got out of the hospital, the kids at school had a lot of questions. It was really hard. My mother also got into therapy, and it came out that she had been abused by her uncle when she was a little girl and had never told anyone about it. She started to realize that a part of her was so terrified that I could be abused that she had just closed off her feelings. This is very sad, because it turns out that the cycle of abuse continued, both with my brother and with me.

Needless to say, there was a lot of pain around our house. My mother told me how sorry she was for not being a part of my life, but she continued to work long hours and still wasn't really there for me.

Then my aunt told me about a therapist, Dr. Patti, she had heard speak at her school about sex abuse. My aunt brought me to my first session with Dr. Patti. I joined the survivors' group, and that's what really began my healing. I was filled with shame and conflicting feelings, and I had to forgive myself big time. The group supported my anger toward my brother. I still can't really imagine ever forgiving my brother. I do not feel any pity for him. As a matter of fact, I'm still really pissed off at him. I am also really angry at my mom. The one person who really came through for me was my aunt. I moved in with her after the hospitalization, and that probably saved my life—at least my emotional life—because she told me again and again that it wasn't my fault, what happened with my brother. She reminded me that my brother and I were just confused and scared.

It's funny, but although my aunt was never all that involved in my family before, she feels the worst. She tells me over and over again how sorry she is that she didn't figure out what was happening and do something. I think she takes it especially hard because she's a social worker who works with teens and thinks she should have known somehow. I know she feels really guilty, but I always ask her how she could have known. I remind her that I wore many masks: the good girl, the good student, the happy kid, the sister who loved her brother. It's that last mask that still confuses me the most.

MY THOUGHTS

Topaz was a very lonely kid. Her mom wasn't around much, and her brother was her only real companion. She was comforted by having him sleep next to her in a home where she felt little closeness and comfort from adults. We can actually see a lot of parallels between Topaz's story and Coral's and Garnet's. Like Topaz, both Coral and Garnet wanted their mothers' support but never got it. We know that Garnet's mother suffered abuse, and so did Topaz's. These mothers weren't close enough to their daughters to intuit the abuse. And Topaz's mother was ignorant of what was happening not only with her daughter but also with her son. All three girls were left on their own at a critical time.

Of course, we also see how sexual abuse and incest cycles through families. It turns out that Topaz's brother felt deeply rejected by his father leaving. Then, when his mother started working after having been pretty accessible to him during the first six years of his life, the feeling of rejection and aloneness intensified. When he was just ten years old, his thirteen-year-old neighbor started paying attention to him, and he craved that attention. Unfortunately, the attention was sexual and totally inappropriate. Topaz's brother revealed in family therapy that the neighbor was also being abused—by his coach. Her brother wanted to break away from the abuser but did not know how. Plus, he continued to get something important from the connection that he wasn't getting anywhere else. It's a pattern we see often: many boys who are abused turn around and abuse someone else. It is interesting that girls who are abused usually turn out to be massively protective of children.

In family therapy, Topaz's brother talked about how, as an adolescent, he was terrified of being gay and he was afraid of girls, so his sister seemed like his least threatening choice. When a girl his age finally showed some interest in him, he no longer needed to sexualize his sister.

The thing that was so confusing for Topaz was that she enjoyed the physical sensations, and that made her ambivalent about stopping him and ashamed when she didn't. The fact is, our bodies are conditioned to respond to sexual touch. But most important to note is that, in most incest situations, the abuser sweetens up the abused first, and this is precisely what Topaz's brother did. By coming to her crying, by wanting to cuddle with and sleep with her, especially when she too was feeling vulnerable and lonely, he gained her trust. This was very confusing. Because Topaz was such a pleaser, she felt sorry for her brother and wanted to make things okay. But it wasn't okay. Her brother knew how and where to touch her to arouse her, and she felt confused by her body. Girls of this age will often say they felt "deceived" by their bodies. No matter how they might be feeling—angry, upset, sad—their bodies are still aroused. That's why girls who have been abused will often hook up with lots of other boys—just for some of those familiar feelings of being touched. Another reason sexual abuse survivors may hook up with boys is because they think that's all they're worth. That's what they've been taught.

Once again, it's striking how the lack of a mother's support can be so damaging to a girl. These mothers never figured out what was going on. But there's no real surprise there, either. Siblings often have a pretty easy time keeping secrets from their parents, especially if their parents are themselves hiding an incest secret. It seems amazing that people can live in such a state of denial, but it happens all the time. As we discussed earlier, often the mother is in a dysfunctional relationship herself and can't face what's going on, or she feels powerless to do anything about it.

A girl recently wrote to my website Girlthrive:

When I was twelve and my brother was sixteen he used to come up to me and squeeze my breasts. He thought this was the funniest thing in the world, that my breasts were growing. I was mortified. When I told my mom, she told him to stop, but he never did and she never pressed the issue. Now that I am fourteen I hate to be touched by anyone. I am jumpy, especially around boys. I always feel as if someone is going to come up and grab my chest. Was this sexual abuse?

Of course it was sexual abuse! Many girls get confused when there's no genital contact, but any unwanted pinch of the butt or chest is sexual abuse, especially if it is allowed to go on without punishment (of the perpetrator), and it can be very distressing to girls who are entering adolescence. Next, we hear from Sage, another girl who was betrayed by her parents, especially her mother.

SAGE

Sage's molester didn't live in her home. He was an older cousin. Unfortunately, he was often left alone to take care of Sage, and her parents were too busy to notice that anything was wrong. He started molesting Sage when she was eleven. She liked having him around because he paid attention to her. They played cards, they ordered pizza for dinner, they played video games. The abuse actually seemed a reasonable price to pay—at least for a while. When she was around thirteen, she started getting more creeped out by it and told her mother. To her mother's credit, she forbade the cousin from ever setting foot in the house again. But she never asked Sage if she was all right, and she made it clear that there would never be any discussion about it. So, her parents never brought it up again and remained aloof as she was growing up.

I first met Sage when she was seventeen and a friend brought her to one of my sex-abuse survivors' groups. She had just disclosed her abuse to a friend, and that friend knew she'd need support. We worked together throughout her senior year of high school, but then, when she turned eighteen, her parents threw her out of the house and told her to fend for herself. Because they'd never really provided even the basics for her, she wasn't all that surprised, but she needed to figure out how to survive.

When she went for an interview to waitress in a topless club and was offered work as a topless dancer instead, she decided to do it because the money was so much better. She says she didn't really feel any shame or embarrassment about dancing topless. She'd learned many years earlier, she says, that feelings were dangerous; they led only to disappointment. She had learned very early on how to shut down her feelings and practically numb herself to the world. Her body may have been dancing, but her mind and her spirit were always somewhere else.

Sage's story not only gives us a glimpse into the world of women who dance topless but confirms what we have been saying about our male-dominated culture and its objectification of young women. It shows how an unsupportive family, sexual abuse, and a culture that views girls as sex objects can compel a girl to feel she is good for only one thing: her sex appeal.

SAGE'S STORY

My Family Threw Me Out

I am nineteen years old and a survivor of child molestation. From the ages of about eleven to thirteen I was made to do things that most kids don't begin to learn about until much later. In fact, the perpetrator was in his teens himself. He was eighteen when he started to molest me, and he was my cousin. He was a really nice guy, friendly, good looking—and he was really fun to be around. But sometimes he would force me to participate in oral sex, masturbation, and passionate kissing. I can remember him exposing his genitals to me and touching my private parts as well.

Looking back, I think I didn't tell right away because I didn't want him to stop coming over. That may sound sick, but, you know, at least Jack paid attention to me. My parents were very young, and they were very involved with each other and partying with their friends. I always felt like I was a bother to them. Jack was always over at the house, and when other people were around he played with me. He'd teach me card games, throw around a ball with me, and play Frisbee with me.

When I was thirteen I finally told my mom the truth about what Jack would do to me when he came over, and she told him never to set foot in the house again. She also told me to stop flirting and walking around in skimpy shorts, implying that what happened was somehow my fault. It's weird, but I kind of missed him. I didn't like how he pushed me sexually, but I did like having him around. At least he was around, which is more than I can say for my parents. For a very long time I was afraid of boys and relationships. I still have never had a boyfriend, and I actually still have never kissed a boy. So you will be surprised when I tell you that I danced topless for a year at a club.

Of course, I can't blame Jack alone for my becoming a topless dancer. My parents had a large part in everything too. And the money was really good. When I graduated from high school, my parents told me to move out and support myself. I shared an apartment with three other girls and was teaching children dance at a weekend program and taking courses during the week. I had a student loan and was a part-time college student, but I knew I couldn't make it through school without a better-paying job, so I started looking for full-time work. I heard you could get great tips as a waitress at this topless club near my apartment. When I went in to interview for a waitressing job, the woman managing the club asked me if I would be interested in topless dancing instead. I had studied modern dance for several years, and I loved to dance. It had never occurred to me to become a topless dancer. She told me I could make three times as much money if I danced and that I shouldn't worry about being unsafe. No one was allowed to touch the dancers. That's how I became a topless dancer at the age of eighteen. To put myself through college. I did it for about a year.

Almost all of the girls and women I worked with at the club had been sexually molested as young girls. No kidding. I know because they told me so. And they all came from families that were totally unsupportive of them. Let's just say most of us did not feel particularly loved growing up.

Let me tell you what it felt like to be a topless dancer. It may sound strange, but in some way it built my self-esteem. On slower nights I'd stand in front of a guy and dance. That's called a table dance. As I danced I would think, "Should I give him a forty-dollar dance or only a ten-dollar dance?" That felt like a lot of power. I knew how to get them to pay. I'd add up my money as I danced. I even enjoyed making them feel small and stupid. They'd ask me if I had a boyfriend and I'd say, "No, but if I did, it certainly wouldn't be you!"

It didn't gross me out to dance. I saved over $10,000 in one year to help pay for college, rent, bills, etc., and I just kept my life and my work totally separate. I never went out with customers. Never. Sometimes when I'd go home after a shift and snuggle with my cats and drink hot cocoa, I'd think, "I don't believe what I did today. I danced naked." But mostly I can't say I had many feelings about anything at the time. I knew I wanted to go to school and pay my bills and not depend on my parents for anything, because they were unreliable. I knew I had no power in my family, but as a dancer I did have power.

Just think of the symbolism. There I was, standing above these guys. I was looking down, and they were looking up to me. These bankers, lawyers, doctors—all they wanted was to talk with a beautiful young woman. They'd show me pictures of their kids, talk about their jobs, or ask about me. If I could keep them talking, I didn't even have to dance. Some nights I made several hundred dollars just talking to these men.

But I could also be really mean. I'd be witty and sarcastic and tell these men they could die wanting me because I would never be with them. I even smacked a few of them who tried to touch me. If a customer tried to touch my nipples I'd rip his hands off me and say, "You're not a very fast learner. Now sit on your hands!" I guess it's as if everything I couldn't say to my cousin as a kid came out with my customers.

There was one weird thing about it, though. I could always tell who was a pedophile. You see, I have a body like a little girl's. I am very petite. When Jack molested me I was barely developed. And if a customer would watch me in a certain way, I could almost feel his pedophilia. I can't explain how, but I just knew. When I had to dance for a pedophile, I'd get really nauseous. No amount of denial would work. I'd freak out and have to take a break.

I quit after a year, when I began to realize what a heavy price I was paying for the money. I was letting men use me as a fantasy object, and it started to get to me. After a while I would look out into the audience and envision the men as animals screaming and trying to touch us—all these young, battle-scarred girls.

Dancing definitely changed me. One of the changes is very obvious. I used to wear more revealing clothing: tight shirts, hip-hugger jeans with a short shirt to show off my pierced belly button. Now I wear overalls most of the time or baggy jeans.

Recently I told my mother that I'd been a topless dancer. She didn't seem shocked or anything, she just said I should be careful and to watch out for illegal behavior. She didn't really seem to care. And she actually said she would like to try it sometime.

I know I'll have a lot of emotional consequences from that work, but I don't want you to have a prejudice against topless dancers. I am not a prostitute, and many of the girls would never be with a customer. The girls who do have sex with customers are almost all abuse survivors who don't feel they're worth better. But they're not bad people.

It's still really difficult for me to get in touch with my feelings. But with Patti's help I filled out college student loan applications, and I just received a student loan and some financial aid. I'm beginning to sort things out and to feel better about myself. Maybe all that dancing was my way of trying to dance out some of my pain.

MY THOUGHTS

Of course, most girls who experience incest don't become topless dancers, but it makes sense that many dancers were molested as girls. They know how to dissociate. Sage used to dissociate the entire time on her job. She tuned in only when she felt her body being violated by a customer. Then she'd respond by either angrily removing his hand or yelling. And, when she sensed a pedophile, she would actually get sick and could not dissociate.

It was a challenge working with Sage because during our time together she was still dancing in the club. This was hard for me, because I could see what a great young woman she was and that there was a part of her that felt violated by her job, but she couldn't bring herself to quit. One day she admitted to herself and to me that she felt trapped and confused, just like when she was younger and molested by her cousin. Emotions started coming back, and she saw the men in the club as predators. The day she admitted that to herself was the day she was finally able to quit. Again, girls may take some detours to their healing, but have faith. You can always come back.

If you are a survivor of sibling abuse, please know you are probably keeping one of the best-kept secrets of all abuse. It is not your fault, you are not dirty, and you are not guilty. If you can, call a hotline, tell your abuser to stop, lock your door, or confide in a trusted relative.

I have worked with so many girls who have survived incest and moved on with their lives. I will tell you that some of them never did forgive their brothers or their cousins or their uncles, and some of that anger actually empowered them to move forward. You do not have to take this from anyone, not even your relatives.

CHAPTER 9

TRUSTING THE WRONG MEN

Abuse by Teachers, Coaches, Clergy, Doctors
(Ivy's Story)

> I kept getting better and better at tennis, and everyone
> was excited for me. What they didn't know was that my
> coach was having sex with me after our practices.
> —*a seventeen-year-old survivor of mentor abuse*

News of sexual abuse started coming out more in the media in
the nineties. The headlines were something like this: "Teacher
Arrested for Molesting a Student," "Coach Caught Sexually
Abusing a Teen Girl," "Rabbi Pleads Guilty to Molesting His
Neighbor." In 1999, Assistant Principal Richard Plass of Stuyve-
sant High School in New York City, one of the top schools in
the country, was arrested. Although there were dramatic photo-
graphs of him being led out of the school in handcuffs, he only
received four years' probation and was given a job in another
New York City high school. It turns out this fifty-five-year-old
man had been molesting a fifteen-year-old female student who
volunteered in his office. Another case that made headlines
back then involved a fortysomething teacher taking his sixteen-
year-old student across state lines to marry her. Then, in 2003,

John H. Dexter, the headmaster of a prominent New York City private school, the Trevor Day School, was arrested for downloading child pornography on school computers.

In August 2016 three investigative journalists from the *Indianapolis Star* broke the story of a doctor who was a serial sexual abuser. USA Gymnastics and Michigan State University failed for years to tell proper authorities of any sexual-abuse allegations against Dr. Larry Nassar, and his abuse had gone on for decades. He was employed there from 1997 through 2016. The several accusations against him at Michigan State went back to 1997 when a university athlete reported to the administration that Dr. Nassar "touched her vaginal area when she sought treatment for an injured hamstring." An Olympic gymnast named Rachael Denhollander read the story and called the investigative journalists to tell them about her abuse as a teen at the hands of Dr. Nassar. By the end of the investigation, more than 170 girls and women had come forward to tell their experiences of sexual abuse perpetrated by Nassar. In late May 2018 the first settlement was reached, and Michigan State agreed to pay $500 million to 332 girls and women who have survived sexual abuse by Dr. Larry Nassar. Also $75 million is being held in trust for other survivors who may come forward. As of the spring of 2018, settlements are still pending through the US Olympic Committee, USA Gymnastics.

Through the years many USA Gymnastics athletes came forward with variations of the same story. Some girls never told anyone until now about the sexual abuse they endured, yet several girls had previously told their parents, their coaches, university officials, other doctors. Some parents did not believe their daughters. USA Gymnastics did nothing, and, in spite of these allegations, for decades the abuse continued.

In January 2018, the survivors had their day in court, and Judge Rosemarie Aquilina gave them the platform to verbalize their experiences out loud to the courtroom and to Nassar himself. As heartbreaking as their stories are, the strength to speak out about their experiences and confront their abuser as a sisterhood of strong girls and women in a safe environment made it possible. They talked about how he lured them into thinking he was their friend, that what he was doing with his "treatments" was all part of the medical care they needed to be better athletes.

The first testimony was from Kyle Stephens. She was the only survivor who was not a gymnast; her parents were friends with Nassar. When twelve years old she was brave enough to tell her parents that Nassar had been sexually abusing her for years in their home. She told, and Dr. Nassar "convinced her parents she was a liar." It turns out that through the years her parents asked her to apologize to Dr. Nassar for saying he did bad things to her; they wanted her to apologize for lying.

This is a familiar outcome. All throughout our book there are times that girls tell and are either not believed or ignored or even blamed. Besides families that are overtly troubled and challenged, there are well-meaning parents who believe priests, teachers, rabbis, and coaches, over their child. These parents choose to believe "powerful" men over their children. Children are often not respected or heard—or believed. So many of these girls told their mothers that the doctor put his ungloved fingers inside their vaginas. But their parents did nothing. They deferred to the doctor. Girl after girl testified, and, as powerful as they all were, I could not help but think, "Why didn't any of these parents go up against the USA Gymnastics? Why didn't any of these parents confront Dr. Nassar?" Now that this truth has been exposed, there are parents of gymnasts suing the USA Gymnastics Corporation for suppressing and concealing their knowledge of known sexual abusers in the USAG program, including Dr. Larry Nassar.

The girls and their parents will bring more lawsuits, and I am hopeful that this case not only helps girls in the future but empowers parents to protect their children. Parents need to trust their children and make sure their children know that no one invades their bodies. Many of these parents seem to be loving, supportive parents who trusted authority figures and, in some cases, did not trust their intuition. By protecting their daughters now, they are helping them heal. Even though many of the girls did not feel safe telling their parents at the time, their parents now have the chance to become their champions, and that love and support can still be powerful in their healing.

Not only are there emotional consequences to this story, there are legal consequences. Larry Nassar was sentenced to over 170 years in prison. The USA Gymnastics board was forced to resign. Politicians are calling for an investigation of USA Gymnastics and the administration of Michigan State University. These girls were the sacrificial lambs. But, with the help of the investigative reporters who broke the story, survivors came through in record numbers and with the speed of light. Brave girls and women once again are the heroines! Sex-abuse survivors are the warriors who are changing the culture every day.

Nassar's case was a public exposure of a demented serial sexual abuser. But sexual abuse by mentors is happening every day in complicated ways. In this chapter we meet a girl whose parents stood by her yet still made her feel ashamed, and we meet a girl who was convinced she was having an "affair" with her abuser. We help you recognize mentor abuse and provide a clear path for you to get out if you are experiencing mentor abuse.

Sexual abuse isn't something that happens only in families, but 90 percent of the time it happens with someone you know and were probably told to trust. Mentor abuse happens in an uneven relationship where the girls are much younger than their mentors, coaches, doctors. Many girls are lured, coaxed, or even forced into sexual liaisons with older mentors, such as priests, rabbis, teachers, coaches, and so one, sometimes in exchange for favorable treatment, sometimes out of infatuation, sometimes entirely against their will. These are men who have some power over the girls' lives and who use their power to coerce girls into crossing inappropriate boundaries.

We have already seen how susceptible to pressure adolescent girls can be. And in Chapter 4 we looked at how having an unsupportive family can make you vulnerable to abuse. So it makes sense that sometimes a girl will fall prey to the manipulation of a man with great influence in her life—and often a very positive influence, as in the case of a coach, teacher, or clergyman. It can be all too easy to fall under his control. You like the attention of your coach, for example. It's very flattering and makes you feel special. But is it okay if he puts his arms around you "to console you" when you're alone in his office? Is it okay if he asks to kiss you? Is it okay to sleep with him if he tells you he loves you? No.

Of course, there's a big difference between the kind of encouraging warmth coaches may exhibit—from an arm around your shoulder after you missed a play to a hug at the end of a defeat—and sexual abuse. For instance, however annoying it may be, a coach who is obsessed with weight and hounds you to lose a few pounds and gain muscle in certain areas of your body to improve your ability at a sport is not sexually abusing you. However, if he laughs and stares at your breasts bouncing up and down as you shoot a basket, or even if he makes lewd comments but never touches you, that is sexual harassment, and it's not okay. Suffice to say that if you are feeling uncomfortable by the attentions of a teacher, clergyman, or coach, it's okay to question the behavior, to say stop, to get help from someone you trust. If you're confused about the line between inappropriateness and abuse, you can flip back to Chapter 2 for clarification. But trust your gut, trust your instinct. If you feel uncomfortable for any reason, tell a trusted friend or adult.

Mentor abuse is also all bound up with our male-dominated culture's obsession with youth and beauty. Remember Lolita? Apparently, many men find adolescent girls "irresistible." They think that when you are in your sports uniform or dressed up for church or trying out new teenage fashions, you are "asking for it." A girl sticking chewing gum behind her knee for an audition (see the story about the director of the *Lolita* remake and Adrian Lyne in Chapter 3) can somehow turn into "a seductress" in the mind of an abusive man.

Just listen to what Cardinal Francis George of Chicago had to say during the meeting of US cardinals with Pope John Paul II in April 2002: "There is a difference between a moral monster like [the Rev. John] Geoghan [who engaged in sex with boys] and someone who perhaps under the influence of alcohol engages with a sixteen- or seventeen-year-old young woman who returns his affection."

Talk about a "Lolita" complex! Don't you know tons of teenage girls who want to sleep with their priests? Aren't all girls just "returning their affections" or "asking for it"? And just think of all those poor, hapless men who can't help themselves! Right?

The fact is, some men in positions of power will misuse that power through sexual abuse. As far as we know, it has been going on since the beginning of human history, and it happens all over the world. But that doesn't mean it's okay or that you have to go along with it.

> When I would go home at night, I would busy myself, distract myself, organize something, make sure I did not have time and space to really think about what my coach was doing.
>
> —a seventeen-year-old mentor-abuse survivor

The biggest difference between incest and sexual abuse by a mentor is that in this case you actually get to go home after the molestation. You do not have to live under the same roof as your abuser, and the sense of violation and shattered trust is not so primal as it is with a parent. But, like any form of sexual abuse, mentor abuse is a huge violation of trust and often leaves girls feeling very unsure about how to form healthy intimate relationships.

In this chapter we'll look at how abusive mentors tend to work, first gaining a girl's trust—and often, especially in the case of clergy, the trust of her parents and family—and then making their way toward a sexual advance. Of course, the abuse is not always premeditated. Some men just lose their sense of boundaries and feel entitled in the moment. At times a man will even apologize—when he's not blaming you for being "irresistible." But it's still abuse, and it's still not okay. To be clear, usually there is grooming, and these men scope out the family situation. If they see a weak link, an uninvolved parent, or perhaps a parent who is overly ambitious for their child to succeed in a sport or activity, these perpetrators will abuse. I have known girls whose coaches abused them after the death of a parent when they knew the girl was particularly vulnerable. An older man and a teenage girl cannot have a healthy sexual relationship, no matter how mature she is or how much it feels like love. There's just too much power in his hands and not nearly enough in hers. Period.

In the case of mentor abuse, there are many different types of predators. We'll hear a variety of short takes in this chapter and read some letters to my website from girls who were abused by their teachers, coaches, rabbis, priests, choral directors, professors, and tutors. Too many girls have kept these secrets. It's time we lift the taboo on speaking out.

Before we hear from the girls, let's stop and take a look at some of the most prevalent myths about mentor abuse:

MYTH: Pedophile clergy are only interested in boys.
TRUTH: The media may have jumped on the story of sexual abuse of boys within the church, but the truth is that, as with all forms of sexual abuse, far more girls than boys are the survivors of sexual abuse by clergy. In fact, according to Mary A. Tolbert, professor of biblical studies at the Pacific School of

Religion, girls are three times more likely to be molested by clergy than boys. She suggests that it is a combination of a profound fear of homosexuality and a devaluing of girls that leads us as a society to be scandalized by the abuse of boys and turn a blind eye to the abuse of girls. A. W. Sipe, a former Catholic priest and psychologist who studied sexuality in the Catholic priesthood for twenty-five years, estimated to the *Boston Globe* that "over twice as many priests are involved with females than males."

Of course, in our male-dominated society, the greatest public outcry is reserved for abuse of boys. When girls are abused, we tend to shake our heads and tsk-tsk; when boys are abused, we are outraged and want justice. And if these boys turn out to be homosexuals? Our culture says, now that would be a high crime!

The truth is, clergy can and do sexually abuse children, and their targets are predominantly girls.

MYTH: It is not against the law for clergy to molest minors.
TRUTH: Clergy are often exempt from laws governing conduct, and the church has always protected its priests against public exposure or criminal charges by moving them from parish to parish. It is very difficult to get the government involved in cases involving clergy.

MYTH: If your priest or other religious or spiritual leader is molesting you, it must be all right in the eyes of God.
TRUTH: Of course this is not true. Sexual abuse is always wrong, no matter what your priest might tell you.

MYTH: Clergy—ministers, priests, and rabbis—can't be sexual deviants, predators, or pedophiles. They are pure and holy, called by God to be leaders within their communities.

TRUTH: People enter the clergy for all kinds of reasons, and, just as in the general population, some clergy are emotionally unstable and prone to sexual abuse. As the continuous and multitudes of scandal within the Catholic Church would suggest, priests are just as capable of abuse as anyone else. And they have a protective private society to protect each other.

MYTH: Your primary-care doctor (sports doctor, chiropractor, dermatologist, eye doctor) needs to do a vaginal exam during your medical checkup. Teen girls are required to have internal pelvic exams.

TRUTH: Obstetricians and gynecologists are the doctors who perform pelvic exams to check for cancer or STDs. You may also have your primary-care doctor and/or nurse practicioner perform this procedure on occasion. This procedure is an internal examination by inserting a metal or plastic device called a speculum into the vagina. Through the open speculum, the examiner can see the inside of the vagina and the cervix. A doctor or nurse may also do a digital exam (usually for first-time mothers during their pregnancy to feel their ovaries and uterus for lumps or other problems) by applying lubricant to her fingers (covered by a medical glove) and inserting two fingers into the vagina while pressing gently on the abdomen. You can always ask for another person to be present in the exam room during your exam. For many *male* physicians, it is customary to have a female nurse or chaperone present *during a pelvic examination of* female patients. You may insist on this. American College of Obstetrics and Gynecology recommends that young women have their first visit with an obstetrician-gynecologist (OB/GYN) between the ages of thirteen and fifteen. For most teens, the first visit will include an external examination of the genitals but not an internal examination of the reproductive organs, which is recommended beginning at age twenty-one for healthy women. The only time an internal pelvic exam will be given to a teen girl is for symptoms of abnormal vaginal bleeding, painful periods, unusual vaginal secretions, or other problems that may be associated with your reproductive health. Again, you can always request another person in the room. And I recommend you do.

MYTH: Male preschool and elementary school teachers are attracted to the field for predatory reasons.
TRUTH: This is another instance of society's gender prejudices: After all, what kind of man would honestly be interested in teaching and nurturing young children? I will tell you, often these are men who are caring nurturers and wonderful examples for young children. The truth is, most of the sexual abuse that goes on in schools is between male teachers and teenage girls.

MYTH: You have to do what your coach tells you to do.
TRUTH: Coaches sometimes exploit their position of power. You never have to have sex with a coach or let him touch you in a sexual way. Period. And it is appropriate to tell a trusted adult if that happens.

MYTH: It's sometimes necessary, as part of the training, for your coach to get a little flirtatious with you, touching you in ways that make you uncomfortable, commenting on your body in a sexualized way.

TRUTH: As we said in the opening to this chapter, if a coach harasses you a bit about losing weight so that you can qualify for a sport, that's not sexual abuse, although it also might not be true or appropriate. If he stares a little too long when you run, that's harassment, even sexual harassment—but it's not sexual abuse. You can still tell your parents and report him for sexual harassment. But if he touches you in any unwanted way, or even just makes sexually loaded remarks, that's abuse and you can report him.

IVY

Now let's meet Ivy, an Orthodox Jewish girl who was molested by her rabbi when she was fifteen years old. I didn't meet Ivy until about six years later, when she was twenty-one. She was going to college in New York City, and one of her friends, a client of mine, brought her to see me. At that point Ivy no longer had much contact with her parents. She described her relationship with her family as "superficial."

She was supporting herself and paying for college with student loans and had stopped observing Judaism, having become suspicious of all rabbis and of religion in general. This is pretty common in cases of clergy abuse. Girls will tend to generalize their bad experiences to all clergy and all religion.

Ivy thought she had pretty much put the abuse behind her, but then, six years after her molestation, she started having nightmares and developed a case of irritable bowel syndrome.

IVY'S STORY

I Tried to Forget

My family was very religiously observant and went to synagogue regularly. My parents were very close to the rabbi and his family. In fact, my best friend growing up was the rabbi's daughter, Sara. We all lived in a small Jewish enclave in Borough Park, Brooklyn, and I would often sleep over at Sara's house. Sara was like a cousin to me, and she would come to my house often as well. We went to camp together, we were classmates, and we shared secrets. Sara did not seem close to her father, who was usually working at the synagogue, and, because he was so religious, he seemed to be observing one Jewish holiday or another, and he was not around much when I was at Sara's house.

One night when I was about fifteen, I was sleeping over at Sara's. Sara was already asleep when I heard footsteps approaching her room. When I looked up, the rabbi was standing over my bed. He looked at me and whispered "sha" (that meant "be quiet" in Hebrew). He was very quiet and sat down next to me on the bed and started petting my hair. I was so nervous, I pretended to fall asleep, hoping that would make him leave.

Before I knew it, he was lying down next to me and rubbing up against me and fondling my breasts. I froze. I prayed he wouldn't notice that I was awake. I began counting to ten over and over again and keeping track of how many times I'd done it. By the time I had counted to ten about twenty-five times, the rabbi had gotten up and left. I just lay there in shock.

I could not sleep and just lay there awake until morning. Sara, on the other hand, appeared to sleep through the whole thing.

When we woke up the next morning and Sara asked what I wanted for breakfast, I made up an excuse not to stay for breakfast and I ran home.

When I got home I told my parents right away what had happened. They did not believe me. They said I must have been dreaming, that our wonderful rabbi was not a "pervert" and wouldn't have done these things. They said I should be ashamed of myself for such an accusation. They then marched me over to the rabbi's house, forcing me to tell my "story" to him. Of course, the rabbi denied everything.

Now comes the twist. Sara must have been listening at the door, because she suddenly burst into the room and confronted her father about how he had molested her for years. In front of me and my family, Sara broke into sobs, saying that she'd been terrified to tell anyone but that she wasn't going to let him get away with molesting her friend, too. Can you believe the adults didn't believe us? Even with Sara there crying and everything? My parents just looked at their beloved rabbi and calmly asked, "Rabbi, how could this be?"

In the face of overwhelming evidence, the rabbi continued to deny that he had ever touched either of us. At that point Sara, who was usually so mild mannered, began to weep uncontrollably. And that's when Sara's father lost his cool and started screaming at Sara violently. It became clear, even to my parents, that there must have been some truth to what Sara and I were saying.

I went over to Sara and hugged her, and she fell into my arms. I kept saying, over and over, "I am so sorry, I didn't know." Suddenly that one night with her father seemed like nothing in comparison to what he'd done to my dear friend, who had been hiding it all these years.

My family took me home and broke off all relations with the rabbi and the synagogue. I told them I wanted to help Sara and report the crime. They forbade me, and they told me to never mention it again. When I would see Sara in the hallways at school, she'd avoid me. My parents forbade me to go over to her house, and she did not even want to walk home from school with me. My family felt shame for me and asked me not to tell anyone. They finally said they believed me, but they didn't want to talk about it. After a few months, the rabbi's family moved to Israel, and I never heard from Sara again. I also never told anyone about Sara or her father or what he did to me. I just buried the experience deep down inside. I became more isolated. I did not trust anyone. I certainly couldn't count on my parents, so I just kind of withdrew into myself.

When I graduated high school, I moved out and enrolled in college. I tried to have as little contact with my family as possible. But six years after this incident I started having nightmares and becoming depressed. That is when my friend brought me to therapy.

MY THOUGHTS

When Ivy came to see me, she pretty quickly made it clear that she didn't want to talk about what happened with the rabbi as much as about how her parents had not allowed her to speak about it after they left the rabbi's house. That's what had hurt the most. Her parents had kept it a secret all these years. When Ivy once approached her mother to talk about the abuse, her mother said, "Look, it only happened once. Put it behind you." This is a very common experience for girls. When you are abused "only" once, most people don't understand why you are upset. But the truth is that one traumatic experience can upset you for years.

If Ivy had been able to process the abuse and keep in touch with Sara, she might have worked through it by the time we met. But she had already experienced six years of repression by then. What Ivy discovered, as do so many other girls, is that there is often lots of unfinished business, even for the survivor who discloses her abuse.

As she described it, the experience had made Ivy very suspicious of religion and of men in positions of power. She had a very hard time trusting her teachers and had problems being intimate with men. Through her therapy, she began to give herself credit for having taken care of herself by bringing the abuse out into the open. The more we worked on rebuilding her confidence in herself, the more she was able to open up to others. She realized that she really had done the right thing by telling and could trust that she was capable of taking care of herself.

The creepy experience with the rabbi, coupled with having her parents not support her or let her speak about it, had caused her to build a wall around herself. She also felt somehow not entitled to be traumatized by the abuse since her mother told her that one experience is not enough to really be upset about. But slowly she realized that the wall had to do with not trusting herself and that by getting in touch with how brave she had been to tell, she was able to regain that trust and allow other people in.

All girls who are sexually abused share some common feelings of shame and mistrust, which can sometimes last for years. Many girls who are abused once or twice feel guilty about even having feelings about it because they know other girls have had it much worse. Of course, girls like Coral (see Chapter 6), after six years of rape, will have some very heavy and complicated feelings and symptoms to deal with. But I am here to tell you that even "just" once is once too many! It's not at all unusual to develop emotional issues from just one abuse experience. You have a right to your feelings. And that doesn't diminish anyone else's right to theirs.

In the continual flow of letters to my website, probably one out of five has to do with some kind of mentor sexual abuse. Often, girls will start out feeling flattered by the attention of their mentor. There can be a kind of natural intimacy between an adolescent girl or young woman and her coach or teacher, especially when a girl is particularly successful and excited by the sport or subject. For example, having your high school English teacher encourage you to submit poetry for publication or a coach invite you to try out for a varsity team can be really exhilarating, even life changing—particularly if you are already feeling vulnerable or don't have a good relationship with your father. And don't feel supported by your mother.

There are other factors that make some girls more vulnerable than others—for example, it may be a part of your cultural tradition to obey your elders, no matter what. Perhaps females have a very low standing in your culture. Girls who are experiencing other traumas—their parents' divorce or a death in the family, where all the adults are focused elsewhere—might be more susceptible to sexual abuse by a trusted mentor. Girls who are going through a depression might be particularly seducible by a coach who says he can guarantee her happiness.

It's easy, then, to project onto your mentor certain protective or parental qualities or to be overwhelmed with gratitude. That is why girls often feel so confused and guilty over mentor abuse. But make no mistake: these men are manipulators wearing the costumes of supporters.

Also, if you were molested as a young child and never told anyone because you felt unsafe in your family, for instance, you might be more susceptible to mentor abuse. But if you were molested early on and told someone and got support and results, chances are your sense of boundaries will be better developed. You know that people support you and believe you, and you'd probably be better at spotting the warning signs (he looks at you a little too longingly, he hangs around a little too often, he invites you out for coffee, etc.). If you are uncomfortable and unsure of your mentor's vibe or intentions, talk about it with a trusted adult. Trust your gut.

One girl wrote to my website for help with her confusion about her coach's inappropriate advances:

Dear Dr. Patti,
I live in Tucson, Arizona, and I am a freshman in high school. I read the other letters on your website and had to write to you. I have never told anyone about this, but something really weird happened to me with my basketball coach. He is no longer working at my school and I have not seen him since he left, but I've been so scared to tell anyone what happened. I am scared that he will come back and find me and say I am lying.

He used to work with me privately and tell me how great I was. He is only in his early twenties and very good-looking. I admit I liked the attention. But one day while we were shooting baskets, he tackled me to the ground and stuck his tongue in my mouth and put his hands up my shirt. I just lay there. I feel so stupid about this now, but I was really freaked out and didn't know what to do. I kept playing basketball after that, but I never stayed after or spent any time alone with him again. It was just that one time. I thought I was over it, but now I am having nightmares. Was I sexually abused? Was it my fault? Should I tell?

Signed,
Suzanne

Yes, Suzanne was sexually abused. No, it was not her fault. She did not know her coach would tongue-kiss her or forcibly touch her breasts. Many girls talk about this kind of thing happening just one time, after which they avoid the person. This is often the best thing to do. It's even better to find a trusted adult to tell. The adult can help you figure out what to do next and can also help you deal with the feelings that come up so that you aren't scarred with fears and mistrust.

Another girl who wrote to my website had a "relationship" with her mentor that started out "nicely" but became abusive over time:

Dear Dr. Patti,

I am twenty years old and just finished my second year of college in the Midwest. I recently ended an "affair" with my eleventh-grade English teacher. I always felt special in Mr. X's classes. I come from a family of overachievers whom I could never measure up to, but he told me I was really smart. He also told me that he loved me and that age did not matter (he's thirty-four). I knew he was married, but he always said his wife didn't understand him and I was the only one who did. He wrote me poetry and bought me gifts and I was very flattered by all the attention.

The affair started by us going out for coffee after school. By the middle of my senior year, we were getting together some-times on the weekends. He would take me to poetry readings and stuff. He said that his wife knew but was never around for him, so it didn't matter. My parents thought it was a little strange that this teacher spent so much time with me, but they liked him, so they didn't seem to mind much. He would stop in and chat with them, and I think they just thought he was a great guy.

Then one Saturday after coffee he took me to a park and told me he was falling in love with me. He said he wanted to kiss me and asked me if it was all right. I said okay. I remember it was a strange feeling, sort of like kissing some old guy from a film or something, someone you watch but would never want to get intimate with.

By the end of my senior year we were spending a lot of time together. That was the same year my parents got divorced and my father moved out. Mr. X really came through for me then. My mother was depressed, and I barely even saw my father, with whom I already had a strained relationship. I told Mr. X every-thing and really leaned on him for emotional support. He was great. He even called my mother and told her not to worry about me, that he'd keep an eye on me.

Slowly, he convinced me to stop seeing most of my friends so we'd have more time together. When I went away to college, he visited me, and that's when we had sex. I didn't want to lose him, so I complied. I also thought he was the only person who would ever love me that much. But, after the first time, I didn't want to do it again. It just felt creepy. But, when I said I didn't want to, he got really angry and forced himself on me, saying he had given up his marriage and moved out and was in love with me. I later found out that none of that was true. I began to get frightened and I wanted to break away, but he was very controlling and I was afraid of what he could do to me. I was afraid he'd tell my parents and they'd freak out. I stopped eating. I became depressed. I didn't want to see Mr. X anymore.

I went to the counseling center at my school and told a counselor about the relationship. She told me it was not consensual and that it amounted to sexual abuse. She also said that she would speak with Mr. X and tell him to stop contacting me or she would report him.

To make a long story short, I told Mr. X what the counselor said and at first he was very angry, but then the weirdest thing happened. He broke down and cried and admitted that he had been with teen girls for ten years. When I told my counselor that, she totally flipped out. She told me to threaten to take him to court if he did not seek help. I was kind of scared of the whole mess and let her contact him. She made sure he got into therapy.

I feel like a coward. I should probably report him so he won't molest other teen girls, but I don't have the courage. I feel so guilty and dirty. Even though my therapist tells me it was not my fault, I feel like I asked for this relationship. Reading the other stories on your website, I see that other girls have forgiven themselves. Why can't I forgive myself?

Signed,
Mary

Mary had a really traumatic experience. She was forced into a romanticized, sexualized relationship with her teacher, a teacher she really liked but didn't want to have a sexual relationship with. Just as pedophiles look for vulnerable children who are alone and unsupervised, sexual-deviant mentors will look for girls who seem somehow unprotected and vulnerable. In this case the therapist was legally a mandated reporter because the girl was underage. He should have been reported.

Mary did not have a strong relationship with her father and barely saw him after he divorced her mother during her senior year. When Mary started to confide in Mr. X, sharing her vulnerability and her sadness, he perhaps surmised that she would be more open to his "comfort." The boundaries in these situations get very confusing. Mentor abuse is very painful, just as incest is, because so often the girl really looks up to and trusts the person who then turns around and sexualizes and abuses her. It only confuses matters if the family also knows and trusts the mentor.

Also, let us be aware that all around us—in films and advertising and magazines and other media—the idea that very young women are attracted to older men is thoroughly normalized. Even in the TV series *Gilmore Girls,* the otherwise outspoken, assertive, brilliant girl character Paris goes off to Yale and has an affair with her sixtysomething professor. We know from earlier episodes that Paris is desperate for the attention she can never get from her parents. Of course girls are always blaming themselves for the situations they land in. But look around you. Look at the culture—specifically at movies—and you easily see how girls are constantly being set up for these "romantic" liaisons with older and oh-so-much-wiser men.

If you are a survivor of mentor abuse or are currently involved with a mentor, please understand that these relationships are not okay, even if they are encouraged all around you. Even if you've been told that it's perfectly normal, that the age difference means nothing, that you're an "old soul" or were connected in a past life—and even if this is a relationship that you don't feel hurt by—you must trust me that you will be hurt by it at some point in your life, because at its root this kind of relationship is all about power.

No matter how "mature" you are or how "ready" you feel, as a teenager you are simply not on an equal footing with an older mentor. Once you are twenty-five or so and have matured into adulthood, it is entirely up to you whom you become intimate with. At that time dating someone ten years your senior may not make as big a difference to you. But, as a teenager, having a relationship with a much older mentor is a whole different story.

To those of you who might currently be involved with a mentor in a sexual relationship, please know that it is best for you to end the relationship as soon as you can. I urge you to take to heart everything we've said in this chapter. Do not blame yourself. It's not your fault, and it's never too late to change your situation.

Often, threatening to report your abuser is enough to stop him. Chances are, you are not the first girl this man has taken advantage of, and mentors are all too often terrified of being exposed or investigated because they know how long the list of their other "affairs" is.

Justice is rarely served in cases of mentor abuse, even though in many states the laws should protect you. But you always have the power to walk away. Remember: Your mentor may be charming and flattering and give you the attention you crave, but the wonderful talents he is offering to nurture in you are yours. He did not create them, and you do not owe him sex in exchange for his kindness. If you are attracted to him, remember that your relationship is not a partnership of equals and never will be.

Times may [finally] have changed, and, in light of the Nassar trial and the brave women who came forward, doctors will start facing consequences for sexual abuse. As women continue coming forward, men will stop getting away with sexual abuse, as they have from the beginning of time. Hopefully this chapter has opened you up to the pitfalls and luring of mentor abuse. It may be painful and confusing in the short run, and you may not even know these are advances. But standing up for yourself and identifying any inappropriate advances from your mentor will save you. And trust me: you won't regret it.

CHAPTER 10

PUSHED TOO FAR

*Acquaintance Sexual Abuse
(Amber's Story, Jasmine's Story)*

I felt as if I was sinking into a drain. I had nothing holding
me up, nothing keeping me afloat. I watched from the
sidelines as he touched me.

—*a fourteen-year-old acquaintance-abuse survivor*

Acquaintance abuse differs from date rape in that, by definition, you already know the abuser before he rapes you, and it
may not involve going on a date at all. You may be friends with
the guy or know him from around the neighborhood. You may
even be attracted to him, but instead of taking it slow with you
and exploring in a way that you can handle, he takes advantage
of your confusion and vulnerability and pushes you much further, sexually, than you are ready to go.

MYTHS AND TRUTHS ABOUT
ACQUAINTANCE ABUSE

Here are some of the most common myths and misunderstandings about adolescent girls and their sexuality. And, to
counter these myths, here are some of the truths I have learned

from in my three decades of talking with hundreds of girls and young women.

MYTH: Young teenage girls have enormous sexual appetites.
TRUTH: Given how complicated puberty is, a statement like this is simply ridiculous. And yet it is widely believed. Here's the truth: Some girls feel arousal and some do not. Many twelve-year-old girls start becoming interested in boys (or girls). They may want to kiss, but they do not necessarily want their genitals touched or to touch someone else's. They have all sorts of thoughts and feelings and lots of fears of the actual sex connection. They are not emotionally ready for consummation of sexual physical contact, and this is the essence of what abuse is—a girl not being ready emotionally to integrate what she may be experiencing physically.

That's where boys and men get confused. A thirteen-year-old girl may dress like Miley Cyrus and be attracted to and intrigued by boys, but that doesn't mean she wants to have sex with them. She may have posters of Justin Bieber on her wall and have romantic fantasies about him, but in reality she doesn't want a teenage boy, no matter how cute he may be, putting his fingers in her vagina or forcing oral sex on her. Usually, a girl's true sexual appetite begins at around age sixteen.

Around the age of sixteen or seventeen a girl is cognitively, emotionally, physically, and spiritually ready for deeper sexual relationships. This is a time when most girls have completed their tasks of emotionally separating and reuniting with their parents and have the mental equipment to manage a relationship that is both emotionally and sexually complex.

MYTH: Young girls enjoy giving boys blow jobs.

TRUTH: There is a great deal of pressure out there for girls to perform oral sex on boys. Nowadays blow jobs are thought of as casually as kissing in much of teen culture. Sometimes giving a blow job is even a rite of passage into a peer group. But underneath the bravado is fear—and even disgust—on the part of the girls. In all my years of working with girls, I cannot remember ever hearing a twelve- to fifteen-year-old say she enjoyed giving boys blow jobs. In fact, a girl that age can experience mild to severe physical discomfort, such as gagging, choking, and nausea, if she tries to perform oral sex. Many girls gag when forced to swallow semen. It can also cause real emotional turmoil. Most girls at this age just aren't ready.

MYTH: Twelve- to fifteen-year-old girls are in command of their sexual appeal and deliberately use it to manipulate boys. They feel sexy, beautiful, and powerful, and want to turn guys on.

TRUTH: Twelve- to fifteen-year-old girls usually feel gawky, awkward, ugly, and often embarrassed about their developing bodies. No matter how they appear to others, they hardly feel sexually attractive. They're busy adjusting to all the changes and mourning some of the losses that come with developing hips and breasts and getting their first menstrual periods. They are navigating new waters, figuring out how to deal with their new bodies and hormonal surges.

At this developmental stage, girls naturally feel confused by their sudden "sex appeal." They may be pushed hard to start experimenting with sex and to conform their emerging sexuality to cultural expectations. They may start to wear makeup and experiment with dressing in a sexier way, and they may seem to go from girl to woman overnight, but few girls can be said to be "in command" of their sexuality even at fifteen—let alone twelve, thirteen, or fourteen.

MYTH: Intercourse feels great at this age.
TRUTH: Intercourse at this age usually hurts and is usually scary. It's simply not something that most twelve- to fifteen-year-old girls desire at this stage in their physical and emotional development, no matter how much they may want attention from boys. Of course, there are the rare cases when two young people really feel in love and ready for this commitment, but this is very unusual. I can't tell you how many times girls who have had intercourse too early (by their own reckoning) have told me that they could not understand the point of it. They say things like, "It hurts. You bleed. Sometimes you even have a hard time walking the next day."

Any girl brought up in a household where she didn't feel valued as a person, where she wasn't supported when she tried to create clear physical boundaries, where she didn't feel vital or important, where she felt invisible, can be vulnerable to sexual abuse, including acquaintance sexual abuse.

Remember Coral talking about feeling proud and pretty in her new little outfit? She also said that after being raped by her father she felt dirty. The rape took away all her comfort and pride in her developing body. It's hard enough just to deal with the feelings that come up during adolescence, but when a girl is sexually assaulted, as Coral was, she'll tend to close off her feelings. The same kind of thing happened to Amber, whom you'll meet in a moment, when she was forced into a sexual relationship too early. As Amber moved through all the normal developmental stages of adolescence—wanting to fit in, feeling awkward and uncomfortable with her changing body, feeling confused about her "sex appeal"—she didn't have a solid base of support at home. She felt at sea with all these new feelings. Along came a good-looking, popular boy, and she succumbed.

AMBER

I met Amber one day when I was speaking to a large group of girls at her school. I remember looking at her and seeing a kind of dazed expression on her face. After the talk, she approached me and told me that some things had happened to her that she had never told anyone. We spoke that day for at least an hour.

Amber told me she was haunted by some weird experiences she'd had with a male counselor at her riding camp a few years earlier. She said he was a really popular guy at camp, and no one knew that he'd molested her. She explained that now she goes out with boys she doesn't even like and is confused about how much attention she seems to need from them. She knew it had something to do with the boy who molested her. She harbored a lot of resentment toward him but also felt guilty because she hadn't stopped him. She was obviously in a state of real emotional turmoil.

Amber described how angry she felt all the time and how she carried her anger into her classes, into her relationship with her parents, and into her relationships with both girls and boys. Although she spoke in a monotone, as do many survivors when they reveal their abuse for the first time, even in that first encounter I could see her body begin to relax.

Shortly thereafter, Amber started coming to my office, and over the next several sessions she filled in the details of what had happened. The molestation took place over two summers, when she was twelve and thirteen. Her anger was palpable. During sessions she would often clench her fists.

We started our work together in the spring of Amber's sophomore year in high school. She was involved with the poetry club at school and was a good student, but she did not derive much joy from her academic success. She had had trouble connecting with boys and with girls and described her quiet and conservative parents as well meaning but incompetent in many ways. Slowly but surely, it became apparent that Amber had a lot of reasons for mistrust.

As an African American living in a predominantly white neighborhood and as an only child, Amber often felt isolated. She lived with her parents and grandparents, who seemed "pretty clueless" about modern teenagers. Amber's father had a small dry-cleaning company and was rarely home, so Amber spent a lot of time with her mother and grandmother. There was no real openness in Amber's home, and, furthermore, there was an expectation of blind respect for elders. It was assumed that Amber would be a "good girl," which included being kind and thoughtful to her elderly grandmother, a bitter woman who herself had lived through some very rough times during the Depression in the South.

Amber had no doubt that she was very loved by her family, but she felt that she needed to play a role to please them. If she acted out, she was always quickly reprimanded by her frightened mother, who was still under the thumb of her own mother. She got the message loud and clear: don't make waves.

When Amber began her "tweens," she wanted to fit in but wasn't at all sure how.

AMBER'S STORY

He Told Me I Was Special

I have been holding in this secret of sexual abuse for years. I have never told my parents or reported this person, but when Dr. Patti came to my school it all came back to me and I had to tell the story of what happened.

I am African American and an only child. My skin is very light. My grandmother on my father's side is also very light skinned. This is a positive thing in my family, to be light skinned, but it is very uncomfortable for me because I don't really fit in anywhere—not with the biracial kids, the black kids, or the white kids.

I have always known my parents loved me, but I could never really be open with them. We live in Staten Island, New York. This is a community with some very wealthy people and some working- and middle-class people, but it is not very integrated. I am not sure why my parents moved to such a white neighborhood, but they did. My family is middle class; my father owns a small dry-cleaning company.

When I was twelve years old, I was already pretty physically developed and felt really awkward. Boys started looking at me differently, and men on the street would whistle. People thought I was at least fifteen. My mother and grandmother both have huge breasts, and I had always prayed that I would not turn out like them. I remember I used to slump my shoulders to try to hide my breasts. This was the same year that I discovered riding horses. When I was on a horse, I felt great. I wasn't self-conscious. I didn't care what anybody thought. I just had a good time.

I started going to the stables near my house after school pretty much every day, and finally my parents scraped up the money to pay for some riding lessons and the tuition for the summer camp at the stables. I didn't have a lot of friends in school, and I noticed at the stables that there was a popular group of girls from my school. There I was with my kinky black hair, different skin, and thick body. All the popular girls seemed to be pretty, skinny, and blonde and rich. Once again, I didn't fit in.

That summer at riding camp that same group of blond, pretty, popular girls was also there, but they talked to me very little. There were some black kids there, but they pretty much ignored me, and I felt kind of isolated. Then Tim came along.

Tim was sixteen and a really good rider. He was also very good-looking, and whenever he could, he showed off his six-pack. He was black and seemed to have crossed the popularity barrier. He was popular with all the kids. Whenever he rode to the stable, all the kids got excited; they thought he was so cool.

He worked part time at the camp and was friends with all the kids. Because I did gymnastics I was really strong, and Tim noticed. I felt great when he asked me to be on his volleyball team and his team in water tag. This was my ticket to acceptance. All the kids knew that Tim included me on his teams.

Suddenly, different girls were asking me to their sleepovers. I was really happy. I started to feel really good about myself and accepted by a popular group for the first time. This was the first time I felt as if I was actually "in" a group. Girls were calling me, and I could feel free to call them. Whenever Tim was around at camp, everyone surrounded him, but he would always talk with me the most.

One day when we kids were all at the beach, Tim was rubbing sand off my back and touched my chest. I felt kind of weird, but I didn't say anything. I figured it was a mistake. After that, Tim started paying a lot of attention to me. He would compliment me on how strong I was and constantly praise me during volleyball or water tag games. I felt really special. My parents could see how happy I was, and they were really pleased with all my new friends. Things were good.

One night there was a campfire at the camp, and, when everyone was sitting close together in the dark, Tim started whispering things to me. He said things like, "Bright Eyes, you know how special you are to me. Here, let's do something and don't worry about it. I really like you."

Then he put my hand on top of his pants. I felt really weird. I was paralyzed and didn't know what to do. But he said, "It's okay, it's our secret." And he kept telling me how special I was. I knew it was probably not normal and it felt weird, but I was hoping it would never happen again.

Things started to escalate with Tim. He would get me alone whenever he could. If I was alone with him in the stables, he would push me down on a haystack and fondle my breasts. Then he'd take my hand forcibly and put it on his crotch. I'm sure I said no, but I'm also sure it was a pretty weak no. Really, I can't tell you exactly what I was thinking because I would find something to focus on and just check out. After each of our encounters, he was really nice to me. He kept trying to get me alone, and I would try to avoid him. In the meantime, the girls were all being really nice to me, but they were always trying to get me to get Tim to come along to the park or the ice cream truck or something. Tim was clearly more interested in being alone with me, but he would come with the group sometimes. In retrospect, I now see that this was his way of keeping me hooked.

The summer ended, and I did not see Tim during the school year because he was away at boarding school. He actually wrote me a letter saying how special I was and how sorry he was if he had done anything to make me uncomfortable. He told me he loved me. I wrote back once or twice, but then we lost contact. I spent that year in middle school feeling accepted. I still didn't like my developing body, but I stayed active in sports and had lots of friends. I had almost blocked out Tim's weird touches when summer rolled around again—the summer before high school.

Sure enough, Tim showed up at camp that summer. At that point I was fully developed and very curious about boys. I had a repulsion and fear about Tim but also a strange excitement. My memories are blurry about this, but I have a sense that I actually wanted to be with him sometimes. I had this fantasy that he really loved me and maybe would be nice to me. But, when he got me alone, all he wanted was to put my hand on his crotch. I would do it, and he would touch mine.

When we were alone together doing all this stuff, I would blank out or think about a movie or anything to get my mind off what was happening. One time he fingered me, and once he forced me to go down on him. I just pretended I was floating above my body, but I felt really awful afterward. Of course, I never told anyone about any of this. I did know I wanted to hold him and kiss him, I wanted him to want to hold my hand and put his arm around me, but I did not want to do the other stuff.

The sexual stuff with Tim went on for the whole summer. I really can't explain why I was never able to stop him. It just became expected behavior from me. I was kind of numb, and I kept fantasizing that he really liked me.

It wasn't until the end of that summer, at thirteen, that I finally told Tim to stop. Things had gone way too far. Even though I would blank out during the sexual encounters, I started having nightmares, and I also wanted to hurt myself. I cut my arms a couple of times with safety pins, and then I realized that it had to stop. When I told him that I wanted to tell someone, he said, "You know, you've let this happen a lot. No one will ever believe you if you say you didn't like it." Tim actually realized I meant business and was no longer going to go along with him, and he became really nasty. He either ignored me or was really sarcastic if he said anything to me at all. At times that he got me alone, he was really mean, telling me that I drove him to do those things to me because I wanted it.

The summer ended and I started high school. I was in a new school with new kids. I felt horrible about myself. When I got really down, I continued to cut my arms with safety pins, and I began to smoke pot. I was repulsed by my own sexuality. I either wanted to feel pain or nothing at all. A part of me felt so guilty and wondered, did I really want Tim to do that stuff to me? I was too ashamed to make new friends. And much of my freshman year was spent inside a shell. I definitely didn't want to go out with boys. I basically buried myself in schoolwork. I'd come straight home after school or maybe hang out a little with the kids I bought pot from. I was lonely and tormented about what had happened, what I let happen.

The summer after my freshman year, I took an accelerated writing course. I spent the summer with other kids who loved to write, and I was able to start to see myself in a better light. I was far away from that camp and Tim.

Then tenth grade started, and I actually started to feel a bit better because I had had a good summer. No one had hurt me. But I was still really shy, insecure, and self-conscious, and I blamed myself for all my sexual encounters with Tim. I was not as self-destructive; at times I wanted to cut my arms, but I smoked pot instead and found myself just feeling angry most of the time. I had never told anyone about that summer, and, even though I felt a bit better about myself, I still felt dirty, guilty, and ashamed.

Then one day there was an assembly about sexual abuse. I went to that assembly, and it changed my life. That is when I met Dr. Patti and started to get counseling. I also started going to her survivors' group, and I realized I wasn't the only girl who'd been sexually abused. Some of the other girls who'd been abused felt the same way I did about boys. I was really afraid. I didn't want boys to touch me, and I definitely didn't want a boyfriend. But when I shared my experience and heard from other girls to stop blaming myself, I realized maybe it wasn't my fault. I knew it was none of the girls in my group's fault about what happened to them. We all started to forgive ourselves.

I still have a lot to deal with. But being free to have so much anger at my parents for not being strong also helps me to stop blaming myself. They're so weak. I am angry that they couldn't tell I was so depressed during my young adolescence. I'm really upset that I had to find counseling on my own. I would even wear sleeveless shirts that showed my cuts up and down my arm. They never even asked about those marks on my arm, and they never suggested that I get help. I don't even tell them I go to therapy.

Dr. Patti lets me pay ten dollars a session, and it makes me feel like it is my private way to heal and deal with my issues. My family is all about not making waves. They always want everything to be just fine.

Only now, through my survivors' group and my sessions with Dr. Patti, am I beginning to realize that I wasn't to blame and that Tim probably did this to lots of other girls, too. For all I know, Tim may still be molesting girls, but I still don't feel strong enough to track him down and go to the authorities. One of the best things I've done, though, is that I've begun writing in a journal. My journal has become my friend. I wrote the following poem to that little twelve-year-old girl who couldn't stop someone from hurting her:

Hear the wind rush
feel the pain
ignore the chill
and hide the scars
count backwards from ten and pretend you're
somewhere else
where all the colors in the world become one.
Now it's over
he's leaving the room
I can breathe
at least until tomorrow...
Maybe then, though, I'll let myself see
that it's all up to me.
I'll clench my fists tightly
and tell the truth.
It was his fault, not mine.

MY THOUGHTS

This was the first time Amber had told her whole story. She let herself go back to the beginning and track how and when it all started. She was able to share her confusion and shame about not stopping the sexual abuse. She talked about feeling guilty and lost and not knowing how to stop Tim from violating her. She believed her abuser when he told her that she must have liked the sexual fooling around and that she obviously wanted him to do these things to her, but it's obvious to her now that she did not want to be sexually molested. She did not want to touch this boy's penis; it did not feel good to her. She was twelve years old. She felt insecure, awkward, and ashamed of her body. With Tim, she was pulled into a pattern, and she did not know how to stop it.

Because Amber did not have parents or friends she could trust, she didn't feel safe disclosing what had happened. Amber did what so many girls do: She pretended that she had forgotten. She tried unsuccessfully to suppress the memories of what happened and turned to hurting herself with safety pins. When that did not numb her, she smoked pot.

Summers were hard for her, with all the associations—the smells, the heat—bringing back memories of what had happened at camp. Through the accelerated English class, Amber was able to feel proud of herself again. She found some inner strength and really applied herself to her schoolwork.

In order to get through the abuse, Amber, like so many girls, dissociated from her body. She described floating above her body, as if she was not participating in the encounters. There are even some blanks in her memory because she so successfully checked out. (This was mentioned as one of the brilliant things girls do to survive in Chapter 6.)

Many girls find ingenious ways like this to cope with their abuse. They feel trapped, and floating away or hovering above their bodies is how they survive. Dissociating helped Amber feel less "disgusting" about what happened. But it didn't stop her pain entirely. As we see so clearly in her story, before she told anyone, she was sitting on a volcano of feelings, which led to some pretty self-destructive behaviors.

It's worth noticing that Amber knew that Tim was bad news. She felt wrong about the encounters from the very beginning, but, like so many girls her age, she acted against her intuition. The drive for social acceptance was stronger than her will to say no. Of course, sometimes saying no doesn't work anyway. But, in many cases of teen acquaintance abuse, the guy is also going through some kind of adolescent angst. If you tell him no, he might become scared and stop, but he also might become more insistent and threatening. It's impossible to predict. You have to trust your gut about whether it's safe to say no. But in all cases, it's best to find a trusted adult and tell. If the kid who abused you goes to your school, he might be forced to go to therapy, or he might even be expelled. You can petition for a legal order of protection, which would force him to stay a certain distance from you at all times. The point is, you have options.

As we saw in Amber's story, it took her a long time to tell anyone, and she has yet to tell her parents. She did not trust her parents to come through for her. Many girls won't go to their parents if they think their parents won't stand up for them. Again, you have to go with your instincts. Once Amber started talking about her abuse, she realized she was cutting her arms simply to feel something. She stopped smoking the pot to self-medicate. She received a scholarship to a college out in California and feels ready for this new chapter in her life.

JASMINE

I met Jasmine when she was sixteen years old. She started coming to our sex-abuse survivors' group at her high school. For the first several meetings she was very quiet. I knew she was Israeli, and I wondered if there was a language barrier. But then after a few group meetings she spoke. Her English was perfect. Jasmine told the group she felt very guilty about taking up group time with her story because many of the girls had been molested by an uncle or father, and her molester was a boy back in Israel. She said she realized that most of the other girls were so much younger than their molesters and had no power but that her abuse was probably her fault because she should have known better.

Then she began to tell her story. Jasmine explained that she had been abused by her friend's brother and felt really guilty and confused about the abuse. He had forced her to give him blow jobs when she was thirteen, and now she felt that was what she was good for and was sexually active. She judged herself as slutty because she internalized this judgment onto herself from her sexual abuse. She knew that she had a reputation for being a slut and felt like she deserved it. Sex and being taken advantage of by boys—this was familiar ground to Jasmine. But now, with the support from the other girls in the group, she was beginning to realize how much guilt and shame she carried around. With encouragement for the other girls, she felt brave enough and it was time to speak up.

JASMINE'S STORY

The Boat

I moved to the United States when I was fourteen years old. I was born in Israel and was sexually molested there by my friend's brother when I was twelve. I already spoke some English when we moved here, so getting acclimated wasn't really all that hard. In fact, I'll be going to college next year—a year early.

I'd say I've always been pretty happy overall. I've always been a good student; I work part time; I have some really close friends; I'm on the track team at school. But the abuse experience is always in the back of my mind, no matter what else is going on. The whole thing is still really confusing to me.

We used to spend summers in this small town near the beach. Down the way lived my friend Izhar. I was an only child, and Izhar, who was a year younger than me, was like a little brother. He had this cool older brother, Jakob, who didn't hang around the littler kids much, but I remember he would sometimes give us these special candies imported from the United States. Jakob was sixteen years old.

Izhar's parents had a big house. It was much more fun than ours, so we always hung out there. The summer I turned twelve, we were playing cards at Izhar's house one day when his brother came in and dared us to play strip poker. I was nervous but I kind of liked him, so I said yes. I was down to my bra and jeans when

I said, "That's enough!" His brother laughed at me, but he didn't push it.

Another time I was over and waiting for Izhar to come home from his guitar lesson, and Jakob invited me into his room. All we did was sit and look through his CDs. But the next time he was alone with me, he asked if he could touch my hair, then my nose and my eyes. He said, "You are so pretty." Then he gave me a bag of those imported candies. Stuff like this went on for a while, I guess. I was nervous, but it was okay. He told me that, even though I was five years younger than him, he really liked me.

Every girl in our town had a crush on Jakob, and I admit I loved the attention. He would be really nice to me and give me those imported candies. Then one time he kissed me and said he really liked me. Before I knew it, he put his fingers down my underwear, and I remember just kind of freaking out inside. I didn't want to scream or anything—that would have been too embarrassing—but I stared at this one painting on the wall. It was a painting of water and a boat. He fooled around with me like this a bunch of times, and I completely memorized everything about that painting—the colors, the boat, the places where the paint got thick and lumpy. I remember wanting to be in that painting. I could imagine myself floating away on that beautiful water in that boat. It was my escape.

I didn't say anything about what was happening with Izhar's brother to my parents. I think I didn't want to bother them. I was pretty close to my parents. My father had lost his job, and my mother was working two jobs to support us. I didn't think my problems with Jakob were really all that important. So I just tried to stay away from him. But I missed Izhar.

The next summer, when I was thirteen, Jakob, Izhar, and I played strip poker a lot. I don't know why I could have a crush on Jakob—I basically pretended that other stuff never happened. I actually was pretty excited at seeing his naked chest. Why? Even though I thought he was cute, I tried never to be alone with him. One time when the game was over, Jakob asked Izhar to run out and get us sodas. That's when Jakob opened his pants and took out his penis. He told me to suck him. I started to cry, and he pushed my shoulders down and put his penis in my mouth. I remember gagging and then vomiting all over the place, all over him, me, my clothes. He pushed me away and yelled at me, saying I was a stupid girl who could not do anything right. That night I went from having a crush on him, pushing away what he had done to me last summer, to being really scared of him and feeling totally disgusting.

I ran home and was sick all night. After that I stayed away from Izhar's house for a long time. But eventually I went back again. I know it seems crazy that I would go back. Jakob apologized and said he wanted me to be his girlfriend. He said he wouldn't do that again. I told him I didn't want to be his girlfriend. He just shrugged and laughed.

A couple of weeks went by, and by now Jakob was ignoring me. But one day I was walking to their house through a path in the woods, and there he was. He told me he wanted me to give him a blow job. "It's nothing," he said. "You can do it without puking, you know." I was really scared. The look on his face was mean.

After that he abused me regularly. I was so confused. I still kind of liked him, but I hated how far he was pushing me, and I didn't know how to stop it. I remember how he would shove my shoulders however he wanted my head and mouth to go, and how

I eventually learned to give him blow jobs and not gag. He would get me alone and make me blow him whenever he could. This went on for the rest of the summer, until I turned fourteen and we moved to the States.

I was happy to move away from Israel, and I thought I'd left all that behind me. The memories started flowing back, though, when I started attending Dr. Patti's groups. I mean, it's not like I ever forgot what happened or anything, but I started realizing that I was still hurting a lot from it. I am so grateful that I will never have to see Jakob again. When I think about what happened to me, I still feel disbelief. In Israel no one talked about anything like this.

After coming to the group for a while, I began to connect what happened back in Israel with some of my weird behavior around boys in the States. Like, I was seeing this guy right after we moved here, and he asked me to give him a blow job. I complied but I did it in an almost robotic way. It was so weird. After that, I broke off the relationship. I was an honor student, always worried about grades, joining all the academic clubs, staying home weekends with my family, but I was not a "good girl" when it came to sex. I never had intercourse or anything, but I went a lot farther than I wanted to go. It was like I had this secret, separate, sexual life that was different from who I was in every other way.

When I was fifteen, I was with different boys. I knew they were using me, so I stopped seeing any boys for a while and spent some time alone. After I started going to the group and hearing the other girls talk, I realized that I did not have to be sexual with boys if I didn't want to be. I really did not want to be with boys. I realized that I wasn't to blame for what had happened with Jakob, and that just because that stuff happened didn't mean I had to let boys push me further than I was comfortable going.

Eventually I got to know a boy from my school, and we became very close friends. After being close for a year, we started going out. We have been dating each other for six months now. We celebrated my eighteenth birthday together. It's the first healthy relationship I've ever had. He is a wonderful guy. He is also Israeli and has been in the States for about five years. When we got really close, I told him about the sexual abuse, and he was so supportive and loving. He did not make me feel dirty at all. He does not pressure me to have sex, and I still don't feel ready. He does these really sweet things for me, like on Valentine's Day he snuck into school early and put this adorable stuffed teddy bear in my locker. He never forces anything on me, and he is very sensitive and gentle. But sometimes when he touches my shoulders I freeze.

For instance, the other night we were watching a video, and, when he came up behind me and put his arms around me, I freaked out. I started to cry hysterically. I realize I still have triggers that remind me of Jakob. Sometimes my body reacts as if it is in trauma, and my mind doesn't even seem connected to my body. But my boyfriend is really understanding. I think what saved me during those interactions with Jakob was that painting on the wall. I really imagined myself floating away on that boat. I was floating away from his hands and his body and his abuse.

MY THOUGHTS

Jasmine is fortunate. She has worked hard to gain insight and forgive herself for the acquaintance abuse she suffered as a young girl. She has a supportive boyfriend, and over time she has learned to trust him and enjoy their closeness. When Jasmine first came into our group, she was timid and frightened. As time went on, she became a lot bolder, and now she shares things more readily. It has been really inspirational for the other girls to see her in this healthy relationship with a guy. Her boyfriend drops her off at the group and picks her up, and they seem really happy. Jasmine has brought a couple of her friends to the group, too—other young women raised in Israel who were molested as children. Jasmine has been a role model for many girls.

> I knew I needed to stop him, but I just froze with my pride in my pocket.
>
> —a sixteen-year-old survivor of acquaintance abuse

Acquaintance abuse is a lot like date rape in that the girl knows the person abusing her and chooses to be with him—but she doesn't choose to be sexual with him. Neither Jasmine nor Amber knew how to end the abuse. They were both preadolescent girls, and they were both vulnerable. Even though neither of them wanted the sexual attention, they both felt it made them special and were confused about whether they wanted to stop it. Amber felt special that a popular boy "wanted" her, and Jasmine felt pride that this "cool" boy paid attention to her.

I have found that girls who suffer acquaintance rape often don't have an open dialogue in their families. They don't feel that their parents will or can help or guide them. This was certainly the case with both Amber's and Jasmine's families. Jasmine's family might have been there for her, but her concern that she was going to be a bother kept her from going to them. This is also very common. It's hard enough for any girl to talk about sex and sexuality with her parents. Especially when a girl is confused about whether she might have "asked for it," she can be too uncomfortable to discuss abuse with her parents.

As with all abuse, if you have suffered acquaintance abuse and are afraid to tell your parents, you can try calling a hotline or telling a trusted adult (a teacher or a friend, for example). You can also write about what happened in your journal. You might rehearse what you would say if you were to tell someone until you find the strength to say it. Even if the abuse happened years ago, writing about it and telling someone about it can make all the difference to how you feel inside. I can assure you that telling will help you feel better. Remember: Acquaintance abuse, even by a boy you like, is never, never your fault. You didn't deserve it. What you do deserve is the support to work through it. It's never too late to tell your story and begin to heal your wounds.

CHAPTER 11

RAPE ALWAYS HURTS

Stranger Rape/Date Rape/Gang Rape
(Iris's Story, Dahlia's Story)

I just don't let anyone get close. I protect myself by not
allowing anyone access to the control panels.

—*an eighteen-year-old rape survivor*

A lot has been written about rape over the past several years
or so. It's easy to forget that it was forty years ago that the first
rape crisis center opened in New York City at St. Vincent's
Hospital. Its founder, social worker Flora Colao, explains,
"Rape was barely talked about then, but we kept getting women
in the hospital who were being randomly raped, women so full
of shame and fear that they were afraid to tell their husbands
or anyone close to them." It took the feminist movement in
the 1970s to define "rape culture," a culture that is made up
of a system of beliefs that encourages male sexual aggression
against females.

We have come some distance since the 1970s. Yes, the laws
back then were so difficult for a woman to prove rape, considering they demanded a witness in order to prosecute! Many
people, women and men, are working hard to change the laws
and the courts. And once again feminists are leading the way.

Women are writing books and songs and poems about rape and running rape crisis centers and hotlines, and we are grateful for all their efforts. But rape is still the most common violent crime committed against women in the United States,[1] and we still have a long way to go. We must make people aware of the impact of rape on women; we must make the crime of rape seen and heard; and, finally, we must prevent it.

One wonderful example of the ways young women are making their voices heard began at Brown University. In 1990, female students at Brown started scrawling the names of their accused rapists on the walls of the women's bathrooms. The attention this garnered drove Brown to require all first-year students to participate in a peer education program against sexual assault. Many other universities now also offer self-defense and rape awareness programs, some voluntary, some mandatory.[2] By 2017 many universities had the "rapist list" on posters and scrawled throughout their campuses: Hamilton, Columbia, Brown, Vanderbilt, Tufts, Notre Dame, Penn State, to name a few.

In 2014 President Barack Obama and Vice President Joe Biden launched the "It's on Us" awareness campaign to help end sex abuse on college campuses through education, responsibility, and consequences

In 2015 Emma Sulkowicz, a Columbia University student, picked up and carried around campus the mattress she was raped on. She was protesting her university's lack of handling her rape report. She didn't know she was going to start a movement. The response on campus was monumental, with girls and guys helping her to carry her mattress. Sexual assault prevention activists spread the word, and soon there was a movement called "Carrying the Weight Together," with students all across the United States carrying mattresses through college campuses protesting campus rape.

Tori Amos sings an extraordinary, haunting song called "I've Never Been to Barbados" about her rape experience. It describes the time when she was nineteen years old and took a ride with a couple of guys who had been at her concert. They pulled over to the side of the road and raped her at gunpoint. In the song, which she sings a cappella, she recounts how the thought that she had never been to Barbados kept playing in her mind while she was being raped. Barbados became her metaphor for living through the ordeal.

So many young female rape survivors approached her after her concerts, she decided she had to do something about rape in America, and that is when she cofounded the Rape, Abuse, and Incest National Network, or RAINN, the largest rape crisis hotline in the country, perhaps in the world.

Over the past twenty years, a number of women have also written memoirs about their experiences of rape. In her book *After Silence: Rape and My Journey Back,* Nancy Venable Raine writes about a stranger rape that took place when she was thirty. Raine was taking out the garbage and left her apartment door open. When she returned to her apartment seconds later, a man raped her at knifepoint. It took her ten years to write about it— ten years in which the rape continued to devastate her.

In *Where I Stopped: Remembering an Adolescent Rape,* Martha Ramsey looks back twenty years to detail her experience of being grabbed off her bicycle on a country road and raped in the woods when she was fourteen years old. She was still haunted by the rape twenty years later, she says, and needed to write about it.

In 2015 Chessy Prout, with the help of a journalist Jenn Abelson, published a book about her rape at St. Paul's, a top prep school. Chessy Prout has made a difference with her story in helping teen girls fight sexual assault in high school by coming forward with details on her rape and the failings of her school to support her. She broke open the rape culture at her school and by doing so became an advocate sexual-abuse survivor.

Finally, as a society, we are "getting it" that girls and women are still at risk, that rape is not rare but in fact rampant. Although most of the books I just mentioned are about stranger rape, perhaps the most widely misunderstood rape crime—both by the general public and by survivors themselves—is date rape. What makes date rape so confusing is that girls think they either should have or could have stopped it. On campus 90 percent of date rape involves alcohol or drugs. Although usually impossible to prevent, date rape is one of the only forms of sexual abuse that you may have a chance to prevent (see the strategies at the end of this chapter). It will take a posse of support, it will take not being drunk or stoned, it will take you and all your posse making sure your drinks are not tampered with. It stinks that you have to be so vigilant to prevent date rape. Remember: rape is rape, and it is never the survivor's fault! One of our goals in this chapter is to give you some tools to protect yourself from date rape. And it all starts with looking at the harsh realities and facing the dangers that can come with dating young men.

RAPE IS AN EPIDEMIC

I feel like my bulletproof vest has been shot through a thousand times, and I try to hold on, but it is all a bloody mess.

—a twenty-year-old date-rape survivor

Girls and young women aged sixteen to twenty-five are at the greatest risk for date rape.[3] In fact, research into date rape on college campuses tells us that between 20 and 25 percent of college girls experience or are threatened with date rape.[4] But RAINN's research also tells us that over 90 percent of campus rape goes unreported.

When you move away from home to begin college or for work, you are still testing the waters. You're figuring out who you are as an independent sexual being, and while you may want to revel in your new freedom and love the idea that you can party all night if you want to, you also have to be smart when it comes to sex and men.

Some girls are more vulnerable to date rape than others. Girls who were abused as children and never dealt with it are at far greater risk of being date-raped. When you are sexually abused and don't get help, the secret that someone sexually violated you still lives inside you and can eat away at you. You might still carry feelings of guilt or feel dirty inside. You might still be wondering, "Why me? I must have done something to bring the abuse on myself."

Depending on the kind of abuse you suffered, you might also feel as if you aren't good for anything else or that you somehow deserve to be treated badly. Many of these thoughts and feelings won't be conscious, but they will affect your behavior and your choices. That's why it's so important to talk about the abuse, write about it, tell a friend, get into a support group, or find a therapist. Even if the abuse happened years ago, you can get a lot of help and perspective by talking about it with trustworthy friends or adults.

Talking about it, you begin to root out that secret and all the ways it may be diminishing you, and you have a far better chance of dealing with whatever may come your way, be it warning signs of an abusive relationship, an attempted seduction by a mentor, or an attempted rape while on a date. When you start talking and get some help, you have a much better chance of being strong and of choosing healthy relationships.

Obviously, not all girls who were abused will be raped as older teenagers or young women, and not all girls who are date-raped were abused when they were younger. But there is definitely an important connection here, and we will be exploring the connection more fully in Iris's and Dahlia's stories later in this chapter.

To all of you who are survivors of sexual abuse and are now attending college or moving into your own apartment for the first time, and finding work, hear this: The abuse you suffered was not your fault. It's never the survivor's fault. Sexual abuse is rarely preventable; most of the time there is simply nothing a child can do about it. Children are at the mercy of adults, and very often the path of least resistance is compliance. But that doesn't mean it was your fault. You have to believe that.

Many, many girls who survive sexual abuse but don't tell, hold their secrets close, feel guilt, and may turn to drugs and alcohol for comfort. They find ways to self-medicate—anything to avoid feeling the pain of what they've been through. That's often where their vulnerability lies—because drugs and alcohol impair our judgment. There are no two ways about it. If you're used to getting high or drunk to numb yourself from an earlier abuse experience, you are less likely to make the safest choices when it comes to going home with a guy. You may think that you have no voice, no agency, that sex is something you don't really have options about, that you have to take whatever the guy expects. Sometimes you may not even be aware that you've been raped. If someone forces himself on you when you say no, you may feel that's just the way it is. That's how out of whack unacknowledged, unhealed abuse can make you. You don't even realize that you are entitled to something much, much better.

IF YOU'VE NEVER BEEN ABUSED, ARE YOU STILL AT RISK?

We're hoping that girls who have never been abused are reading this, too. No matter how loving a family you may have come from, no matter how great and supportive your dad or brothers or uncles, you've got to understand: Chivalry does not exist, especially when it comes to young men. There is a strong rape culture on college campuses (more in Chapter 12). You cannot expect boys to protect you; you can't count on them to respect your boundaries or to stop when you say stop. You need to be able to count on yourself.

In my work I've spoken with hundreds of boys, and I can tell you what they tell me: when a girl is drunk off her ass and fooling around, "coming on to me," these boys feel they have the "right" to fuck them. That's the way they see it, girls—as their right.

I know this sounds harsh. I have had lots of people tell me it's not fair to paint all young men as potential predators. But I

have to tell you the truth as I know it. Given the opportunity—
the right time, the right place, with drugs or alcohol present—
most young men could force themselves on a girl, especially if
they feel they are being led on and believe the girl "wants it."
And remember that 96 percent of abuse is perpetrated by men.
Again, our culture supports misogyny.

Some enlightened young men do exist. We know that some
young men volunteer to provide escort services to young women
on college campuses. It warmed my heart to see and hear so
many young men marching with women at the women's marches.
Men were chanting, "Whose body? Her body!" Even as the rape
culture changes and some men are becoming enlightened, the
trouble remains: all boys and men are exposed to the same movies, videos, and books as the rest of us. They are a part of the
male culture that has its Humbert Humbert believing that Lolita "wanted it" when she was just twelve. They share the same
locker-room mentality, where boys put another notch on their
belt for every girl they fuck. That makes them the "mac daddy."
This sexual violence against women will change only when men
join the fight. According to Donald G. McPherson, the executive
director of the Sports Leadership Institute at Adelphi University
in New York, an organization reaching out to male youth, "Boys
and men must be involved in the fight against violence toward
women because men are the perpetrators. As long as they per-
petuate misogyny, there will be violence against women."

That's where the danger lies for girls. You may enjoy looking
sexy, you may want to be sexual, and you may be turned on by
a guy. But if you don't want to have intercourse with him or give
him a blow job, you can't count on him to respect you when
you say no. You have to be prepared for this male-entitlement

mentality that says, "She asked for it." Of course you have the right not to have sex; you have the right to draw your own boundary lines. You may really enjoy kissing, touching, and holding, but if you don't want intercourse, don't go off drunk or stoned with a guy. Accurate statistics on rape are hard enough to come by and of course fluctuate from year to year, but the National Crime Victimization Survey kept by the US Department of Justice each year tells us that the vast majority of all reported rapes occur between people who know each other. You have to be smart about things and be prepared to protect yourself.

Unfortunately, there is an increasing number of women who blame women for date rape—for not being savvy enough to stop it. For all the awareness that has grown up around rape over the past several years, there is a real backlash, too. Katie Roiphe, the daughter of renowned feminist Anne Roiphe, has written books and articles and has been all over the Internet with her message that girls on college campuses must be asking for it if they are raped. She says it's your fault. In her book *The Morning After,* Roiphe casts doubt on the idea that young women mean no when they say no. She claims that no is sometimes part of the mating dance and that you can't ask a boy to understand the difference between a no that means maybe and a no that really means no. Recently, there have been many stories online, on blogs, and on Twitter about girls being date-raped. Yet it seems, as one sex-abuse story comes out, one backlash story comes out as well. Be aware of the backlash against the #MeToo movement, claiming that girls and women lie, that now men can't even hug a friend without being called a predator.

Then there's the old and disturbing saying "If you can't stop the rape, you may as well lie back and enjoy it." This type of thinking only fuels people's woman-hating attitudes toward rape, and particularly date rape, and makes it that much harder to change public policy and the law.

There is already so much misunderstanding about rape. There's confusion about whether it differs from sexual abuse. There's confusion about date rape versus stranger rape, and whether one is worse than the other. There's confusion about whether a girl has a right to say no to intercourse when she has otherwise been fooling around with a guy. There is confusion about whether you can be raped by your intimate partner. Some even say it's not really date rape if you meet a guy at a party, hook up, and then he forces you to have sex with him.

Let's be clear here: Any time a woman resists having sex but is forced to do it anyway, that is rape or sexual abuse. Whether you say no, push the person away, cry, or try to run, if you are forced to have sex against your will, that is rape. And one way sex is against your will is if you are too drunk or stoned to even resist.

Many girls ask me whether being forced into oral sex is rape. In my opinion and in the opinion of other professionals, the answer is yes. While this might not hold up in a court of law because the legal definition may be more restrictive, any forced sexual entry is rape. That means if someone forces his penis into your mouth or forces anything into your vagina or anus, it is rape.

Let's get to some myths and truths.

MYTH: Rape and sexual abuse are different.
TRUTH: While rape may occur as part of a longtime pattern of sexual abuse, rape can also be a one-time experience with a date, acquaintance, or stranger. Incest and other forms of long-term sexual abuse involve an ongoing relationship with the

abuser and usually go on for some time. Sexual abuse usually involves coercion, false promises, or some kind of seduction. That said, again any forced sexual connection is sex abuse.

Although after a rape you may have some of the same feelings of violation, as well as fear and shame, as you would after long periods of abuse, the two can cause different emotional scars. Sexual abuse by someone you know usually involves tangled issues of shame, guilt, and responsibility. Some of the aftereffects of stranger rape may be fear of the unknown, of the dark, of being alone, and a general mistrust of strangers, whereas incest causes a general mistrust of the people closest to you and of intimate relationships.

MYTH: You can't rape your own girlfriend or wife. That wouldn't be rape.
TRUTH: Rape does indeed happen between girlfriend and boyfriend, husband and wife. Men who force their girlfriends or wives into having sex are committing rape, period. The laws are blurry, and in some countries marital rape is legal, but it is still rape.[5]

MYTH: Alcohol and drugs may sometimes be involved in date rapes, but not usually.
TRUTH: According to Robin Warshaw in *I Never Called It Rape,* published in 1994, alcohol, drugs, or both are known to be involved in at least 75 percent of date rapes.[6] In 2018 the National Council of Alcoholism and Drug Dependence stated that 90 percent of acquaintance rape and sexual assault on college campuses involves alcohol.

MYTH: If a young woman comes on to a guy and wants to be sexual, she has no right to draw the line at intercourse or oral sex. If she's flirting heavily, she's "asking for it."

TRUTH: Just like young men, young women have the right to enjoy their sensuality and sexuality, including intense hooking up, and still say no to intercourse or oral sex. No one has the right to demand any kind of sex or coercion into sexual acts from another person, under any circumstances.

MYTH: These days most rapes get reported.

TRUTH: Very few rapes get reported.[7] According to RAINN, as of 2018 two out of three rapes go unreported.

MYTH: Rape is against the law, so if you report a rape, there's a good chance that justice will be served.

TRUTH: The laws are still in flux, and most rapists are put back out on the streets, even after many arrests.[8] In December 2004, the Justice for All Act was finally passed. This law provides approximately $1 billion in funding over five years to eliminate the rape kit backlog and improve the collection and processing of DNA in solving more rape cases. It is also known as the Debbie Smith Law, named for a woman who survived a stranger rape and fought for more than fifteen years to get this law passed. Nevertheless, as of 2018, RAINN reports that, out of 1,000 rapes, 994 rapists will go free.

MYTH: Having an alcoholic blackout means you pass out, so you wouldn't even remember if you'd been raped.

TRUTH: It's true that you won't remember anything that happened to you during an alcoholic blackout, but you don't pass out. In fact, you could be wide awake throughout. Alcoholic blackouts are periods of intoxication where you may seem awake and alert but your brain is unable to form or store new information and experiences; in other words, you are out of it, even though your eyes are open.

MYTH: Date rape drugs are hard to come by.
TRUTH: Date rape drugs are actually remarkably easy to get. They are used to incapacitate you and make you prey to sexual attack, and they can take away memory, not unlike an alcoholic blackout. However, with date rape drugs, which are usually slipped into your drink and have no taste, you are passed out. You may wake up and have a strange sense that something happened or have no memory at all. There is also not just one date rape drug. The familiar name heard on the streets and on college campuses is "roofies," short for Rohypnol, but you should also know that Ativan, Xanax, and Benadryl—all commonly found on college campuses and easily obtainable—are also used to induce a blackout for the purpose of date rape. There are almost a hundred slang names for these drugs, including mind erasers, forget pill, R2, bump, black hole, Special K, super acid.

MYTH: Stranger rape is more traumatic than date rape.
TRUTH: Generalizations like that are impossible to make. All rape is traumatic. Women who are raped will have approximately the same symptoms, both physical and emotional, regardless of the type of rape. Stranger rape may make a woman fearful of walking alone or taking risks, but date rape is a major betrayal of trust. Who's to say which one is the more damaging?

THE DIFFERENCE BETWEEN STRANGER RAPE AND DATE RAPE

Stranger rape is a terrifying violation that leaves many women frightened not only of strangers but of all relationships. It can leave you feeling unprotected and unsupported by society, much as the incest survivor feels unprotected and unsupported by her family.

The biggest difference between stranger rape and other forms of sexual abuse is that being raped by a stranger doesn't usually cause the deep feelings of guilt and self-blame that come with being raped by someone you agreed to be with. With stranger rape, it's much easier to understand that it wasn't your fault. But that does not take away the deep feelings of violation.

Another difference with stranger rape is that you usually fear for your life. There are more murders reported in random stranger rape than in any form of sexual abuse between people who know each other, whether incest, acquaintance rape, or date rape. In her book *Lucky,* Alice Sebold describes seeing a pink hair tie in the leaves on the floor of the tunnel in which she was brutally raped by a stranger at nineteen. She remembered that a girl had been raped and murdered in that same tunnel and felt "lucky" that she got out alive.

One of my clients had a similar experience. When she was raped at knifepoint by a stranger who broke into her apartment, all she could think about was her baby daughter. She was twenty-eight at the time and had just returned from a class. Her daughter was at day care. The rapist, who had gagged her and tied her up before raping her at knifepoint, told her repeatedly that he would kill her if she did not comply. She was more afraid of being killed than of the rape itself.

With incest, most girls know they will not be killed. They know the person raping them; they have a context. There is no context in stranger rape—just fear.

While the statistics on stranger rape are little better than those for any other kind of sexual abuse—as with other forms, most women don't want anyone to know—most professionals agree that stranger rape is reported more often than date or acquaintance rape because there is less self-blame and confusion about responsibility with stranger rape.

WHAT TO DO IF YOU WANT THE OPTION TO REPORT A RAPE

The first thing to do is not shower. It may feel absolutely awful to have to wait, but if you want the police to have evidence of the rape, you simply can't wash. Try to find a loved one or friend to come over and be with you and take you to the hospital. Once you get to the hospital, they will call the hospital's rape crisis unit.

In the 1970s nurses and feminists led the anti-rape movement as advocates for survivors of rape, and they developed rape kits in hospital emergency rooms and for rape crisis units. Those units include advocates and specialized nurses. Things may vary by state, but usually you will be met by a rape crisis counselor/advocate, who will walk you through the process of being examined and be there with you and for you throughout the examination. At that time, you and your rape crisis advocate or friend or loved one should request a sexual assault nurse examiner be assigned to you. These are nurses with specialized training to provide trauma-informed, patient-specific evaluation and treatment, which can include forensic evidence collection. These nurses will also test for and give treatment for sexually trans-mitted diseases and the human immunodeficiency virus (HIV) and for pregnancy prevention. The hospital will then ask to col-lect what's called a "rape kit." Rape kits are intended to assist in the criminal prosecution or to collect evidence for prosecution of sexual assault cases; the goal is to prove rape with DNA.

Many girls get very nervous at the prospect of having to go through this procedure and don't know what their rights are. That's where the advocate can help you. Basically, no one can force you to get a rape kit; the hospital will not col-lect one without your consent. Remember that. The choice is yours. Also, getting the rape kit doesn't commit you to press-ing charges; it only gathers evidence that might be extremely useful, and will sometimes be necessary, should you decide to prosecute. In any case, you can also expect follow-up services with community-based sexual assault advocacy, and medical and law enforcement partners.

Even though some girls do get the rape kit, they do not of-ten choose to go to court because of the added trauma. Please know if you do decide to prosecute after the rape kit, the rape crisis advocate and sexual assault nurse are both prepared to testify in a criminal or civil trial as expert witnesses if neces-sary. You should never feel pressured to prosecute. The girls I know who have gone to court against their abusers are usually protecting a younger sister or friend.

If you do decide to get the rape kit, you should know what to expect. First of all, remember that you have the right to have your rape crisis advocate or loved one with you (or both) at all times. You also have the right to stop the process at any point.

WHAT IS A RAPE KIT?

1. You will be asked to disrobe, and a nurse will bag each article of your clothing—including, of course, your panties—to send to the crime lab.

2. Your pubic hair will be combed for any foreign hairs, and a sample of ten to fifteen of your own pubic hairs will be collected for comparison.

3. You will be examined for visible blood or semen stains. If such stains are found, samples will be collected.

4. You will be given a vaginal exam similar to a routine gynecological exam. The nurse will use a speculum and swab your vagina and cervix.

5. Your fingernails will also be examined for blood, hair, or foreign tissue. If the nurse sees any foreign matter, she will also swab under your nails. A sample nail clipping may also be taken.

6. Your mouth will be swabbed for saliva.

7. If you report anal penetration, your anus may be swabbed as well.

8. The nurse will take a blood sample to check for infections and pregnancy.

9. And finally, a head hair sample (ten to fifteen hairs) will be taken.[9]

Whether or not you go to the hospital, you can still decide to press charges. Many times, for varying reasons, rapes are reported without a rape kit. Should you decide to report the rape or any other sexual abuse, here's what you can expect from the legal system (procedures vary from state to state, but this is more or less the sequence of events):

1. A detective will meet with you to take a report. You will be asked to describe what happened and to describe the suspect. (Remember, the decision to go ahead or stop is always yours. You can always request to have a trusted loved one with you during questioning.)

2. The detective will follow up with an investigation and may talk to witnesses and the person who assaulted you, if that person can be found. That person may or may not be arrested.

3. The detective will send a report to the district attorney's office, and an attorney and advocate will be assigned to your case.

4. If an arrest is made, the defendant may be able to post bail.

5. The case will usually take a few years to prosecute.

Needless to say, this is a very quick sketch. If you want to know more about the complicated process of prosecuting sexual-abuse and rape cases, check the Resource Center at the back of this book for further information, where you will find lawyers specializing in this.

DATE RAPE

When you are just walking down the street or riding your bike in the park or sleeping in your apartment and someone rapes you, there's no question that you didn't do anything to bring the rape on yourself.

With date rape, it could be different, and you may have more choices than you think. I never blame the survivor of date rape. Even if you are fooling around and you want to stop him but you become mute from fear and cannot speak, even if you say no quietly and then do not have the courage or strength to stop him, even if you invite him to your room and start to want sex and then change your mind during sex and tell him to stop, even if you feel intense pressure to perform oral sex on him and he pushed you to it and you did not want it. Let's get agency and avoid date rape at all costs, if at all possible. Again, I am not saying you don't have the right to fool around, but have your posse with you, have a designated gal pal or good guy pal to make sure you all leave together. Watch your drink while you are out. Stay away from drunken frat parties.

Several of my clients suffered date rapes between the ages of eighteen and twenty. The two you will hear from were both nineteen when they were date-raped. Iris's date rape was her first and only experience of rape. Dahlia was date-raped after being violently gang-raped by acquaintances when she was fourteen. Both girls have come through these experiences to the other side, and they hope you will learn from their stories how important it is to take care of yourself. Understanding that you have the potential power to protect yourself from date rape by keeping your wits about you, by not getting so stoned or drunk that your decision making is impaired, having friends there to back you up, all can possibly protect you from date rape. That said, rape is rape, forced sexual contact is sexual abuse. It is never the survivor's fault.

IRIS

I met Iris when she was twenty-two and a senior in college. She had been raped three years earlier but had only recently come to terms with the fact that it even was a rape. In fact, it was a male friend (one of the good guys) who convinced her that what she had experienced was date rape.

Since the rape, she had been in a string of bad relationships with men who did not appreciate her. She came to therapy because she had a sense that her rape three years earlier had affected how she made choices in relationships. She also wanted to deal with her history of emotional abuse and connect the dots as to why she kept picking such losers.

Iris had not been sexually abused as a child physically, but her older brother had subjected her to emotional abuse, verbal sexual abuse, and physical violence. Iris comes from an Irish Catholic family. She is the younger of two children; her brother is seven years her senior.

Both of their parents worked, and her brother was left in charge of her beginning when she was seven and he was fourteen. That was when he started abusing her verbally. He would repeatedly taunt her. He would choke her, pinch her, make sexual comments about her breasts, her hips, and her rear end, and constantly tell her that she was a "worthless, ugly piece of shit." By constantly talking to her in sexual terms and touching her in inappropriate ways, her brother taught her that she had no right to any boundaries, physical or emotional.

As a child, Iris didn't know how to stop the sexual innuendoes or the inappropriate touching. Of course, in front of their parents, her brother behaved like an angel. Her parents trusted and praised their son, and, when Iris complained about how he mistreated her, they ignored her.

When Iris began dating at around fifteen, she seemed to seek out males who would treat her badly. In hindsight, of course, that's no surprise. That's what she knew; that's what she felt she deserved. She put herself into many situations she should never have been in and struggled throughout adolescence with the feeling that she didn't deserve good relationships.

Fast forward. Iris is now twenty-two and graduating at the top of her class from a prestigious university. She came in to see me because of her recurring nightmares, heightened anxiety, and depressive feelings. She had hit bottom and wanted to understand why she kept having dreams about the rape.

In Iris's story, she tells what it's like to be out partying with your friends and what can happen as you get more and more drunk or high, how your judgment can blur, and how quickly your situation can escalate and become dangerous.

She talks about how she would get "buzzed" to deal with her insecurities and her very human need to fit in, and then she describes the date rape and its aftermath in precise detail. She does not gloss over her rape in any way. I warn you, this is rough stuff. This is the unvarnished story of a date rape.

IRIS'S STORY

But I Thought He Liked Me

I was nineteen years old and had just finished my first year of college. A group of us were going out to celebrate the end of exams and the beginning of summer. We met at a club I had never been to. I loved the magic that took place when you entered a club.

Through those guarded portals lay another world, a planet with an atmosphere all its own. Our group of three young women and two young men entered a room with swarms of people dancing to music, and I squinted as my eyes adjusted to the darkness. My head was fuzzy from the drinking I'd already done that night.

Our group met up with some other friends I did not know. There were people everywhere, drinking, talking, popping pills. I was immediately attracted to a guy named Michael. He smiled a sweet, boyish smile when introduced to me, and I noted how handsome he was. He had large, dark eyes and a narrow goatee. I smiled back at him, more from self-consciousness than anything else. When I'd left the house that night I'd thought I looked good, but when I looked at the people around me, they seemed to have stepped out of the pages of a fashion magazine. I felt like an impostor in the velvet-drenched, smoky scene. For more courage, I got another drink at the bar.

The bartender was a friend of a friend and had made us something special on the house. Sweet, fruity drinks usually made me sick, but I took a large gulp. It went down surprisingly smoothly, and I swallowed the rest of it quickly before my buzz had a chance to disappear. I wanted to drown myself in the stuff, let the pink liquid rise above my head as I danced and the alcohol pounded in my brain as if keeping time, my limbs gaining courage with every sip. Michael came over and danced with me. He was holding my back and swaying slowly from side to side, and my body responded. He was strong, and my lightness felt secure in his arms. The music got faster, and I started to move on my own in a sensual, drunken haze. He smiled down at me, grinding back. I was absorbed in the moment, in a capsule, all by myself. No external reality existed for me. All I knew at that moment was how good I felt, how good and free and light.

We stopped dancing and got another drink and started talking, and I found him as charming and funny as he was handsome.

My friends then joined us. Ezra, a guy I had some classes with, came over and put his arm around me. He had been Michael's friend since high school, and after a while Ezra and Michael said, "Wanna get out of here?" I said good night to my girlfriend, who was also pretty drunk, and she winked at me, and we left.

My head was spinning wildly now, and I was starting to lose my balance. I should have listened to what my body was telling me, to have them drop me off at home so I could sleep the drunkenness off. I was drunk and tired, but I trusted Ezra and I was attracted to Michael. I was dizzier than ever, slightly nauseous, and stumbling, but I still thought I was all right. Michael and Ezra took me by the arms and held me up, and we stood there, in front of the club, waiting for a taxi to take us home.

The next thing I knew, I was in bed in my apartment with no idea how I'd gotten there. My head felt like a swarming beehive, and, as I opened my eyes, I saw Ezra crouched over me. He kissed me, the dry, alcoholic taste of his mouth mingling with mine, but I was dizzy. I wasn't aroused. I couldn't feel anything. Then, as quickly as he had begun, Ezra stopped kissing me. He pulled his face away from mine and looked down at me again. Michael came over. "I'm sorry," he said, starting to make his way down my body. "I just have to eat you."

I was so confused, the words meant nothing to me. I couldn't respond. Then Ezra appeared above me. I could feel my legs being pried apart and Michael sticking his face between them as Ezra shoved his tongue in my mouth. My body was numb and I felt nothing, as if my nerve endings had been severed. As the drunken fog in my head began to clear, I realized what was happening.

With the little strength I had, I got up and away from them and ran into the bathroom.

I was crying hysterically when Ezra came in. "What's the matter, baby?" he asked. I couldn't stop crying, couldn't talk, my body was shaking as I tried to speak. I tried to explain to him that I didn't know what was happening, that I was drunk and didn't want to do this. "Don't cry, baby, don't cry. I thought you liked Michael. You really want us to stop?" I nodded my head yes, suddenly exhausted, and he said okay, leaving me alone in the bathroom. The next thing I knew I was lying on the bathroom floor alone, with closed eyes, having passed out again. My body was leaden, too heavy to move, and I wasn't sure where I was. The alcohol seemed thicker in my bloodstream now, moving slow as syrup, disorienting me. Before I could figure out where I was next, I felt my underwear being pulled off my body.

Realizing this was no dream, I opened my eyes and found Ezra gone. I had been dragged out of the bathroom and pulled to the floor in the bedroom, and Michael was kneeling in front of me. He was pulling my legs up around him and shoving his penis inside me. I was so tired I was paralyzed. I felt like a rag doll, a limp creature with no skeletal structure or will of my own. It felt as if he was splitting me in half. I was torn between numbness and pain, and I asked him to stop. I opened my mouth to say no, but he rammed his tongue into my mouth hard. He kept pounding into me. I faded in and out, unable to stay awake. I kept trying to push him off me, I kept crying and struggling, and at one point I managed to get away.

I ran into the kitchen and hid behind the refrigerator. I was huddled back there shaking like a frightened animal. He followed me in and pulled me from behind it, lifting me like a feather and slamming me back down onto his penis. He propped me up against the countertop, driving me up and down on him like a butter churn, slamming my spine into the rough tile. Finally, he carried me back to bed to finish what he'd started. I realized I wasn't going to get away, and I almost willed my body to stay limp so I could disappear.

When he was done, he rolled over. I was allowed to fall back to sleep. I passed out from fear, exhaustion, and shock. When I woke up, the sun was up, and I heard noises in the apartment. I found myself on the floor. Michael was at the edge of the bed. He seemed large and awkward, mean spirited, uninterested. He was putting on his shoes.

"Hey, do you have a T-shirt I can borrow?" he asked.

I looked at him for a minute, confused, before lifting myself up from the floor. I rummaged through my dresser drawers for something that would fit him. "Thanks," he said, barely glancing up. Suddenly I felt ashamed. He continued dressing. I felt stupid and pathetic, and frightened at the same time. He wasn't friendly; he wasn't nice at all. He grabbed his knapsack from the messy floor, littered with clothes—my clothes from the night before.

"See ya," he said, slamming the door behind him.

I stood for a moment watching the door, amazed that he could have disappeared so quickly. Tears were suddenly falling from my burning eyes. I smelled like smoke and my mouth was dry and pasty, my vagina was bruised and burning, and bleeding. There was dried blood all over my legs. The remnants of the alcohol were nauseating me. My inner thighs ached, and my lower back stung. I saw bruises on my upper chest and my legs. I crawled back into bed, trying to figure out what had happened. All I wanted was for someone to tell me it would all be all right. I wanted to be held tenderly. I pulled the covers high over my head and lay like that for a long time, until I finally cried myself to sleep.

It took me a long time afterward to recognize what had happened to me. Unable to face the truth, I said to myself that I had been "rejected," a much easier pill to swallow than having been date-raped. I didn't talk about the experience to anyone. I basically put the incident in the back of my mind. I would run into Ezra from time to time, but he acted as if nothing had happened.

About one year after the incident I was describing it to a friend, and he said, "Iris, you were raped!" I can honestly say that it hadn't hit me until then. I had been date-raped.

Three years after the incident, at twenty-two, I began therapy. I didn't know where to start. So I started to rehash the abuse I had experienced at the hands of my older brother. I began to understand that I had believed his lies; I had believed that no one would want me, so I was susceptible to any attention. In retrospect I think I kept drinking that night because I was insecure and wanted Michael to like me. I came to therapy because I knew I needed to change. I was feeling insecure about graduating and finding a job, I was having nightmares, and my therapist explained that I needed to appreciate myself before I could commit to any relationship.

In the past two years, my therapy has been a journey to some places I didn't want to go. But I am finding that the more I talk about my childhood abuse at the hands of my brother and the lack of support from my parents, the more I am able to begin to stop blaming myself. As children we have little to no control over the violations of our families—verbal, sexual, or physical—yet as young women we can choose friends and lovers who do not treat us as our families did.

I have since learned that I do have boundaries; I have since learned that it is my responsibility, and no one else's, to make sure people respect me. As a child I could not control my destiny. I could not get my parents to see the demoralization I had suffered at the hands of my brother. But as an adult I get to choose to be around good people. I don't have to speak with my brother. I can limit my time with my parents if they are unsupportive. Slowly but surely, I am putting the rape behind me. I am learning that I am worth more. I have begun to heal.

MY THOUGHTS

Iris very much wanted to share her story to help other young women avoid the mistake she made. She wants girls to know that they should not get drunk or stoned to the point they make themselves vulnerable to danger. We also learn from her story that sometimes young women don't watch out for each other.

As she tells us, Iris did not have high self-esteem, and, even though she was not physically molested as a child, the torment she suffered from the verbal, emotional, and physical abuse by her brother brought her to a point where she believed she deserved very little in relationships. It is no wonder Iris responded to the attention of these two males. After all those years of being told how ugly she was, just a crumb of positive attention felt great.

You'll recall that she knew, as she was getting drunk, that she didn't have all her faculties, but she trusted her "friend" Ezra. In fact, she drank so much that she passed out and came in and out of consciousness during the rape. She was so ashamed, she didn't even want to blame the rape on Ezra and Michael; it was easier to tell herself she'd been rejected by Michael.

I've seen many other girls who've blamed themselves for date rapes. They figure they're old enough that they should be able to keep things from getting out of hand. That's why date rape on college campuses is such a huge problem. Within the past several years, date rape on college campuses has been identified as the number one problem, with date and acquaintance rape topping the list of violent crimes against women on college campuses. This is why the Obama/Biden team founded the "It's on Us" program. And although in the past several years we have made some progress by bringing this crime to the forefront, it remains a huge problem.

Many college girls are testing their new freedom; they do want to go out and get drunk and have a good time; they may even really be into the guy who takes them home. But that doesn't mean they asked to be raped. If a girl resists or says no or tries to run and a guy overpowers her, that is rape. All the backlash in the world doesn't change that fact.

Ask yourself a few questions: Is Iris's story so different from what could have happened to you on a night of partying? Do you and your friends keep each other's backs? Do you keep an eye on your drink at all times to be sure no one tampers with it? If you are going home with a guy do you text your friends, let them know where you are, and ask them to check in on you?

ACQUAINTANCE RAPE / GANG RAPE

quick, call the cops
I've just been cocked blocked
Knocked out by a rock
My body was in shock
a flock of guys just left me alone
coughing up a bloody song
how could I whimper without a fight
I was weak and the cuffs were too tight

—*an eighteen-year-old gang-rape survivor*

Amber's experience, in Chapter 10, of being manipulated into a molestation relationship with a counselor at summer camp, we noted the difference between acquaintance sexual abuse and incest. In this chapter, we've been talking about some of the differences between stranger rape and date rape. But there is also a difference between acquaintance rape and date rape.

Acquaintance rape usually refers to a situation where someone you know rapes you, but not on a date. Usually you did not choose to be out or alone with this person. You may have ended up with him after being out in a group and never had any intention of being with him alone. Of course, at some basic level rape is rape, but getting raped after choosing to be with a guy feels a lot different from being raped by a guy you never had any interest in or attraction to in the first place. The former is more confusing, and you can really begin to question your judgment. It's upsetting in an entirely different way than when a stranger attacks you. Nevertheless, acquaintance rape can be just as traumatic.

DAHLIA

When Dahlia was raped by some boys from school, she didn't even know any of their names. She'd only seen them in the halls at school. A girlfriend had brought her along to meet up with them in a park and then left her alone with these boys she didn't know.

Dahlia was only fourteen at the time. She grew up in San Francisco, in the upscale Pacific Heights area. Her father was very uptight, a successful banker and businessman. He made her feel worthless with his withering criticism. She was expected to get straight As and excel in sports. He also bullied her mother and younger brother. Dahlia never leaned on her mother for support; she just felt sorry for her. From a very young age, Dahlia learned to do everything she could to be perfect. She spoke softly and was always sweet and agreeable.

When she was eleven and her brother was eight, her parents got a messy divorce. Her father jerked her mother around about money, and her mother slipped into a quiet depression. Her brother became needy and demanding of both parents, and Dahlia, being the good girl, slipped into the background. She hardly ever saw her father and mostly just threw herself into her schoolwork and the track team.

Through Dahlia's riveting story we learn how low self-image and constantly being in the background of her family can leave a girl vulnerable to rape and eating disorders.

DAHLIA'S STORY

I Was Scared They Would Kill Me

When I went to therapy at twenty, I felt like such an idiot. Not only was I raped once, I was raped twice! The first time I was clueless, but when I was nineteen I should have known better. Actually, I did know better. I knew I should have stopped drinking after the fifth drink. But I am insecure and the drinking made me relax, so I kept going. A big mistake.

I am what some kids call a "mixed breed." Not a very nice way of saying I am half Chinese (my mom's Chinese) and half Irish Catholic (from my dad). I am kind of light skinned for an Asian and have light brown hair. I call it mousy brown. I have always felt like kind of a freak, never really fitting in with either the Asian kids or the white kids.

My school was very rich and white. I always felt like I stood out. I guess you could say I still have a pretty bad self-image.

People are always telling me how thin I am, but I don't agree. I think I'm much too fat. But I am trying to change those feelings. Track has always helped me to feel stronger and centered, but, when I started to run to lose weight, it took some of the joy out of running. I am working on that, too.

I have always been a shy kid. When my parents separated when I was twelve, I was actually relieved. My father had the ability to scare the shit out of me just by entering the room. He never hit me or anything, but he was joyless, stern, and very judgmental. My mother is a sweetheart. I was really proud of her for breaking up with my father and going back to college at thirty-five. Asking for a divorce was the first time I ever saw her really stand up to my dad.

So there I was. Twelve years old, a shy kid without a lot of friends. I spent most of my time alone, drawing in my sketchbook or writing in my journal. My seventh-grade year was mostly about helping my mom around the house and getting used to not having my father around to scare me, and my mom spent a lot of time calming my brother down. The year I entered eighth grade, I met another eighth-grader on the track team, a girl named Lee Ann. Lee Ann was everything I wasn't. She was brazen, funny, self-assured, and she even hung out with boys in the tenth and eleventh grades.

I wanted friends, I wanted to be invited along to things, so when Lee Ann asked me to go to the diner with her after track to get a sandwich, I said yes. Lee Ann then suggested that we go meet up with some guys she knew at Speedway Meadow in Golden Gate Park. Golden Gate Park is a huge park in the western part of San Francisco. It runs more than forty city blocks out toward the ocean and has lots of different areas: beautiful ponds, trails, fields, and lots of woods.

We all met up at the meadow at dusk. At first, I was enjoying hanging out with these guys, even though I felt out of place. I had only seen them in the halls of school. They were all popular varsity football players and seemed pretty cool.

After a while Lee Ann announced that she had to go. When I tried to leave with her, one of the boys knocked me down. Weird. I thought it was an accident, but then Lee Ann turned to look and saw me on the ground and just left me there. That's when I got scared. As I got up, another boy grabbed me by the arm. I tried to yank myself free, I told them I was leaving, but one of the boys took off his sock and stuffed it in my mouth. I couldn't make a sound. I think I was in shock.

The three boys dragged me into a secluded woody area. It was dark by then. One boy pushed me down, another pulled down my pants, and the third unzipped his pants and forced his penis into me. I remember the boys laughing. Then one boy started jerking off, his sperm hitting me on my head, while the third boy took his turn with me. Even though this all probably lasted about fifteen minutes, it felt like hours.

When they were all done, they threatened to kill me if I told. They said they'd hurt my little brother and my mother. They recited my address and phone number and told me they'd be watching me "all the time." Then they left me with the sock stuffed in my mouth, my pants and underpants all ripped and bloody, and gunk all over my hair and face.

I am not sure how I got myself up and got home, but I did. I was so relieved that no one was home when I got there. I headed straight for the shower, still feeling numb. In the shower I finally started realizing what had happened. I began to sob and just sat at the bottom of the shower, holding myself and rocking back and forth.

When my mother and brother came home a little while later, my mom called up the stairs. I quickly threw on some clothes and came down to join them as if nothing had happened. My mom asked about the bruise on my forehead, but I just told her that I had fallen during track and not to worry. My mom, having no reason to suspect anything, believed me.

I couldn't sleep that night. I felt as if I was crawling out of my skin. I looked at my bruises and remembered them pushing and pushing until my skin was scraped bare. They'd taken all my hope and ripped it out of me. When my mom came up that night to kiss me good night, I almost jumped out of my skin in fear. I told her I felt sick.

That night I woke up in a cold sweat. I had come down with a fever, and my mom agreed that I should stay home for a couple of days. I was terrified to go to school; I was terrified the boys would find me in the halls and torment me. I believed they would come after me again, and I was terrified that they would come after my family if I told. After the brutality of the gang rape, and their laughter, I figured they were capable of anything, even killing. What did I know? I was just a young kid.

Even though I was scared to go back to school, I wanted to see Lee Ann and say to her, "Fuck you for leaving me alone with those assholes in the park." I didn't know if she knew or had even maybe set me up. I mean, the way she'd turned and looked and then ridden off on her bike. I thought she must have known they were going to do something to me.

I lay there in bed thinking about their sick smiles and laughter, the spitting, the jerking off, and I just cried and cried.

Meanwhile my mother was crying herself to sleep every night. It's a really shameful thing in Asian culture to get divorced, and my mother's family had shunned her and actually taken my father's side. I certainly wasn't going to burden my mom with my problems. I believed I was her lifeline.

On Friday I finally went to school. I saw Lee Ann in the halls, and she said hi really nonchalantly. I couldn't believe it. I was practically shaking the whole time, but I did draw up the courage to ask her why she had left me alone with those assholes in the park. She said, "Oh, they said they had a great time with you!" That froze me. I just avoided Lee Ann from then on. I didn't know whom I could trust.

I spent months being petrified that these guys would do something to me or to my family if I told. I retreated into my own little hell. I never spoke to Lee Ann, but I avoided everyone, really. I always looked over my shoulder for those asshole boys, and I tried to always leave my classes with classmates and to never walk alone in the halls.

The boys did see me a couple of times. Once they even followed me home, jeering and whispering, "Better not tell, bitch." One time they cornered me at my locker when the halls were deserted. They pushed me up against the locker and threatened me again, saying they were watching me and my little brother and that I should watch my back. After school ended for the year they seemed to leave me alone. Who knows? Maybe they'd raped another girl by then. But I was still frightened all the time.

I felt out of control. Now running track was not enough. I needed to control something else, and about the only other thing I could control was my eating. So I started to count every calorie of everything I put into my mouth, and then I would vomit after almost every meal. I bought cookbooks and read the calorie content of all foods; I figured out ways to pretend I had eaten what was on my plate by putting food in napkins at the dinner table. And I think this little bit of control saved me from going totally crazy.

Meanwhile, my mother was pretty clueless. My father was always away on business, so I barely saw him, and my brother was having a lot of trouble in school, so nobody was really paying attention to me. I used to cover up my body with double layers of T-shirts and everything, so I guess nobody really knew how thin I had become. No one knew, either, that I would puke after every meal. I know it sounds awful, but the vomiting felt like getting rid of all the bad stuff that had been building up inside me.

I was scared and tormented by the rape, but I never told anyone what had happened to me. I continued to do well in school, avoided most kids, and finished eighth grade.

The next fall, I started ninth grade, and about thirty new kids entered our public school from the next town over. I made the varsity track team and actually started to become friends with a couple of new girls at school. I would still see the boys who raped me in the halls at school from time to time—they were seniors now and they thought they ruled the school—but they had stopped paying any attention to me. I was still scared to death inside, but I found great comfort in being obsessed with food and weight and calories.

Ninth grade was when my body started to betray me. Even though my period had started when I was twelve, it stopped with my eating problem. But now my breasts had started growing and boys were checking me out. This made me totally anxious. Whenever a guy would look at me or try to hang out with me, I would panic. I tried never to walk the halls alone. I always tried to be with one of the new kids. My reputation at school was that I was some guy-hating weirdo. Some kids even started rumors that I was gay. That didn't bother me so much, but the stares from guys did, so I ate even less. Still, nobody noticed. My mother was busy with college, and most of my friends were almost as obsessed with calories as I was.

My little world at the time revolved around eating and purging, around counting calories and checking for pinchable flesh. I was determined never to have any flesh that could be pinched. I figured that if I didn't look like a woman, if I had no curves, no breasts, no flesh, maybe I wouldn't be rape-able, maybe I wouldn't be sexual. Maybe I would disappear.

Finally, my mother became concerned. She finally noticed that I had become reclusive and frail and less and less communicative. She tried to talk to me, tried to get me to eat. But I would get defensive, and my mom and I started fighting a lot. She was doing better, and I was pissed. I was pissed if she tried to tell me what to eat and what not to eat. I hated her commenting on my body and felt invaded when she said anything about my looks.

Then one day at track practice, I passed out on the field and had to be taken to the emergency room of our local hospital. I weighed just eighty-seven pounds. I was immediately given an IV and came in and out of consciousness. I think they were sedating me, and the IV was making me nauseous. After two days they transferred me, or I should say my mother committed me, to a psychiatric hospital. I hated that place. I had to go to group therapy with boys, kids were hooking up on the unit while the staff wasn't looking, and girls were vomiting and taking enemas to keep their weight down and then drinking gallons of water and not peeing for weigh-in. Wow, I was learning all kinds of tricks in the hospital.

I really wanted to get out. The social worker kept asking me over and over why I was so depressed, why I was anorexic and bulimic, why, why, why. I hated her. Finally, one day in a family therapy session I blurted it all out about the rape. It was me and my mother and the social worker. My mother leapt from her chair and grabbed hold of me. It felt really good to finally let out the secret, but I made them promise it wouldn't go past that room.

Three weeks after that meeting, I left the psych hospital. I had my new survival techniques (enemas, water retention) and felt a mixture of relief and terror that I had told. Even though I'd asked her not to, my mother told my father, and they insisted that I press charges. I told them that was impossible. I was too scared. I told them that the boys weren't reachable anymore, that they'd graduated and gone to college and moved out of town. But my parents insisted.

Before the boys were notified or any charges pressed, I was grilled by the attorney and everything got dredged up again, and I went into a major depression. My anorexia was in high gear because I felt all over again that all my power was being taken away from me.

When we showed up for another appointment with the lawyer, I fainted and needed another hospitalization. This time I was put into a regular hospital, and my weight was "normal" at ninety-two pounds, so I was released with a sedative. I begged my parents to drop the case. They agreed.

After the case was dropped, I made a deal with myself that I would keep myself so busy I wouldn't have time to think or remember anything. I refused therapy. I became obsessed with track, school, and, of course, calories. Now I knew the price of going under the required ninety-two pounds. It was tricky, but I managed to maintain that "healthy" weight. I somehow finished high school with honors and got accepted into an Ivy League college with a track scholarship. I had put the gang rape way down deep into a dark place that I never went to.

My first year at college went smoothly, and then, the summer after my freshman year, I got raped again. This time it was a date rape. The next thing I knew I was sitting in Dr. Patti's office, with my roommate who brought me there.

MY THOUGHTS

The summer of her freshman year, Dahlia was out on a date with a guy she'd just met. She was nervous and had drunk herself into oblivion. They started fooling around a little, but when he wanted to keep going, she said no. This time she screamed. It didn't matter. He raped her anyway. Dahlia waited a couple of days to tell, then she told her roommate, who was also an abuse survivor. Her roommate was one of my clients and brought her in to see me. We immediately began to peel away the layers of Dahlia's traumas.

It has been two years since that first session, and Dahlia still struggles with her weight. She is afraid of relationships with males, but at least now she has a good female friend, her roommate. Dahlia is still haunted that she never went through with the case against the sick boys who gang-raped her, but the truth is she is still not strong enough to do so. Not all girls have the strength to report their rapists or molesters. And that has to be all right, too.

Of course, we all want to see justice done, but sometimes justice is served when a girl can sleep through the night without a nightmare. Although Dahlia still struggles with her eating disorder and still gets depressed, she has not been out drunk with a guy since her date rape. And in our last session she talked about accepting a date with a really nice guy she met at school. That's justice, too.

WHERE WILL IT END?

Rape is an epidemic, and although the laws have gotten better over the years, they do not protect women from rape. Police follow-up on rape is terrible. According to the website and organization End the Backlog, there are hundreds of thousands of untested rape kits in crime labs and police stations. Survivors can take from four to six hours to complete the rape kit, and many of these courageous girls and women never receive any follow-up. Most rapists are never caught, and if they are they're rarely prosecuted, and if they're prosecuted they almost never go to jail, and if they go to jail they're usually back on the street at the speed of light (see the Resource Center for more updates on rape kits).

At this point, unfortunately, we cannot depend on the police or the courts to protect us from rape. And our culture doesn't help. There is more pornography available now than ever before, not to mention the general "pornographization" of young women. It's no surprise that the director of many Britney Spears videos is Gregory Dark, a well-known hard-core pornographic-movie director. The Britney Spears of the world are ever present, making it even more difficult for young women to actually enjoy being sexy without the shadow of explicit sexual provocation hanging over them. Women of color are especially depicted in sexualized ways. The rap and hip hop movement have perpetrated this sexualizing of young women through music videos where half-naked young women surround the fully dressed rapper, all vying for his attention. These young women are depicted as hungry for this man, and the sexy seduction is all they have.

Young women have the right to love their bodies, to enjoy their sexuality, to connect love and sex. And many young women do. But there's never been a greater need to be smart about it. It is not only men who are susceptible to those sexualized images. Boys are susceptible to sexualized images of young girls and are demanding sex at younger and younger ages.

Again, there are boys and men out there who respect and champion girls and women. Feminist mothers are bringing up their sons to honor girls and women, and we hope that things are changing. Be clear that I am in no way blaming girls and women for date rape. That said, there are ways to be smart and to take steps to stay as safe as you can. Remember these pointers and pass them on to your friends:

1. Keep your wits about you when you are out. Do not get stoned or drunk to the point of oblivion.
2. When you do go out with friends, make sure they have your back. Always have one friend aware that you are partying, and take turns being on call for each other.
3. If you are out partying and the guy you are with is also drunk or stoned, do not go off alone with him unless you are ready to defend yourself from a rape. That may sound alarmist, but let's face it, girls, this is our culture. Of course, not all boys or men are rapists in waiting, but why play with fire when there are possible ways to protect yourself?
4. Understand that alcohol and drugs impair your judgment.
5. Never leave your drink unattended so that a drug could be put in it.
6. Never go off alone with a guy you don't know. It's just not safe. If you meet a guy and like him, your best bet

is to go out with him several times in a group before going anywhere with him alone.

7. Make your intentions clear. If you are not interested in sex, let the guy you are with know that. Remember, you are entitled to set the boundaries on physical contact.

8. Check in on your girlfriends to make sure they are safe. Help your friend if it looks like she is getting drunk and about to go off with a guy she just met—intervene and take her home. Build this sisterhood of strength and caring, and invite the good guys in too.

9. Try to stay in a public place

10. And, last but not least, do not blame yourself for date rape.

As far as stranger rape goes, there is not that much you can do to protect yourself because of the randomness of the crime. Needless to say, you are less likely to get raped in the afternoon on a busy street than at 2:00 A.M. walking alone on a deserted street. Large parking garages are notorious for rapes, so always try to park in a crowded, well-lit, preferably outdoor lot. Walk tall and proud. Don't be looking at your smartphone oblivious to your surroundings, or deep in conversation. Don't look vulnerable. This cannot always prevent a random rape, but it may help. Take a self-defense class. This will make you feel more in control of your body. Some girls who have been date-raped even report that when they snapped to and became aware that they were being forced into sex, they had enough physical strength to push the guy off and get away. That said, during stranger rape, especially if he has a weapon, all the strength or self-defense skills in the world might not help you.

But it can be very empowering to know that you have some skills to fight back if a guy is trying to force sex on you.

Most importantly, be there for your friends. If your friend is raped, be there for her; but also be there to help each other to have a good time when you are out partying. Always have a designated girl to stay sober and be on the watch. Look out for each other, girls. Support each other, and enlist the good guys to stand tall with you. Know your agency, it is there!

CHAPTER 12

STOP CALLING US *WHORES*

Prostitution Is Sexual Abuse
(Ruby Rose's Story)

For many years feminist activists, politicians, and writers have been bringing our attention to the violence and exploitation prostitutes face every day. "Old school" feminist Gloria Steinem says, "Sexual violation—body invasion is much more traumatic than any other violation." And yet there are young women who identify themselves pro-prostitution feminists who deny that prostitution is abuse and call it "sex work." Pro-prostitution feminists believe that women choose sex work. And, of course, much of the male-dominant culture says that prostitution is a perfectly legitimate "choice" of profession for a woman.

Meanwhile, as the debate rages, young girls and young women are being brought into "the life" of prostitution in a kind of national emergency. There's no ambiguity about it: Putting a teenage girl to work selling sex or buying that sex from her is abuse, whether she seems to "choose" it or not. There's simply no way a minor makes such a choice freely. It's always about someone taking away her power.

We hope that even third-wave feminists will agree that girls who are trafficked for sex do not choose to be prostitutes. Yet a large majority of prostitutes were originally sexually trafficked. As we will learn with Ruby Rose, sex trafficking is when a girl is kidnapped and drugged, or lured and drugged. She is raped on average anywhere from six to thirty times a day. The pimps treat these girls as if they are rag dolls; the more drugged they are, the better. In 2006 the FBI estimated that more than 100,000 children and young women aged nine to nineteen were sex trafficked in the United States. In 2018 that number has risen to over 300,000. What has been a worldwide epidemic for decades, selling children—mostly girls—for sex, is now an epidemic in the United States. These are not only girls who are runaways, girls from broken homes, girls on drugs. Many of the teen girls who are lured into the world of sex trafficking are middle-class girls from caring homes. These are the same invisible girls who are on the soccer team, good students in college. These are girls from Texas, New York, Illinois, California.[10] Ruby Rose was lucky that she was only abducted for two days before her aunt rescued her. Yet her life in prostitution began with sex trafficking.

Carol Smolenski, an old-school feminist, founded ECPAT (End Child Prostitution, Child Pornography and Trafficking) USA in 1990 to stop sexual trafficking and to protect every child's basic human right to grow up free from sexual exploitation and trafficking. Her organization is educating youth who are targeted by pimps. ECPAT USA is conducting workshops in New York City public schools, helping girls have healthy online identities and making teens aware of the predators online. Girls who are suffering sex abuse and are feeling desperate with no way out are easy prey for the sexual trafficker or the pimp abuser online (more in the Resource Center).

Pimp culture permeates the sex trafficking industry. Men are making the money off the backs of teen girls. Some girls are abducted from the streets, others are lured with the promise of a new life, a fun life, an adventure. And, again, 96 percent of sexual predators and abusers are men, and that includes men who are paying for sex with teen girls and young women.

When I wrote the first edition of *Invisible Girls*, I had been working with girls all over New York City, and few of them had been sexually trafficked or involved in prostitution. It is, frankly, an area I neglected with the first edition. But I've had the opportunity to work with the girls and staff of the GEMS program in New York City. GEMS, which stands for Girls Educational & Mentoring Services, works with young women prostitutes ages twelve to twenty-one, helping them get off the streets by providing services, including housing and court support. GEMS was started in 1999 by a young woman named Rachel Lloyd. Rachel was sexually exploited and abused as a teenager and has come through her abuse to thrive and help change the culture around prostitution. GEMS began at a kitchen table and now has funding and helps hundreds of girls. When I donated copies of *Invisible Girls* to GEMS, the feedback from the staff was that their girls felt just like the girls in the book. As I started to work with some of the girls from GEMS, I realized that each of these girls is just like any other girl who survives sex abuse, the same as any other girl whose mother rejects or disbelieves her, the same as any other invisible girl who is being sexually exploited and sexually abused. They are righteous and strong and resilient— and they, too, heal from sexual abuse.

As I talked with more and more girls "in the life," I knew these voices needed to be heard.

One night about I was watching the news and saw a young woman talking about "sex work" in Colorado. She was claiming to feel "empowered" as a sex worker and talking about how she "chose" to do this work. My jaw dropped practically to the floor. This young woman had been a client of mine more than ten years earlier, when she had been raped by the telephone repairman—but even then she had insisted that she had wanted to give him a blow job and that it was not rape. She was fifteen years old, and he was in his thirties. She had also talked about an uncle who had molested her years before.

She was very resistant to therapy and to my strong insistence that she'd been abused by the phone repairman. I urged her to report this dangerous predator. She told me she would never return to therapy, and she didn't. When I told her parents, they seemed fairly indifferent. I called the phone company and reported it, but they said without any corroboration they would not do anything. I tried to reach out to her several times, and then she and her family moved out of state and I never saw or heard from her again. Until that night ten years later when I saw her on TV talking about her "sex work."

It's no wonder the whole issue gets kind of murky or that it gets whitewashed. Popular culture uses the word *pimp* quite freely: People pimp their cars, their rooms—a song called "It's Hard Out Here for a Pimp" won a Grammy Award in 2005, for heaven's sake. Some self-identified third-wave feminists are contributing to our numbness, arguing, as I mentioned, for the use of the term *sex worker* instead of *prostitute*, to give the work a kind of dignity. But, in my view—and the view of the girls I speak to who have been "in the life" and the staff who work with them and the lawmakers who are changing the laws to protect them and the activists out there on the front lines trying to change the culture—there's nothing all right about teenagers selling their precious bodies for sex. It's degrading work, with men buying the right to invade a girl's or woman's body and play out their own, often-violent fantasies on young women, many of whom are the age of their own daughters!

We are numbing ourselves to the reality that pimps and johns are predators—and abusers—and they are taking very young girls and putting them directly in harm's way and serious life-and-death danger. Girls in prostitution generally won't surface for a statistical study, but I often hear anecdotally from the girls "in the life" that almost all of the girls who go into prostitution have been sexually abused. Of course, we also know from Sage's story in Chapter 8 that many topless dancers are also survivors of sexual abuse. It's not girls' instinct to sell their flesh. Girls and women do it because they've been so degraded by other life experiences that this seems, somehow, the best option—or the only option.

Other feminists are bringing to light the reality that prostitution is sex abuse. In her anthology *Prostitution, Trafficking, and Traumatic Stress,* psychologist and anti-pornography/anti-prostitution activist Melissa Farley interviews women who have left "the life," and most of them claim a history of sexual abuse. In her book, feminist theorists, psychologists, and researchers all draw the same conclusion: prostitution is a form of sexual abuse, such violent crimes against women are all part of a male-dominated culture, and prostitution is basically for the profit and pleasure of men at the expense of women.

And remember that these studies reflect the experiences of women in their twenties, thirties, and older. Here we are talking about teenage girls, invisible until they are picked up and arrested and treated like criminals for prostituting. In 2008, New York State passed a Safe Harbor for Exploited Youth Act, which decriminalized prostitution in children under eighteen. Activists at GEMS led the fight alongside feminists and politicians and lawmakers. Now local districts are required to provide crisis intervention services, community-based programming, counseling, and emergency services as well as long-term housing solutions for exploited youth. What this bill recognizes is that these children are "victims," not criminals, and that we as a society are responsible for providing them with basic social services. This bill will save the lives of many invisible girls "in the life." In 2016 twenty-eight states have enacted this law. The 2016 statistics show that 93 percent of sex-trafficked youth are females fourteen to seventeen years old. The statistics of sex-trafficked girls and of prostitution are almost identical.

SOMEBODY'S DAUGHTER

As I listened and learned about the lives of young prostitutes, it became so clear: The fifty-year-old man who pays for sex with a sixteen-year-old prostitute is not so different from the uncle who gives his niece expensive gifts for sex. The man who repeatedly rapes his daughter or stepdaughter under the threat of denying everything—or worse—is no different from the pimp who keeps girls working for him under the threat of injury—or worse.

In this country, we don't lock up johns, we lock up prostitutes. That tells us pretty much everything we need to know. Perhaps these men are not going home and molesting their daughters, but how much better is it that they're paying for sex with girls of twelve, thirteen, fourteen, fifteen, or sixteen? At the time that then–New York governor Elliot Spitzer was caught up in a prostitution ring, his own daughters were fifteen and seventeen years old. The prostitute he was caught with was nineteen. What makes his story even more tragic, for all of us, is that Spitzer, as attorney general (prior to becoming governor), was responsible for breaking up several large prostitution rings and was one of the most outspoken political advocates for changing laws to punish johns and pimps. He devastated the violence-against-women movement when he was caught himself. With a nineteen-year-old.

In 1999 Sweden passed laws to protect prostitutes and punish johns, and in only two years they saw a decline of 50 percent in the number of women prostitutes and 75 percent in the number of men buying sex.[11] Norway and Iceland adopted similar legislation in 2009, and leading British politicians have called for the same. In 2015 the European Parliament announced its goal to reduce the demand for prostitution by punishing the clients. Here at home, some states have taken cues from Europe. In 2018 in California, the Los Angeles County Regional Human Trafficking Task Force arrested more than five hundred pimps and johns. In spite of some progress, though, the statistics are terrifying: 80 percent of the world population of prostitutes are female and aged thirteen to twenty-five; 90 percent of all prostitutes are dependent on a pimp. The breakdown of arrests is 70 percent female prostitutes and madams, 20 percent male prostitutes and pimps, and 10 percent johns.

MYTHS AND TRUTHS ABOUT TEENAGE PROSTITUTION

To get these myths and truths down accurately, I asked one of my girls out of "the life" to write these with me.

MYTH: Young girls enjoy the sex in prostitution—or at the very least they don't mind it.

TRUTH: Prostitutes usually go into an alternate world when they are performing or participating in sex acts. They "check out."

MYTH: Some teen girls choose prostitution.
TRUTH: Pimps recruit girls 98 percent of the time. If a pimp does not put a girl "in the life," her mother, uncle, father, boyfriend may.

MYTH: Teen girls make a lot of money as prostitutes.
TRUTH: Almost all their money goes to their pimp.

MYTH: Pimps are usually nice to "their girls."
TRUTH: They are nice in the beginning to lure the girl, which lasts about two weeks to a month. Often there is physical violence between a pimp and his girls.

MYTH: You can always choose to get out.
TRUTH: It can be life threatening to get out of "the life." Many girls become completely trapped, threatened with beatings, cut with knives, raped, and even killed when they try to leave.

MYTH: Girls feel sexy and powerful being prostitutes.
TRUTH: Prostitution demeans girls. Their bodies are scrutinized, they are told they are ugly, fat, too skinny—you name it, they are called it. It is humiliating. I have never spoken to a girl who really felt sexy or powerful when she was in "the life."

MYTH: There is no rough sex in teenage prostitution. The johns see to that.

TRUTH: Johns rape, beat, cut, strangle, spit on, ejaculate on, and smack girls around—and sometimes kill—and the girls have no protection. They are told to just "take it."

Of course, the biggest myth of all is that prostitution is not a form of sexual abuse. Looking at these myths and truths, you can see the same dynamics taking place with prostitutes and their pimps and johns that takes place with all other girls and their sexual abusers. The pimp becomes the father/brother/uncle; the pimp becomes that one beloved family member who violates a girl's trust.

DIFFERENT CIRCUMSTANCES, SAME OLD COERCION: "DO IT FOR DADDY"

In the beginning, pimps tell girls many of the same things their fathers/uncles/brothers/stepfathers tell them: "You are beautiful, I need you, I will teach you the real way to be a woman." "Do it for Daddy. I promise you whatever you want." "You are so special, and this is our little secret."

Pimps lure girls the same way uncles offer candy, the same way fathers like Garnet's tell them they're princesses and that Daddy needs them to make him happy, the same way that Sage's cousin was the only one in her family to pay attention to her when her parents were totally preoccupied with their own lives.

Girls who turn to prostitution come from circumstances where no one protected them. Their families have already done the damage to the girls' sense of self. Their families have already made them feel that they are not special, smart, worthy, or beautiful. That's why pimps can so easily convince or control them. They are desperate to find "strong" adults to take care of them.

When you come right down to it, there's just not a lot of difference where you're abused or by whom. Whether the abuse takes place in a middle-class bedroom decorated with pink-flowered wallpaper and shelves of stuffed animals or a cheap motel with urine-stained floors or a topless dancing club or the backseat of a car in an alleyway, girls are being abused and we don't see it.

As with the girl who is being sexually abused by her coach, uncle, brother, father, stepfather, there is a lot of secrecy in the world of a girl "in the life." This girl may very well be going to school every day and facing her peers with her secret, the same way the incest survivor keeps her secret from her peers. The shame and secrecy are the same.

These are the same invisible girls who are on the soccer team and the only positive attention they get is from their coach. These are the same invisible girls whose mothers tell them that they "must have asked for it" by being too seductive to their stepdads, the same girls at the top private schools whose fathers sneak into their beds at night and rape them.

It does not matter whether you come from money or you are poor or if you are black or white-Muslim or Jewish: if your family has already made you feel that you are not worthy, you begin to believe it, and when someone comes along and tells you are beautiful/special/wonderful and showers you with attention and gifts, or offers you money when you desperately need it, you are vulnerable and want so much to believe them.

And if your father has already molested you or your uncle has told you you're only good for sex, and your mother has found out and told you it is your fault and you deserved it, you may begin to believe it. You may believe you are only good for sex, only good for being used.

I have known girls to be suicidal because they really believed that was their only worth, and I have had other girls tell me that they may as well trick, because that is all they ever "succeeded" at. These girls use the same words as sexually abused girls. "I check out anyway." "I stare at the ceiling and then before I realize it, it's done." "I go into my own private world."

One very big difference can be around how the abuse is enforced. With prostitution there is often the threat of violence; with incest it's coercion, the promise of gifts or special privileges or love.

PIMPS AND FRATS

Another arena where girls are invisibly abused sexually is in fraternity houses on college campuses. In fact, the similarities between pimp culture and frat house culture are startling.

It's pretty common in fraternities to try to get girls drunk and take advantage of them. Some frats have even been found to practice a particularly despicable form of gang rape called "pulling the train," where a girl who is high on drugs or looking for acceptance is dragged into a bedroom and raped by a whole bunch of brothers in turn. They line up like a train and rape this girl over and over and over again. I first discovered this practice in a book called *Fraternity Gang Rape*. Author and college professor Peggy Reeves Sanday was told about this practice by a female student who had passed out drunk at a Thursday night frat party and was raped by six frat boys who took her up to a room, lined up, and forced themselves on her. Sanday then went on to investigate this kind of rape and found that it's happening all over.

In 2014 police investigated a number of rapes at a frat party where University of Wisconsin–Milwaukee frat brothers were color-coding drinks to roofie and rape women. Another despicable act of sexual violence against women that takes place in frats is called the "pig roast." This is a secret game in which new fraternity members compete to earn points for having sex with overweight women. Only in 2018 did Cornell University, an Ivy League school, denounce this ritual and admit it is contributing to the rape culture on campus.

Just as in pimp culture, where girls' bodies are scrutinized and where girls are often "treated to," or hooked on, powerful drugs to make them more dependent and compliant, frat boys often use "roofies," or Rohypnol, a hypnotic sedative and muscle relaxant, to get girls into a kind of trance state, so that they can abuse and rape them without their conscious awareness. Just as "in the life," where pimps set girls up for forced sex with one man after another, lots of frats practice some form of the rape train. Just the way pimps manipulate, demoralize, and exploit girls, frat boys do the same.

But sometimes girls get out. And, just like survivors everywhere, they want to tell their stories. They need to tell their stories as part of their healing.

THE BRIGHT, BEAUTIFUL GIRLS "IN THE LIFE"

In 1979 an organization called Children of the Night began to rescue teenage girls and boys from life on the streets as prostitutes. By 2017 Children of the Night had rescued more than 10,000 children and teens from prostitution in the United States. And other programs, like GEMS, are also popping up to help these kids. College campuses all over the world now hold annual Take Back the Night demonstrations, where students light candles, have speakers, and protest sexual abuse. In 2014

EROC (End Rape on Campus) was formed by a group of young women. In San Francisco a former prostitute started the SAGE Project (Standing Against Global Exploitation), which has been around for two decades, helping girls get off the streets and providing them with trauma recovery, housing, and legal advocacy.

We're making progress, but we have such a long way to go. Our male-dominated culture still does not support saving girls and punishing pimps and johns. Our media still incessantly depict young women as "liking" to be "Lolitas," using their sexuality to lure older men. We've still got work to do.

Most of the girls I've met through my work with GEMS were survivors of sex abuse and trauma before pimps pulled them into "the life." One of the most interesting things I found is how similar these girls are to the girls whose fathers, brothers, and uncles molested them. They, too, were trapped, they were betrayed, they were forced into sex. Girls "in the life" are no different from any other invisible girl. Not in any ways that matter.

If you were to talk to a girl from GEMS—most of them from economically challenged homes, girls of color, from the most urban parts of New York City—and then meet a Caucasian, "all-American" incest survivor from a wealthy home in the rural Midwest, you would find so many commonalities. For starters, most incest survivors talk about not sleeping through the night. They say that they never know when they may hear their fathers' footsteps coming to their room. Girls in the life talk about being "on call" for their pimps, not sleeping more than a few hours at a time, never knowing when they could be called to work.

One summer my thrivership fund, Girlthrive, Inc., sponsored a retreat for sexually abused girls. I posted the opportunity on my blog at www.invisiblegirlsthrive.com, and it attracted girls from all over the country, both survivors of date rape and incest and coach abuse and girls who were getting out of prostitution. When these girls were brought together, their degree of mutual understanding and support and recognition was simply amazing. They shared so many common feelings—of guilt and worthlessness, of rejection by their mothers and betrayal by all—and what was most impressive was they all had a deep kindness and inner strength. As one GEMS girl said to an incest survivor, "You are amazing—you have been through so much and you are so strong." Then another incest survivor turned to a GEMS girl and said, "How can our mothers not know how great we can be?"

All these girls are invisible girls. No one would ever know from looking at them what they have been through.

There are differences, of course, and one has to do with what we expect from "nice" girls from "good" homes versus what we expect from girls who have been forced into prostitution who often come from low-income, single-parent homes or foster homes and marginal communities. Our culture does not expect these economically poorer girls, who have ended up in "the life" to go to college or succeed. The culture tends to write them off. But, just as we don't really know much about the inner lives of girls being abused behind the closed doors of their private homes, we don't know much about the inner lives of sexually exploited girls "in the life," either.

Once these girls have the chance to get out of "the life," once they are in a more stable environment, be it a program like GEMS, a positive foster home, group home, or with a trusted family member, and when they are given the same opportunity to talk about their experiences of sexual abuse and to come out from under our accusations of being "hoes" and "sluts," when they begin to realize that the way they were exploited was abuse and not their fault, their own aspirations begin to bloom.

It may surprise you to know that these invisible girls often also develop some of the same emotional survival techniques as girls from schools and homes filled with opportunity, namely, escape through academics and activities. Many of them are very successful in school and with guidance can be accepted to prestigious colleges, just like girls from privilege. Listen to Ruby Rose's story and you'll see.

RUBY ROSE: FROM THE STREETS TO COLUMBIA UNIVERSITY

When I met Ruby Rose, she was fifteen years old. It had been several months since her arrest for prostitution. Ruby Rose is a cappuccino-skinned Dominican beauty, with intricate, braided hair and beads the colors of the rainbow. She has an infectious laugh and the kind of presence that makes you stop and listen to whatever she has to say. She is graduating from high school this year and has already been accepted with generous scholarships at her three top-choice schools. She is planning on attending Columbia University, President Obama's alma mater, when all the details of financial aid are worked out.

Believe me when I say prostitution would be the furthest thing you could imagine when meeting Ruby Rose. She plays the violin and the piano, she was the president of the debate team and the cheerleading team, and she is a gymnastics pro.

Ruby Rose's mother was a highly educated woman, a nurse with a full-time job in an urban hospital, when she was diagnosed with paranoid schizophrenia. She was in her late twenties and Ruby Rose was just three years old, her brother one year old. Ruby Rose's father abandoned them, and from the age of three Ruby Rose had to try to take care of her mother and her brother on her own. Even then, she says, she knew her mother's lashing out and beating them for no reason was terribly wrong, but she had nowhere to go, and this was her mother. She had to stay.

Her mother's illness was controlled with medication, but she did not take it regularly. By the time the children were eleven and thirteen, someone in the community called children's services, and Ruby Rose and her brother were placed in two separate foster homes for a short time. By then the damage had been done. One of her mother's boyfriends, whom she was told to call her "uncle," had sexually abused her starting at age nine. By fourteen she had come into "the life."

Ruby Rose doesn't know where her mother is these days. She doesn't know if her mother is living in a shelter or on the street. She has not been in touch for the past several months. She worries about her mother but tries to put it out of her mind.

RUBY ROSE'S STORY

Flipping Tacos Never Felt So Good

I love my mother. I do not really understand her sickness. I can remember my mother playing with me and my brother—she was happy and funny and loving. She read to me and played with me—she held me and my brother on her lap. But she also had lots of mood swings. It's hard for me to hate my mother or blame her for all the abuse I suffered at the hands of her boyfriends—she has a sickness, she cannot help herself. She hears voices, telling her crazy things.

When my brother and I were very little, my mother worked, and we always had dinners together. She made sure we had baths and clean clothes. But, when her sickness got worse, she would forget to feed us or bathe us. But my brother and I still wanted to stay with her.

When I started kindergarten my brother was only four years old, and I was afraid to leave him at home alone with my mother. At that time, my mother slept a lot, and I was always worried about my little brother being alone with her like that. When I think back on it now, I guess I was like a little adult trying to make everything all right. It was such a relief when my brother and I were in the same school. We would walk to school together the ten blocks from our apartment in Harlem.

Things were pretty bad at home. Sometimes my mother would just beat us for no reason. When she did not take her medication, she was psychotic—she heard voices and the voices told her to hit us sometimes, and sometimes she thought people were talking about her and saying bad things. She used to make me go to the bodega [corner store] for her because she thought that the guy there was after her.

I don't remember the specifics until I was about nine years old. My mother had lots of different "boyfriends." Even though I was just a kid, some of them were attracted to me, and many of them would come into my bedroom and touch me. I told my mother, but she said not to worry about it.

She had one particular boyfriend who she knew liked me. I was ten then. He used to pick me up in the middle of the night and bring me to his disgusting, dirty apartment in Staten Island and rape me. After he raped me he would give me money to give to my mother "for the rent." Sometimes I would be fast asleep and she would wake me up at around 1:00 in the morning and tell me to go with "Uncle Jason," and even though I would cry and say he was hurting me and raping me, she told me, "We need the rent money—he likes you—just deal with it."

I never really slept well because I never knew when she would come and wake me up and tell me to go with "Jason." Sometimes she'd wake me up and beat me with the belt, or one of her "boyfriends" would come into my bed.

My brother used to also wake up if he heard footsteps coming toward our room, and he would tell me to go out the window and down the fire escape. I often was roaming the streets in the middle of the night. I have to say, I was a little scared, but I felt safer on the streets than in my bedroom. It was one of these nights at about 3:00 in the morning, I heard my mother screaming that she was coming to my bed to beat me. My brother stood in the doorway and I escaped down the fire escape. Often my brother took a beating for the both of us—he said at least he was not being sexually abused, and he felt so helpless—this was one way he helped me.

I started walking down the street as I often did. I just walked. The streets were deserted. A van pulled up next to me and a man said, "Get in." I said no and kept walking. I picked up my pace, saw there was no store open to run into. Before I knew what was happening, a man's hand was on my shoulder. He shoved my face to the window of the van, another man opened the window and put a gun to my head—I was then shoved into the van. The man with the gun kept the gun to my head, opened my mouth, and stuffed pills down my throat. They raped me in the van and then took me to Philadelphia and put me in a hotel room, where one man after another came in and did things to me that I would love to forget. Because I was drugged up I kind of do forget some things, and because I had already been abused by my "uncle" and other of my mother's boyfriends, I had already taught myself to "disappear" during the abuse.

After three days I woke up in a hospital outside of Philadelphia. The next thing I knew, my aunt who had just finished a tour in the army was at my bedside. Because she was in the military, she was able to locate me through a military GPS. I was badly bruised, my breasts and vagina were bruised and aching. My aunt was going back on a tour with the army, so believe it or not I was sent back to my mother's home.

Pretty much everyone at school had heard about what happened to me, and also on the streets they already knew my brother and I were not really taken care of. I started to get a reputation as a "ho." People in the neighborhood said they knew who the thugs were and they could come and get me again. I was smoking a lot of pot at this point and really trying to be numb. More than anything I was afraid that the thugs would come back for me. That's when I met Darren.

Darren was in his thirties. He was clean cut and nice—he told me he would protect me. He told me that he knew the thugs and that he could promise to keep them away from me. He told me he would be like a daddy to me—the daddy I never had. He told me I was sweet and pretty and not a "ho." He was really kind—he took me to dinner at a nice restaurant—he called me, he got me a cell phone.

After a few weeks he asked if he could be my boyfriend. Looking back now I can see how crazy all this was, but you have to understand, by this point my body was covered with bruises and burns from my mother and the men who abducted me, I was stoned most of the time, I did not really give a shit about any-thing. Most days I just wanted to disappear. So of course I was happy that Darren was nice to me.

Then we started "dating." He told me I was such a "beautiful young flower," and he wanted to take photos of me. Of course, I was totally taken in and I did let him take photos. A few weeks after that he told me that if I really loved him, I would be with his "friend." By this time my self-esteem was nonexistent. Someone had called social services again, and my brother and I were placed in another foster home, but I was MIA most of the time.

Darren put my pictures up on craigslist. He then would drive me to different men's apartments and they would have sex with me. These men were usually older, some of them were obscene and nasty, but the ones who were cops (lots of cops go to prosti-tutes) were never abusive. Some of them said I reminded them of their daughters. Yes, that was creepy.

By this point I had been getting molested for so many years that I had this mental escape route I would use to deal with it. I would transport myself to a Hawaiian spa resort. I would picture myself on a beautiful beach with big palm trees and mangos—I would pick the mangos and eat them. There was beautiful, crystal-clear water—the color of turquoise. I would be in a really nice bathing suit and so would my brother, because he was usually there with me. The very best part would be swimming with the dolphins. My brother and I would be swimming with the dolphins and the dolphins would kiss me and protect me. I would float with them through the water. And then the sun would set. By that time the john would be finished with me. . . .

One afternoon I was walking on the street after leaving one john's apartment—it was a school day—and the police picked me up and took me to the station. They figured it out that I was being prostituted. At first I was really scared—I was fifteen years old, been abused since I cannot even remember the first time, my mother was totally MIA, I had been cutting school all the time, smoking pot, numbing myself out as much as I could.

I was placed in another foster home and sent to court. A court advocate from GEMS met me there and helped me not go to a detention center. I agreed to go to the program at GEMS and attend the therapy groups with other girls who got out of "the life." I started sessions with Dr. Patti and began to understand that I did have worth and I had the power to stay healthy and strong and out of "the life." Then my aunt finished her tour in the army, and she filed papers to be mine and my brother's foster mother.

We moved to another neighborhood and moved in with my aunt. I started to catch up with school, I joined lots of clubs, picked up the violin, which is something I had started learning as a small child. I also played the piano by ear. One day I was sitting in the music room at school, playing the piano, and the school orchestra leader came in and recruited me. I love music, and I loved playing with the school orchestra. I also love the energy it takes to do gymnastics—I have been captain of my school's gymnastics team for the past year.

I am making my body strong again in positive ways. I have a real job now working at Taco Bell, and I have to say that flipping tacos never felt so good. I wear that corny hat with pride!

I am healing the wounds that I've been trying to cope with. I love having my life. I appreciate each day that I realize I am free. I love knitting, writing, singing, dancing, learning, reading, swimming, doing yoga, and spending time with people I care about. I love making positive connections and going forward with my life.

I am really proud that I attended the retreat that Girlthrive sponsored last summer for teen girl survivors of sexual abuse. Dr. Patti ran some groups with us, and it was pretty amazing to be with a group of girls who have been through incest and other kinds of sexual abuse and to believe for the first time that I was sexually abused.

I did not choose to be a prostitute. I was trapped in a life, then "in the life." I am beginning to trust myself, to love myself. I will never be trapped again. I can only move forward full force!

MY THOUGHTS

We cannot change the culture quickly enough. We have to stop calling girls who are prostitutes *whores*. We have to start prosecuting pimps and johns. They need to go to jail for sexual abuse. As a culture we need to open our eyes and see when girls are being exploited, and we need to take action. We can write letters to elected officials. But most importantly we need to stop calling these girls *hookers* with so much judgment and disdain. We need to remember Ruby Rose. We can remember how her mother was there for her until her psychotic breakdown. We can remember how, at the age of eleven, Ruby Rose learned to escape through her bedroom window to prevent another ride in the car to her mother's "boyfriend's" dirty apartment where she would be raped "for the rent money." We can remember that prostitution is sexual abuse.

PART FOUR

THE ROAD BACK

CHAPTER 13

DIFFERENT PATHS TO HEALING

All the men who have crossed my path have hurt me, invading the journey I was supposed to be on. I have been tampered with and washed up. I am clearing out a new path now.

—a twenty-year-old incest and rape survivor

As we've seen, there are many different paths to healing. You've heard from many girls by now, and although their experiences vary, each of them told how they were able to move on in their lives once they spoke out about their abuse. This was their primary means to healing. When you release something that you have held deep inside, you feel lighter, you feel hopeful, you let go of a burden that you have been carrying.

Throughout this book, we have seen how powerful and healing it can be to tell your story, and, as you move through the various feelings, you might want to take some further action. Much of this book is about dealing with your sexual abuse once you have already left your home, because that's when most girls have their first real opportunity to get some perspective and to heal. As much as I understand how difficult and perhaps impossible it can be to leave home before you are eighteen, one important purpose of this book is to open new pathways for you, pathways you might not have known about before. If you are still living at home, make a list of all the adults you know, and figure out who might take you in, who would support you, and who would help you get away from your abuser. Use your sixth sense. You'll know if you have the option to leave.

Trying to move out before you're eighteen might involve you in a court case, but if you feel you have a good option for getting away from your abuser, you might choose to go ahead anyway. If you are being molested and feel trapped, please know that there are organizations out there that will help you if you choose to leave. Check our Resource Center. I understand that it is so difficult for a girl to leave before she graduates high school and moves out to college or an apartment. But please know you can get out. I have known girls who told and had teachers take them in, neighbors, friends' parents.

Beyond telling and getting away, however, there are an awful lot of myths out there about how to move on or get "justice." People may tell you to report the crime or confront your abuser—or even to forgive him. I don't necessarily advocate any of these things. I think counseling of some kind can be enormously useful, but the bottom line is that the main way to heal is to find people who will support you, to talk about what happened, and to ground yourself in the reality that the abuse was not your fault, that you have nothing to be ashamed of, and that you deserve great love and happiness in your life. But I would be remiss were I not to at least look at some of the paths that some girls take and to give you some information.

SHOULD YOU REPORT THE CRIME?

Throughout this book, we've been talking about how important it is to tell someone what happened to you, to choose wisely whom you tell, and to get support. You should know that, no matter what kind of sexual abuse you've endured, you may be encouraged to report what happened to the police. That's not necessarily the kind of telling that is important for your healing. Many girls who have been sexually abused don't want to get the police involved. They don't want to press charges and have to face the legal system. And that's completely understandable.

Some instances of sexual abuse, especially if they happened in the distant past, would be too hard to prove. When the abuser is a family member, girls are often pressured by their family not to press charges and cause the family embarrassment. Girls also know that they'd need iron wills to be able to withstand all the interviews, get on the witness stand, tell their stories publicly, and undergo brutal cross-examination that dredges up every intimate detail of their life, to make no mention of low prosecution rates. Every girl has to ask herself whether it's worth reporting the crime in her particular case. For many, the answer will be no, and that is okay.

Many girls who choose to report end up feeling violated all over again by the criminal justice system. The process can really stink. The one good reason I can think of to report your abuse and press charges is if your abuser is likely to be a danger to other girls. As Pearl tells us in her story in this chapter, for example, she became afraid that her uncle was abusing her younger sister. She stepped forward and told in the hopes that she could stop him.

Pearl told her guidance counselor about her uncle, and her counselor called the police, as he was required to do. Police came to the school and spoke with Pearl. They also interviewed me, because she had disclosed the abuse to me and given me

extensive details. They took my verbal and written word as evidence, and I was considered a witness to the disclosure.

With the support of her family, Pearl pressed charges
against her uncle. An order of protection was issued that pro-
hibited him from coming within ten feet of Pearl. Her uncle
then pleaded guilty to the charges, and the case was settled out
of court. This was a positive thing for Pearl. Going to court is a
very difficult part of the process for a girl—having to face your
abuser, tell your story over and over again in detail, and have
all the intimate details of your life become public property.

In Pearl's uncle's case, because the abuse had taken place
seven years prior to the disclosure, he received only a very
light sentence: probation and mandatory counseling for a year.
It seems that he never went after Pearl's sister again, but now
other girls have made allegations of sexual abuse against him.
Was it worth it for Pearl to report the abuse and press charges
against her uncle? Maybe. It did prove to her that her parents
were squarely in her corner, and that in itself helped her heal
from the abuse. But then there was Garnet, who also reported
the abuse; nothing was done because her father managed to
convince the police that he was innocent and her sister refused
to corroborate the abuse—and then ended up living on the
streets as a prostitute.

I have a client who did report an acquaintance rape to
the police. They pressured her to wear a wire and meet with
the rapist, and at that meeting he once again attempted to rape
her. The police intervened, but even with a witness and good
solid proof, this rapist was jailed for only six months.

And then there is Emily, whom you'll read about in
this chapter through her mother's story and who, during a

custody trial in family court, did report her father's abuse. The judge allowed his visitation rights to continue—albeit under supervision—until further information could be gathered.

Many counselors and police detectives will tell you that it's always best to report the crime. That may serve them and give them useful data. And it may be right for you. But you must never let anyone force you to report abuse. And the people around you should support your choice. If they don't, remind them that it is your choice. If you think there's little chance that you can prove that the abuse took place (if it was years ago, or there were no witnesses and you didn't undergo a medical exam), you have to ask yourself what is to be gained by reporting. Only you can make the right choice for you. I feel the same way about your confronting your abuser. If you don't want to, don't. This is about your healing and no one else's.

All that said, the criminal justice system is far more responsive to and respectful of women now than it was, say, thirty years ago. It is not, however, strong enough in protecting females. Women are still subjected to a misogynistic culture. And girls and women of color have the added intersectional problem of being black or brown and a woman; thus, they suffer racism and sexism. One of my clients, a beautiful, strong African American, nineteen years old, went to the police to report her biological father for incest. She was convinced to sign a waiver. The waiver said she would not press legal charges against her father if given an order of protection then and there. She told me that the detectives were male and white. And this was right outside of Newark, New Jersey, an integrated urban community! If you decide that prosecuting is a part of speaking your truth and healing, then use the criminal justice system well. Be prepared, have advocates, and know that, no matter what happens in court, you have spoken your truth and it was not your fault. The legal route is certainly not for everyone. Only you can decide if it's right for you. The Resource Center at the back of this book has more information.

SHOULD YOU CONFRONT YOUR ABUSER?

> You fat fuck of a blood-sucking villain. The time has come for me to squash my mosquitoes, and you, buddy, are the first to go.
>
> —a seventeen-year-old rape survivor

This quote is from a poem in a rape survivor's journal. She never confronted the rapist, but she sure is confrontational in her writing, and that has been a huge factor in her healing. There are many types of confrontation. The most important thing is that you confront, in your own mind, the truth that your abuser is the guilty party.

Many girls ask whether they should confront their abuser directly. My short answer is no.

That said, if you somehow end up in the court system, either by choice or because your parents insist on it, you will be forced to see your abuser in court, to look at him and speak about what happened. You may have been told or read somewhere that confronting your abuser, in person, in a letter, in a phone call, will help you heal. That has not been my experience at all. Confronting your abuser could have almost nothing to do with healing. I have seen many cases where girls were pushed to confront their abusers and it only hurt them more. If you choose to confront your abuser, never do it to get an apology or response from him. Only do it because you want to get it out of your system. His response will likely disappoint you. Sometimes it makes you feel retraumatized. I think it's simply a fallacy that, by telling the abuser what he did to you and airing your feelings, you will somehow feel better. Much of the time your abuser will just deny everything anyway. It took more than 170 brave girls to confront their abuser in a court of law in the Dr. Nassar case. There is always comfort in numbers, yet most cases may not have that many survivors coming forward. This could be why incest is the least confronted or reported crime.

You remember Garnet, whose father completely dismissed her when she confronted him. He told her no one would believe her. That's when she started to feel totally despondent and turned to drugs, drinking, and self-harm. She had hoped that confronting him would bring her relief, and all she got was violated all over again.

If you feel the need to say something to your abuser directly, you could try writing a letter and burning it. You could write songs and poetry. But don't ever expect your abuser to make you feel better, because he never will. Even if you confront him and he cries and apologizes, things won't necessarily get better. He may still have an emotional hook into you and have the ability to even make you begin to feel sorry for him, which will only lead to greater confusion. Healing is about you, healing is about forgiving yourself, releasing your pain and trauma. It is never about the abuser. The goal is for the abuser to become smaller and smaller and smaller and for you to become stronger and stronger and stronger.

I'll say it again: You do not need to confront your abuser to heal from sexual abuse, and I don't recommend it. Most of the time, your best bet is to get away and work through your process away from him. I have worked with hundreds of girls who have healed without ever directly confronting their abusers.

SHOULD YOU FORGIVE YOUR ABUSER?

I wanted so many times to simply have faith, to give my soul over to the care of something else, someone else, because there were times when it just felt too filthy for me to hold anymore. But then there was always some rule like "Turn the other cheek" or "Forgive and forget." Some concept of forgiveness that I couldn't even wrap my brain around. It seemed so incomprehensible. How do you "forgive" someone for taking away your childhood, your wonder and your innocence and your "first time" and your chance to discover yourself without dark pits and chasms opening up underneath you on the path? Maybe some people can forgive, but I always knew in my gut that I wouldn't. It felt like a cop-out, like maybe if I avoided feeling angry about this, then my world would stay the way it was on the surface, ordinary and cheerleader-y. I am angry and I know I don't have to "walk a mile in my stepfather's shoes." I don't give a damn about his pain or "why" he did what he did to me.

—*a twenty-two-year-old incest survivor*

I cannot tell you how many young women survivors come to me having been told by a well-intentioned therapist or clergyperson to forgive their abuser. I say no. No, no, and no. The only person you need to forgive for your healing is yourself. That is your life journey, to forgive and love yourself. I have seen too many girls who tried to forgive ending up right back where they started, believing they were at fault in the abuse. As far as I'm concerned, forgiveness is just a kind of gift to your abuser. He is 100 percent responsible for what happened to you. You don't owe him a thing.

Of course, you need to make peace with your own faith, and if your faith tells you that you need to forgive in order to come through, I would never want to stop you from doing that. But I will tell you that I believe clinically and psychologically that forgiveness is not necessary for healing. There is so much pressure out there to forgive, so many books, blogs, websites telling you it is the only way to heal. Again, if you feel it will help you, then go ahead and forgive, but do it for you, not for your abuser. And again, forgive yourself.

It's almost always best to make a clean break, surround yourself with supportive people, express your emotions to people you can trust, and not worry about confrontation or forgiveness or getting closure in that way. With good support, you will get over this, you will thrive and love and be loved. You will find passion in life, friends, and happiness. It's not something your abuser can do for you. You don't have to allow him any more space in your heart or any more access to your body or soul.

Your mother may have forgiven your father or stepfather for molesting you. Your abuser may have served his (usually pitifully brief) time and then come back home to live with you. Maybe your parents dragged you to family therapy and forced you to learn to "forgive." I have to tell you, I think this is criminal. I have seen it wound girls deeply and spill over into how they feel about themselves for years. If you find yourself in this scenario, please try to find people to support you. And try to find another home to live in, rather than live in the home where your abuser is back with your mother's support. When you have the opportunity to move out, you will have the choice not to be part of a family that forgives the father who raped you. Having to live under the same roof as your abuser because your mother has forgiven him and promises things will be different is retraumatizing. I highly recommend if this happens to leave.

One girl told me that, after she told her mother about her father molesting her, her mother begged her not to go to the authorities. Her mother promised to put up a curtain for privacy in their small apartment so that she could almost have her own room. Honestly, if you cannot find a relative or friend to take you in, it is my opinion that living in a group home or foster home could be less painful than having to sit at the dinner table with your abuser because your mother has forgiven him. I have known girls who ended up living their last year of high school with a teacher's family because her teacher could not tolerate her student having to live under the roof of her abuser with a mother who chose her husband over her daughter. So many of my clients have what they call their "chosen family." These are their dearest friends, who are there with support, understanding, and love. You too will find your "chosen family."

SHOULD YOU GO FOR THERAPY?

When my therapist told me the incest was not my fault
and that my father was evil, I just sat there and cried.

—*an eighteen-year-old incest survivor*

At many points along this journey, you may find yourself wanting to talk to a professional. Fortunately, there's more and more help out there. There are hotlines, crisis counselors, social workers, and therapists, just for starters. In fact, in most states now there are rape crisis centers where you will receive free counseling. Our Resource Center has more options.

You might want to start with a hotline. The fact that the person on the other end of the phone doesn't know you can make it a lot less scary to open up. I have known girls who have called hotlines many times, even twenty times, before they were ready to tell someone they knew. The volunteers answering the phones are often survivors themselves and lend a very understanding ear. They won't advise you unless you ask for specific advice; they'll just listen to you and support you.

If you're ready for face-to-face counseling, just be sure that the counselor is someone you trust completely. Of course, it doesn't have to be a professional therapist. This person could be a teacher, tutor, or principal. Just find someone who cares about you.

Do be sure and understand that if you are under eighteen and there is still abuse taking place in your home, any teacher or counselor you tell at your school is obligated to report the abuse—they are mandated reporters. If you know the counselor or if she is very experienced and sensitive, she will help you with the report, but she will be obligated, legally, to make a report. If you really want to speak to that trusted counselor and are not ready to have the crime reported, you can make up a story about a "friend" "out of the country" who needs your support and you can receive comfort and advice. If you are no longer in danger, mandated reporters don't have that legal obligation, and you may feel freer to open up.

Even though I am a therapist, I want to tell you that therapy is not the only way to heal. If you open up and find support and love, you will find healing. There are also some pretty amazing novels, films, websites, and blogs listed in our Resource Center that may really resonate with you and be part of your path to healing. And remember—running, singing, talking, playing, drawing, painting, dancing, and all the other ways you express yourself help you heal. Let it go, get it out, and you will move on. Telling someone trusted is part of the path to releasing the trauma.

If you do choose some form of therapy, the most important thing is to feel comfortable with your therapist. No matter how much training or how many degrees your therapist has, if you don't like her or him, the therapy probably won't help you. Sometimes the experience of being in counseling with a therapist you can't relate to can make you feel even more isolated. If you feel that your therapist has too much power or control over you, you may re-experience the abuse feelings. If that's the case, don't stick around. Even if your parents are forcing therapy on you, they can't pick the person you are going to feel the most comfortable with. Only you can do that. So keep interviewing until you find the right person. Trust your instincts. If you feel comfortable, if you feel warmth and caring, if the therapist is willing to slide her payment scale for you, it does not matter what degree the therapist has. She does not need a PhD or an MD. She should have special training and experience, but the relationship is the most important part of the healing journey in therapy.

HELPFUL HINTS FOR FINDING A THERAPIST

1. Make sure you "click" with the therapist and feel unconditionally supported. If the therapist tells you to leave this stuff in the past and not talk about it, run—don't walk—out of the office.

2. Keep looking until you find someone you can afford. Many clinics offer free or low-cost counseling to sexual-abuse survivors.

3. Find a female therapist if you possibly can. You might not feel all that comfortable talking about sex with a man, but this is a decision you have to make. That said, some incest survivors have told me that having a kind, sensitive supportive male therapist has helped them to trust men again.

4. Never allow yourself to be forced to talk about anything you're not ready for. If you do not want to recount an experience, don't.

5. If you are under eighteen and currently surviving incest, your therapist will be legally bound to report the crime, but a good therapist will consult you and work it out with you before she does anything. She should make sure you have a safe place to stay with a relative or friend's family before you report the crime just in case your mother rejects you.

6. Be aware that everything said in your sessions should be kept confidential, even from your parents, unless you are a harm to yourself or others. But if you are under eighteen, your legal rights to confidentiality vary from state to state, and you may not have that legal

right. HIPAA are forms you can sign beginning at age eighteen guaranteeing your privacy rights.
7. Take your time. Find the right counselor. Get well. Allow yourself the time to heal.

One of my sixteen-year-old clients defines therapy beautifully. She says that she comes in and dumps all her problems on the floor as if scattering papers. We pick one up, we look at it, we put it down. We pick up another, we work it through, we rip it up, we throw it away. And at the end of the session, we gather up all these papers and put them in a special box, up on a shelf, and leave it in my office until the next session.

One of the great benefits of therapy is that in many ways it is a one-way relationship. You do not have to worry about the therapist. She is there to help you, never to burden you with any of her personal problems. She is there for you. Therapy should provide you with a space to vent, release, process, and heal.

Healing does not necessarily come from reporting or confronting your abuser, and it certainly does not come from forgiving him. Don't let anyone pressure you into doing any of these things. Healing comes from speaking about your experience, letting out your secrets. It is a process, a process of forgiving yourself. Healing comes from loving yourself and trusting yourself. Healing comes when you realize that your abuser is to blame, when you are able to slough off the feelings of shame and guilt. This is a very different process for every girl and every young woman. This is your life, and you deserve to walk your own path in healing.

CHAPTER 14

SUPPORTIVE FAMILIES SPEAK OUT

(Jannie's Mother's Story, Emily's Mother's Story, Pearl's Story)

When my husband found out that his brother had molested our daughter, he went to his home, pushed him to the floor, and started to bash his head in.

—*a mother of an incest survivor*

So far we have heard a lot about families who sit by and do nothing to protect their daughters from abuse. We have heard about parents who loved their daughters but were blind to what was going on, mothers with their own unresolved childhood sexual abuse who married men who then molested their daughters, mothers who stood by their husbands even after the abuse was reported, fathers who were so evil that they raped their daughters and told them it was their right to do so.

Needless to say, most people do not want girls to be raped, molested, and harmed, and most parents don't let such things happen; they would never tolerate anyone hurting their child. Most of us feel rage toward molesters, rapists, and abusers.

The following stories bring us into the worlds of some of these betrayed families. As you'll see, many girls do have allies within their families. And you may be surprised to learn that often it takes parents much longer to heal than it does

275

daughters. Girls are incredibly resilient, but long after their own scars of abuse have healed, their parents are often still dealing with theirs. Nonetheless, the single most important thing the parent of a sexually abused girl can do is show unconditional support.

Jannie's father literally had a heart attack after hearing about her abuse and trying to confront the abuser. Her mother still believes his heart finally gave out because he could not bear his daughter's abuse or the injustice that followed.

JANNIE'S MOTHER'S STORY

A Mother's Loss

"They were mean to me. They made me do things I didn't want to do." These words will haunt me for the rest of my life.

When my daughter Jannie was nine years old, she went to spend a weekend at her friend Amy's summer home in a chic area of the Jersey Shore, a hundred miles away from our Upper West Side Manhattan home. Jannie had really been looking forward to this weekend away, the last summer weekend before school. We knew Amy's parents and certainly trusted them with the care of our only child, but I hadn't wanted her to go. Before she left I explained that we could not pick her up if she wasn't having a good time and said that we'd see her in three days. She seemed to understand.

When Jannie got home three days later, she went straight to her room and curled up on her bed. She made me come with her and begged me to stay with her until she fell asleep. Just before she dozed off she uttered these haunting words: "They were so mean to me. They made me do things I didn't want to." I asked her what they made her do, but she wouldn't answer. She made me check under the bed for "men" and assure her that no one could enter her window (on the twelfth floor!). This was very atypical behavior for Jannie, and I again asked her what had happened, but again she did not answer. I thought perhaps they'd made her eat peas and carrots or something trivial like that. I remember being a bit annoyed and acting abrupt.

Jannie woke up the next morning and went off to school just fine. She seemed all right. And for eight years she never mentioned that weekend again. I will never forgive myself for being so flip and maybe making her feel that she couldn't talk to me. I can't stop thinking about how I didn't press the issue or beg her to tell me what she meant by those ominous words. It taught me that you should never trivialize what a child says to you.

Jannie's adolescent years were very rocky. She had learning problems and hence some of the other problems that typically result—feeling a bit left out socially, bouts with depression. We were a loving family, but I guess our love wasn't enough to take away Jannie's depression.

At age sixteen Jannie made a suicide attempt and was hospitalized. It was in a family therapy session in the hospital that we learned what had happened to Jannie on that weekend so many years before. The hospital reassured her of her safety telling.

Amy's father had brutally raped and sodomized Jannie. She had just turned nine years old. He told her that if she was a good girl and never ever told anyone, he would not do it again. He told her that it was a very private, important secret and that harm would come to her family if she told. He pricked his finger with a pin and then pricked hers, and then put their fingers together and explained that this gave them a blood connection. He exploited my poor little girl's insecurity over being adopted. How sick is that? He also said that because she was adopted, she could be taken away from us if she told.

Well, she believed this man, this so-called pillar of the church and community. And she never told until she had to because she was crawling out of her skin.

When my husband heard Jannie describe the rape, he totally lost it. He made us go to their house straight from the hospital, and he practically broke his hand banging on the door. They let us in, of course, and my husband lunged at the father. His wife and I had to pull him off. At that point we noticed their daughter Amy crawl under the table. My husband was so enraged he had a heart attack.

After his hospitalization, we began legal proceedings. As helpful and nice as all the police and lawyers were, they made it clear that our daughter would have to testify. Initially, she agreed. But she became so frightened to face Amy's father in a trial that she cut her wrists. At that point we agreed with the doctors that Jannie could not go through with it.

Jannie also asked us not to tell our friends; she needed her privacy. So my husband and I could confide only in our therapists. Once when we saw the abuser on the street, my husband spat at him. We spent many sleepless nights together trying to figure out how to punish this man. For a few years, my husband would go down to the Fulton Fish Market on Sundays and get some dead fish and put them outside the door of his home. The dead fish was an Italian threat that someone was to be killed. He also sent him threatening letters.

I sank deep into a depression and felt I was the worst mother in the world. I felt doubly guilty because we had adopted Jannie. We were so blessed to have her, and then I did not protect her.

A few years after Jannie's breakdown, my husband died—of a second heart attack. He was just fifty-two years old. I believe he simply couldn't live without seeing justice done. I sometimes wish that I could just kill this horrible man myself. I have had thoughts of cutting off his penis and shoving it down his throat. I am still filled with rage and confusion all these years after my daughter was raped.

The good news is that Jannie is a happy person. She is twenty-seven now and working. She has graduated from college, has friends and a social life, and she is not nearly as scarred from this abuse as I am. Thank God.

MY THOUGHTS

Jannie was off at college when her mom, Samantha, became my client. She has worked very hard in her therapy to try to forgive herself. As she said, her feelings of rage turned inward, into depression, while her husband's turned outward. Tragically, his rage ended up killing him, or at least hastening his death. He simply could not live with the knowledge that this monster who had brutalized his daughter was free.

When the police questioned Samantha and her husband, they also went to the home of the abuser. They questioned his teen daughter and asked whether she had ever been abused; she said no. Because Jannie would not testify, the police dropped the entire case. Samantha was always tormented, believing the monster was also molesting his own daughter. Recently, the man and his wife moved away from New York, and the one comfort Samantha has is that neither she nor her daughter will ever have to see him again. This family stood by their daughter, even when it meant not getting the justice they thought she (and they) deserved. The support and love from her parents was a huge part of Jannie's recovery.

Another mother of a fifteen-year-old client and incest survivor had me mesmerized with her extraordinary story. This mother acted like a lioness protecting her young.

For much of Emily's childhood, her parents were both heavy drinkers. Emily had a pretty rough time, but she did feel love from her parents. Her mother entered AA when Emily was ten years old and then divorced her father three years later, when he wouldn't stop drinking. Emily had visits with her father every other weekend. When Emily was fourteen, her parents had a custody hearing because her father wanted more time with his daughter, and Emily told the court officer that on her visits to her father he had been forcing sex on her. Here is what happened, in her mother's words:

EMILY'S MOTHER'S STORY

I'll Kill Him

I was in a drunken fog for many years. Only since I've been sober, for the past four years, have I finally begun to see clearly. I knew my ex-husband was still a drunk, but I never, ever suspected him of molesting our daughter. When Emily told the court officer that she didn't want to visit her father anymore because he was molesting her, you know what I did? I went up to her and slapped her hard across the face. Hmm...that was crazy. I was definitely feeling crazy at that moment.

Instead of recoiling or slapping me back, Emily grabbed me and hugged me. She said, "Mom, it's true." Well, I just lost it. I jumped over the courtroom railing and ran to my ex and began to pummel him. The court officers had to pull me off him. Then they wrote up an order of protection for him against me, until the sex-abuse allegations were substantiated. As if that weren't outrageous enough, then the court told us that my daughter would have to continue to have visits with her father, but that they would be supervised. I was fit to be tied.

Later that day, my daughter actually went back to school. She was so relieved to have the truth out, she told me she could deal with anything. I went home in a fog. Almost robotically, as if under a hypnotic spell, I went upstairs to my room, took out my (licensed) gun, loaded it (with three bullets, just in case I missed), put on a trench coat and tucked the gun under my coat, and started heading back to my car. I was planning to go to my ex's home and kill him in cold blood. There was no doubt in my mind. He had to die.

Just as I was getting into my car, my sister pulled up in front of my house. Turns out Emily had phoned her, worried about my state. I told my sister that I was on my way to kill my ex because he had molested Emily. Actually, I can't really remember exactly what I said. I was blind with rage, but my sister tells me I spoke in a dead monotone. When I told her I was going to kill him, she slapped me, and hard. She explained that I was in shock and needed the slap to snap out of it. We sat down and she made me give her the gun. Then we both sobbed into each other's arms.

MY THOUGHTS

I treated Emily and her mother for a while. It's been five years since the incident at the court, and Emily's mother never did follow through on her threat. But she still lives in a kind of jail—not a typical jail cell, but the jail of guilt for having been so blind. She was an alcoholic and not the mother she should have been. She won't let herself off the hook.

Emily is far better off emotionally than her mother. She is in college and has had therapy. She has close friends and a love for poetry that has helped her to deal with her parents and her upbringing. Emily's father was never put on trial. Emily was just too frightened to go through with it. But they did get her father to sign a legal document stating that he agreed to leave the state, register as a sex offender, be on probation for the next twelve years, and never contact Emily again.

Over the five years, Emily has not spoken to her father once. She has done a lot of work to heal herself from the abuse, but she says that the most important path to her deep healing was her mother's love and support.

LISTEN UP, PARENTS

> When my mother believed me, I knew I would be all right.
>
> —a sixteen-year-old survivor of mentor abuse

It is often the case that, when sex-abuse survivors see their families begin to deal with feelings of betrayal, their own healing begins. Just the acknowledgment and the support can make a girl begin to feel it's not all her fault. That's why it's so important for parents to show support and to believe in their daughters. But they also have to keep a grip on themselves. Even though they may feel enraged at the violation of their child, even though they may want blood or justice, they have to understand that it was the daughter who was abused and that her wishes need to be respected. That may mean not talking about the abuse to the extended family. It may mean not going to trial if doing so feels like another violation.

In the previous two stories, one mother went into a serious depression, the other became homicidal, and one father actually died of a broken heart, but in both stories the parents understood that their daughters did not feel strong enough to go through the criminal justice system and did not force them to go to trial. That was one of the best ways they could show their support.

In my many years of work, I have witnessed many parents and daughters experience very deep pain. But there are many other ways in which families show support—not just through going to therapy or discussing everything with great emotion. Sometimes a family quietly supports a daughter through its actions. The first action is simply believing her.

Pearl's was one such family. I met Pearl when she was sixteen years old. She was a new member of our sex-abuse support group and did not speak for the first few weeks. Pearl is a petite Filipino girl from a strict and religious family. She is quiet and shy and driven academically. When she finally did share in our group, she said she knew she wanted to protect her sister from their pedophile uncle. Pearl tells a story of a very supportive family who believed her and stood by her, even when it meant going against both their culture—which prizes privacy above all—and their large, extended family.

PEARL'S STORY

Church Songs

I am sixteen years old and Filipino. I was born in the United States, but a lot of my relatives immigrated to the States within the past twenty years. We are a tightly knit family. We celebrate holidays together, we babysit for cousins, we hang out together. I guess you could say our parents depend on each other to keep all our lives running smoothly.

My uncle started molesting me when I was seven years old and continued to do so until I was thirteen. I tried very hard to block out the abuse. I got involved as a peer counselor at school, I was on the honor roll and involved in my church, and I began dating a little. I thought I was fine.

Uncle Jim had always been my favorite uncle, and his daughter, who was five years older than me, had always been like a sister to me. But one day things changed. We were over at his house, and he asked me to come to his room. When I walked in, he was wearing only underpants. That was already weird for me, considering my parents' modesty, and I was pretty scared. Then he asked me to come closer to him. Reluctantly, I approached him. He took out his penis and put it in my hand. It felt disgusting. I wanted to die. But I stood there paralyzed. Then he put it in my mouth. He said it wasn't going to hurt. He told me to not be afraid and said that he loved me. Then he said, "This is our little secret."

After that I tried to avoid him, but several times he came to my school to pick me up, telling my teacher that my parents had sent him. I didn't want to make a scene, so I just got in the back seat of his car. But then he'd take out his penis and begin masturbating.

He'd keep telling me how special I was and that he loved me and that I should touch him. I'd just sit there frozen, looking out the window and trying to blank out until he dropped me off at home.

He used to bring me gifts and money in front of my parents, and of course I accepted them. I wish I had never accepted anything from him. This is one reason I feel so guilty. To this day it really bothers me that I accepted his gifts. He never threatened my life, but I was afraid of him. His words were very powerful. I knew that what was going on was extremely wrong, but I wasn't sure how to stop it. Mostly I wanted to get away from him, but the little part of me that felt special wanted to stay, and I kept thinking maybe he would stop. I guess that is why I felt so responsible for and guilty about what happened.

By the time I turned thirteen, I could no longer be in a room with him without feeling sick. My body had started to develop, and I'd started getting my period. Maybe unconsciously I began to feel the beginnings of womanhood. Whatever it was, I started taking action. I told Uncle Jim he could not be alone with me. He became really nasty and threatened to "get me" when I wasn't looking. But I stayed away from him. I hated and feared him.

I began to have dreams about my uncle. I would wake up in a cold sweat of fear. Then the smell of cigarettes started triggering all these awful feelings and memories. I remembered how it used to feel when he'd touch me or whisper in my ear. I'd think about how he used to make these disgusting gestures. And it all came back to me. A week after hearing Dr. Patti speak at my school about sexual abuse, we had a family celebration. As always, my uncle tried to hug me too tightly, and after I wrenched out of his embrace I saw him hugging my twelve-year-old sister the same way. Then, right before my eyes, I saw him touch her breast.

I knew then and there that I had to stop him. When my uncle started molesting my little sister, I had a choice: to save her or to keep my extended family together. I chose to save my sister.

I tried to think of ways to stop him from getting to my sister. I wanted to tell my parents, but I didn't know how. My parents and I were always pretty close. My parents are traditional in lots of ways and very conservative about sexuality. As much as I love them, I am very aware of pleasing them and being a "good girl." So there are lots of things I don't tell my mom, and the sexual abuse was one of them. But it always felt like this huge, ugly secret.

When Dr. Patti came to my school and started talking about sexual abuse, she explained that it is never the child's fault. For the first time I began to realize that maybe my uncle had been manipulating me all that time and that he was entirely to blame. I was ready to tell my secret. It was hard for me to talk in the sexual-abuse support groups, but after hearing all these horrible stories from these other girls, too, I felt I could share my experience. Hearing so many other girls who I never would have dreamed were abused made me feel less alone. You could just tell from their stories that their abuse wasn't their fault. Maybe mine wasn't my fault, either.

On my sixteenth birthday, I went to see the counselor at my school with the support of Dr. Patti and the other girls behind me. I knew I could do it. I knew from Dr. Patti that when I told my counselor he would call the police—because the abuse happened less than six years ago and involved two minors, the school had to report it—but I knew I had to do something. When I told him, of course, he said he'd have to get the principal. I was so scared and upset. I didn't know what was going to happen. I asked my friends to stay with me.

The next thing I knew, the police showed up at my school. They talked with me and asked me lots of questions, and then they called my parents. My father came to the school. His just being there, so awkward, so out of his element, was startling enough for me. But then, with the help of my counselor and principal, I told my father about my uncle, and my father began to cry. I had never seen him cry before. He asked me why I hadn't told them. I told him I was scared, and by then I was sobbing, too. I felt so ashamed that I couldn't look at him. I was sure he thought of me as less of a person.

At home, my mother made me feel much worse. She didn't say anything, she just looked at me in horror, and then she slapped my face. Thankfully, she called a close family friend for support, and, when her friend came over, she told my mother that she had been sexually abused by her brother-in-law when she was a teenager and had attempted suicide. Then my mother looked me in the eye with a new understanding, and I knew that she believed me. At that moment, I felt my mother's love. But I also knew that she could not deal with what was happening.

The next few hours were very intense. My mother called Uncle Jim's wife, her sister, and told her what had happened. My aunt said she did not believe me. While they were on the phone, the police arrived at my uncle's place of work, and he was taken to the police station for questioning. While all this was going on, I could hardly look at my parents. My father was crying, and my mother was shaking all over. My poor little sister came home to all this pandemonium. When she found out what was going on, she said that Uncle Jim had given her the creeps for a long time.

Needless to say, family relations were severely strained. My aunt and cousin sided with my uncle. My mother stopped calling her sister, and my cousin wouldn't speak to me. I felt like I had lost my older sister. My dad seemed really embarrassed around me, and my mother tried very hard not to hold anything against me, but there were times when she would just look at me and shake her head and say, "How did this happen? How did you not tell me?"

My sister came to me and said, "Thank you, Pearl. You know, I've always been kind of disgusted by Uncle Jim, but I thought it was my imagination that he was touching my breast when he hugged me. I didn't know he had touched you, but I was really scared." Hearing my sister's words made it all worth it to me. I could give up my relationship with my cousin, I could even live with my mother's ambivalence, if I managed to save my sister from Uncle Jim's abuse.

It's been a year since I disclosed the abuse to my family. I am seventeen now and a lot has changed for me. I don't think about my uncle as much, and when I do I know how to deal with the feelings that come up through journal writing, going to group, and doing these relaxation exercises Dr. Patti taught me. I still have a lot of feelings about what happened with my uncle, but the strongest emotion is not fear. I still don't speak to my cousin, but I am not as sad about it as I was a year ago. I sleep better. I feel happier. I feel so relieved that I don't have to worry anymore about anyone finding out. All the important people in my life know. I am not hiding anything anymore. It really feels like a weight I have been carrying around is off my shoulders.

My dad never talks about the abuse. My mom sometimes mumbles that she wishes she could see her sister, and sometimes she even slips and blames me for letting things with my uncle go on for so long. But last week in church I felt my mother reach for my hand while singing her favorite hymn, and it felt so real to me. We don't have this huge secret between us anymore.

MY THOUGHTS

Pearl is a success story in many ways, but her family's support was certainly key to her healing. Although they had to go through some difficult feelings to get there, they stood by Pearl even when it meant losing connections with important family members. Although Pearl had haunting memories of her abuse, those memories led her to get help. It's even somewhat surprising that her mother and father were so fully supportive and willing to confront the uncle. Most Asian cultures strenuously protect the family image and guard family secrets. Also, in the cultural hierarchy, boys are more respected than girls, and we might have expected her parents to try to hide Pearl's abuse to protect the honor of her respected uncle. He was one of the first family members to immigrate to the United States and was held in very high esteem. That's why it's all the more remarkable that Pearl's parents were willing to become estranged from him and the extended family. Filipino women tend to go to great pains to make sure that the men "look good" to the world and in the community, and Filipino as well as many Spanish families will go to great lengths to avoid *chismosa,* or gossip about the family.

Of course, Pearl will never forget her mother's slap, but it seems that with the slap her mother released her anger and shock and then was able to face Pearl. Her father simply never discusses the abuse. Although the Filipino culture is considered a matriarchy, it still teaches girls and women to defer to boys and men, especially in the family. Parents of many cultural persuasions can be expected to be anxious to deny that their child has been abused, especially by a relative. It just brings up too many tricky emotions.

One of the things many girls have told me is that it often isn't until their parents can look them in the eye again that they feel they can look in the mirror. Girls can stay stuck in their shame when their parents are stuck in their own grief, shock, despair, and pity. Daughters need to know that they are not the three Ds: dirty, damaged, defective. They need their parents to be able to look them in the eye—and work out their discomfort away from their daughters—so that they can help their daughters feel all right in their own skins again.

In her book *Lucky*, Alice Sebold talks about her first encounter with her mother after she had to phone her and tell her she had been brutally raped by a stranger in the park the night before. She said that when she saw her mother, with all her fresh energy, she knew she could handle things and get through the rest of the day.

Ironically, teen girls and young women can rebound from trauma more quickly than their loving parents do. But it is the loving parents who speed up the healing, just by their love.

CHAPTER 15

FINDING YOUR SUPPORT POSSE

When you are a survivor of sexual abuse, and especially of incest, trust is hard to come by. You can start to believe that no one in the world will help you. Your abuser has put the blame on you or convinced you that what he is doing is right. Just as Coral's father told her, men tell girls that sex is a rite of passage, "like a bat mitzvah." You may feel too isolated to know that there really is help and support out there.

As strange as it may seem to you, most families would be completely devastated if their daughters were abused, and, frankly, so would most people. For all the crass commercials and obscene music videos out there, there's also a tremendous movement against the tide of abuse, and it's beginning to work. By telling your truth, you are adding force to that movement. There are more women judges, more women lawyers, more feminists, both male and female, in the criminal justice system, more advocates for children. And more people than ever are willing to speak out loud and in public about sexual abuse. When the news broke that Harvey Weinstein was a serial sexual abuser, many other survivor voices came forward. We all need to keep the #MeToo movement powerful and alive, because we know that sexual-abuse survivors are stronger than their abusers. The more we speak out in support of those reclaiming their voices, the more we end the culture around sexual abuse.

We are also seeing more and more grassroots efforts at change—from individuals to organizations, schools, hospitals, crisis centers, and websites. As I see it, each of these represents a piece of that mosaic we spoke about earlier—the incredible mosaic of our movement to combat sexual abuse.

There are women and men, mothers and fathers, teachers and counselors, nurses and doctors, lawyers and judges across the country reaching out to young people trying to make a difference. There are rape crisis centers at most colleges and universities. There are groups for survivors as well as individual counseling. And, as sexist as much of the music culture is, some feminist musicians have come out with songs about their abuse, including Tori Amos, who started the Rape and Incest National Network (RAINN), and Ani DiFranco, who sings about women's empowerment and started her own record label, Righteous Babe Records, because she would not be packaged by the corporate music industry.

Young women are putting out beautiful videos celebrating womanhood in all its glorious power, strength, and diversity! Colbie Caillat released "Try," a beautiful song and video in 2014. Lyrics include "you don't have to try so hard, you don't have to give it all away, take your makeup off, let your hair down, take a breath, look in the mirror at yourself, don't you like yourself, 'cause I like you." The girls and women in the video make strong statements about the pressures of living up to beauty standards while they celebrate themselves. Solange's 2016 release of "Don't Touch My Hair" is the antithesis of the sexualization of black and brown women that is so prevalent in music videos. Solange calmly sings, "Don't touch my hair, don't touch soul, when it's the rhythm I know, don't touch my pride, they say the glory's all mine, don't test my mouth, they say the truth is my sound." She and the other women of color in the video are all strong and proud. Young Muslim independent artist Mona Haydar released a powerful music video "Hijabi—Wrap My Hijab" in 2017 with women from all over the world proudly wearing their hijabs. Some lyrics include "all around the world love women every shade, be so liberated, make a feminist planet, all haters get banished." Although the music video industry is still primarily run by men and sexualizes girls and women, these young women are speaking out against misogyny loud and clear!

BOYS WILL BE BOYS...NOT ALWAYS

Long before the media blitz around sex abuse, there have even been some men from major rock bands who have come forward to take a very visible stand against rape. At the 1999 MTV awards, the Beastie Boys condemned Limp Bizkit for the several rapes that happened at Woodstock 1999. They attributed the rapes to the lyrics of a Limp Bizkit song played at the festival that actually encouraged men to rape women. The Red Hot Chili Peppers have taken a stand, too, through their support of RAINN, which by the way has a man for president! Film director Tim Roth has also championed the issue of preventing sexual abuse of girls. His movie The War Zone is about a boy who wanted to kill his father for molesting his sister. In 2018 director Michel Hazanavicius launched the #WeToo hashtag for men in support of women fighting sexual harassment and abuse. He wanted to make sure supportive men's voices were heard loud and clear. There are some organizations for men to stop violence against girls and women (see our Resource Center).

Boys and young men are under tremendous pressure to

adopt the role of the "mac daddy" even though most girls just want to take things slow and have the time and space to explore their sexuality, and don't just want to "fuck." Those boys who want sincere friendships with girls are put down as wimps.

There are young men volunteering at rape crisis hotlines and helping escort girls on campus at night. And more and more fathers are showing their wives and daughters respect as equals and taking pride in their daughters' physical strength and accomplishments. Men of all ages are marching with women to stop violence against women.

Yes, we have a long way to go in changing our sexist culture, but there are many people out there helping us move to a better place. They are doing it in response to the outrageous truths that girls and women have been willing to share. Every time a survivor breaks the taboo of sexual abuse and speaks out, she helps the culture of boys and men by teaching everyone what sexual abuse does to a person, the pain that's involved, the displaced emotions of shame and guilt. This is a bottom-up movement all the way. Now conversations about sexual misconduct, rape, and sexual violation are going on all around us. Finally, the culture seems to be beginning to listen. Every girl who tells her truth and heals from sexual abuse helps another girl to tell her story and heal.

LIFE GOES ON

You may never be able to heal the damage done in your family. You may hate your abuser forever; you may struggle with forgiving your mother for letting the incest or other abuse happen. You may even need to separate from your family and create a new one. Girls often have to create new chosen families and new support systems that they can count on as they move forward.

But please know help is out there. You'll be surprised at how many people will join you in your anger at your abuser, join you in your healing process. Yes, getting your posse together can take time. You sometimes need great patience. But don't give up. If at first you don't get the response you are looking for from the people you tell, find others. Join a survivors' group. Talk to an aunt or a cousin or someone you can really trust. Call a hotline. Find parts of our book that are a comfort and keep going back to those sections that help you. You will find your support system.

All sexual-abuse survivors are righteous and strong. Remember sexual abuse knows no color or faith, no wealth or poverty, and healing knows no boundaries! You are beautiful, you are strong, you are determined. You have agency! Your abuse is just a part of you, a part of your past. It does not define you. It is something that was done to you. You cannot undo it, but you can heal from it and lead a wonderful, blessed life filled with success, love, fulfillment, power, creativity, and healing. There are people out there who will help you—good people who will love you and whom you will love. Always know you are so much more than what was done to you. Thank you for joining us on this journey of surviving and thriving after sexual abuse. You can move out of the darkness of abuse into the light of life.

Remember the brave girl who told us:

Out of all the piles of dirt, garbage, and shit we have been handed, we can grow a patch daisies.

I know it's true. I see girls do it every day, and I can see your beautiful gardens growing already.

CHAPTER 16

FLOWERS BLOOM

Updates on Zinnia, Lily, Coral, Garnet, Topaz, Sage, Ivy, Jasmine, Iris, Dahlia, Pearl, Ruby Rose

This book was ten years in the making, and, with subsequent editions, fifteen. Over the course of these years, many of the girls who shared their stories in the book have come back to see me. Even though many have moved to different States and some even to different countries, we've stayed in touch. They have grown, changed, and gotten way beyond their abuse. I was the first person most of these beautiful girls shared their experiences with. It's a strong link that connects us, even when we are out of touch.

The girls in the stories you have witnessed have continued and moved past their abuse. No matter what abuse you have suffered through—incest, rape, or mentor abuse—you too will have a life filled with love and hope. And if you have joined us in these journeys and you have not been abused, our hope is that our words have brought you a depth of understanding. None of us can sit back as witnesses to the misogyny in the world. We all need to link hands in the sisterhood of protecting and respecting all girls and women. There is life after sexual abuse. I see it every day. And here's your chance to see it with me. The flowers have bloomed.

Zinnia, who escaped her torture by cataloging flowers and building beautiful homes in the woods has actually become a social justice lawyer. She prosecutes pedophiles and helps girls and women in the court system. She is happily coupled with another woman, and they live and work together with their three cats and two dogs in a farmhouse in Montana.

Lily, the girl who survived abuse by imagining herself as a superhero, called me a few years ago about her first social work case. She had successfully fought to have an abused survivor removed from her abuser-father's home and was feeling really victorious about her work. She was partnered with a woman who she called the love of her life for five years at the time of her call.

Coral, whose father raped her for so many years in Holland, is happily married with twin daughters and three cats. She and her husband are restoring their historical home in Vermont. Her mother divorced her father. Coral has set up boundaries with her mother, and she has totally cut her abuser out of her life. Coral continues to compose music and give music lessons to children.

Garnet, the girl whose father raped both her and her sister, came back a couple of years after she wrote her story. She is a preschool teacher. Her sister, who, you'll recall, had been living on the streets as a prostitute, is now living with Garnet and her husband. She showed up on Garnet's doorstep one day, and Garnet has helped her get off drugs. She remains in a drug treatment day program, and she and Garnet joined forces in pursuing charges against their father. They have a court date to prosecute their father. Neither one is in touch with their mother.

Topaz, who was molested by her brother, came back to therapy a few years ago. She came out as gay when she turned twenty. Because she had fallen in love with a fabulous woman, she was worried she would screw up this great relationship. With a few months of therapy, she got on track. She is an artist and is now living with her girlfriend, who is also an artist, in Williamsburg, Brooklyn.

Sage, the topless dancer, came to see me five years after our therapy ended. She'd move to another state, gotten married, and had a baby. She told me how much she loved her husband and how she has made a family totally different from her family of origin. At the time of her visit, she was twenty-nine and working part time teaching art to children. Seeing her doing so well, I was overwhelmed with joy that generations of abuse in Sage's family had stopped, and I was so moved when Sage let me hold her daughter. She said, "Patti, I can't tell you how much joy I get from my daughter and the knowledge that she'll never be abused like I was."

Ivy, who was molested by her friend's father, the rabbi, had a rough start at college. She took a year off and lived in Israel. She enrolled in Tel Aviv University and graduated with honors. She is happily single, working at a tech start-up and living in Haifa, Israel.

Amber, who suffered from acquaintance abuse at her camp when she was twelve, has become a florist. She called to tell me she just gave birth to a healthy baby boy. She lives and works in Paris with her husband.

Jasmine, who was sexually abused in Israel, has graduated from college, lives in New York, and works at the United Nations. She earned her PhD in international relations, and she ended up marrying the boy she dated in high school eight years after they met.

Iris, who was brutally date-raped, ended up becoming a journalist. She travels the world and writes about different cultures. She is kick-ass assertive and happily single.

Dahlia, who was gang-raped and spent years battling anorexia, has started volunteering at a rape hotline while in graduate school pursuing a career in journalism. She has conquered her eating disorder. She waitresses to make extra money and has learned to stand up for herself with inappropriate diners. She says each time she does this she feels stronger.

Ruby Rose, who left "the life," has graduated with honors with her pre-med bachelor's degree. Girlthrive sponsored a summer in Peru for her to attend a medical training program. She is attending an Ivy League medical school where she is specializing in woman's health. She is a tenacious young woman!

Pearl, whose uncle molested her, has graduated college, where she majored in art and design. After reporting her uncle when she was seventeen years old, other girls and women from his community whom he had abused came forward. He is serving eight years in prison for the molestation of Pearl and three other girls. Pearl has left that behind her and is a website designer living in Brooklyn, New York, with her younger sister, who is forever grateful to Pearl for saving her from abuse!

All these girls have found strength in becoming visible. They have told their truths. Every time a girl comes forward with her truth, opening Pandora's box with her story of sexual abuse, she too becomes visible. By telling your story, you not only ensure your own healing, but you help other girls to come forward, too. Together, we are inching our way toward a future where men can no longer get away with sexually abusing girls and women.

It is the girls and the women, the mothers and daughters, the aunts, sisters, and nieces—there is nothing more powerful than the chorus of girls and women coming together with such fierce determination, all in the name of sisterhood. Together, we will transform that pile of shit into a huge field of daisies. I know we can.

CHAPTER 17

FIVE YEARS OF E-MAILS AND LETTERS FROM AROUND THE WORLD

Girls Become More and More Visible Every Day

GIRLS' STRENGTH AND HEALING

For me, one of the most extraordinary parts of the experience of publishing this book has been the connections I have made with girls and their allies from all over the world. I continue to receive amazing e-mails, letters, and phone calls from girls and young women who are opening up about their sexual abuse. They're not just writing to thank me for my book, but being extraordinarily loving and open about their truth.

I find it so profound that, no matter where it happens or to whom or how or when or how often, sexual abuse has the same impact. As you can tell from their letters, at least for a time so many girls carry guilt around with them like rocks in their pockets. If they don't blame themselves outright, they at least live with a ton of confusion about what happened to them and why. It is so important that we all work together to change this. I can't repeat this often enough: Sexual abuse is never the survivor's fault!! Never, never, never.

Most of these girls and women originally wrote to tell me how *Invisible Girls* changed their lives. They wanted to share their opening up, their new strength and resolve. They wanted me to hear their stories of fighting back and making their way back to life.

They add to the chorus of voices already in the book, but from the perspective of having had the chance to read other girls' stories and reflect on what those stories and my advice meant to them. They have been changed by reading the stories of the deep, involved work of my clients who experienced sexual abuse and came through it to thrive. They found comfort in my clinical guidance throughout the book, and now they join those girls in wanting to become visible and stop suffering in silence. Together, girls like this, girls like you, are releasing their traumas and healing, changing the culture, and making girls stronger and more righteous every day!

There's also an extraordinary eloquence and grace in the ways girls get through abuse. Here are their stories, in their words. (I have edited some of the letters and changed the locations to protect the identities of the girls.) Here is proof positive of how wonderful, amazing, and resilient girls can be. I am blessed to know you all.

THEIR STORIES

These are just a handful of the amazing e-mails I receive. I have tried to include the many different topics people write to me about, including brother-sister incest, date rape, father-daughter incest, mothers' responses, lovers' questions, sex trafficking, as well as healing letters. All the e-mails are remarkable; this is just a few of the gems.

Most of the girls who write to me about brother-sister abuse are quite young, and in most of these cases the sister finds out that her brother was also abused at some point in his life. Often the brother's abuse of the sister goes on for years without any-one knowing. And it's often the girl who puts a stop to it when she reaches adolescence and begins to come into her own. She's starting to move forward into relationships of her own and somehow finds the strength to interrupt the abuse. Or it stops when the brother gets a girlfriend or boyfriend.

He Can Never Hurt Me Again

Hey, Dr. Patti,

I am writing to you from England. I just finished reading *Invisible Girls*, and it has given me so much insight into sexual abuse and the effects it has on its survivors. Growing up I always felt like I was the only person I knew who was being or had been sexu-ally abused, but after reading your book I realized that really I probably do know other girls that have been abused, it's just that they're as good at hiding it as I am!

There was so much in the book that made me think, "Hey, that's exactly how I feel" or "That's what I do." I found that really encouraging, even just to know that other abuse survivors strug-gle with low self-esteem, fear of sex and intimacy, panic attacks, poor relationships with their mothers, and perfectionism.

It's also really good to know that I don't have to forgive him to heal. Someday I might be able to, but right now I can't. I hate him! He doesn't deserve my forgiveness. Whenever I see him I can't help making really sarcastic and mean comments. My mum keeps saying that all I do is sit there and rip him off, but, trust me, that's a lot better than what I would like to do to him! She also says it's like I don't like him or something. Gee, I wonder why!

Reading Topaz's story, I saw so many similarities between her life and mine! Her parents getting divorced and then not having any contact with her dad, her mum not being there when she was younger due to work and being left home alone with her brother. Just like Topaz, I didn't talk about personal things with my mum or really connect to her. The only thing she ever seemed that concerned with was my schoolwork. And about Topaz's mum and brother fighting—my brother was always fighting with my mum and pretty much everyone else. I actually kind of felt sorry for him. We were really different, and he never really fitted in.

One thing that really jumped out at me was the part where Topaz said, "This was probably the most confusing time in my life. As much as my body was reacting, in my mind I knew it was gross, it was wrong, and yet I didn't stop it." I totally related to this statement, it was like I had said it, like it had come out of my mouth. It wasn't until my brother got a serious girlfriend that he left me alone physically, but there was still that constant fear that he would start again.

When the physical abuse finished, the verbal abuse would start. He would always talk about how I looked and tell me in detail what he had done with his girlfriend. When he moved out for university was when I finally got away from it all.

Reading *Invisible Girls* helps me to see that I am safe now. I am away from him, and he can never hurt me again, even if I see him. I am visible to myself. Thank you and all the girls who shared their stories.

XO,
Nera

Something we didn't address in *Invisible Girls* is teenage pregnancy. I know girls who got pregnant as young as fourteen or fifteen here in New York City, and I receive heartbreaking e-mails from girls who live in rural areas and tell me they gave birth to their "daddy's" baby. Even in the most awful situation, these girls seem to surpass their circumstance and love their babies with all their hearts. They become the protective mother they never had.

I Love My Baby Girl

Dear Dr. Patti,

When I was fourteen, I told my mom that my uncle had been forcing himself on me on and off for two years. She said it was my fault and yelled at me for being a big flirt. I got pregnant when I was fifteen. The father was my boyfriend. He was twenty-seven at the time. I knew I would have the baby (a beautiful girl) and, even though my mom pressured me to marry the dad when I turned seventeen, I refused. My baby is my whole life. Sometimes I think she's the only person who ever really loved me. I love her and she just loves me back. Nothing twisted or weird.

I'm no longer with my baby's father, and things are pretty hard for me and her. (My mom is almost totally out of the picture now.) I get really lonely sometimes, and it's also hard for me to leave her with other people. I am like a fierce hawk who won't let anyone mess with her baby birds. A friend gave me a copy of *Invisible Girls*, and I'm beginning to put things together—like maybe I got involved with an older guy because I thought he would take care of me and protect me after the abuse and my mother not supporting me and all (my uncle is her brother, by the way). He was a pretty good guy, but he had a lot of problems, too. Things are really hard right now, but I'm back in school (this school has a nursery, which is amazing), and I am just trying to get my life together. Reading about the other girls has really helped me feel a lot less alone, and it is helping me stop feeling like I should have or could have done something to stop my uncle or get my mother to believe that it wasn't my fault.

Thanks.
Destiny

I love hearing from girls who discover the book on a trip to the bookstore and find themselves sitting on the floor of the store just reading and reading. Many of these girls tell me they didn't necessarily buy the book that first day but went back for it later, even a week later or more. I cannot tell you the thrill it gives me to know that on any random day a girl may stumble onto our book and find hope and healing.

Reading and Healing

Dear Dr. Patti,

I live in downtown Minneapolis. About two weeks ago I saw your book at a bookstore and just picked it up and bought it, like for some reason I knew I should read it. When I got to the chapter about incest with a brother, I wept and wept and was relieved in a way to know that it was not my fault and that I wasn't a sick and gross person for being physically aroused by that.

I finally called a counselor last week who read your book, and she gave me some really awesome advice. I also called one of my good friends and shared with her on a deeper level just how humiliated I was and how deep it really was. I have always felt that the abuse was my fault because I never said no, my voice was always stuck in my throat. I avoided him, I tried to keep him away from me at all costs, but I never could say no, I only went numb. I knew no one would help me. I was always too scared. But reading your book I realized that maybe it wasn't my fault and that I was abused by this man since he was so much older than me. Why is that so terrifying to admit? Also that I may have been abused by several men rather than just my brother? It is much easier to blame myself, but I just hated myself. I always thought I was so gross and ugly.

But, Dr. Patti, for the first time in a long time, I feel hope. I feel like there is hope for me, and I am going to continue to work on this and let it come out. I have about twenty years of rage stuffed into my heart.

Whenever I start to blame myself, I open up *Invisible Girls* and find stories of other girls like me. Of course, I know it wasn't their fault, and that gives me hope.

Thank you, Dr. Patti. God bless you and the girls, thank you.

Sharon

I knew that Chapter 6, "Girls' Genius," was monumental. We were among the first to tell the clinical community and the community of survivors that dissociation is a healthy tool that girls use to get through sexual abuse. We made it clear that this is a mechanism of creativity that girls are able to tap into while they are being abused. We got to see deep inside the alternate worlds girls create to live through their abuse. You see, girls really are geniuses at getting through their abuse. I often get beautiful thank-you e-mails from girls and women who want to tell me that they, too, have created these worlds and it is such a comfort to be acknowledged for their strength.

My World of Make-Believe

Dear Dr. Patti,

I would first like to say thank you for writing *Invisible Girls*. I am a twenty-six-year-old woman living in Alaska. I have read almost the whole book over the last three days, and it has giving me such a different view about my past. The part of your book that helped me the most was the stories written by Zinnia and Lily. You see, I was abused by one of my parents' sons for a long period of time. I have to word it the way I did because I can't use the b-word without getting physically ill. Because of what happened I created my own world. I always felt safe there, and I could go there whenever I needed. I always thought I was crazy because of this. And knowing that I had this other world in my mind made me feel as if I was completely alone. Knowing that there are others out there who do this as well, who can stand up and tell it to the world, makes me think that there may be hope for me too. Thank you for your time and again, thank you for *Invisible Girls*.

Rachel

I am always so encouraged to hear from girls who have found solace by talking to counselors who understand about sexual abuse and who help girls realize it is not their fault. As I talked about in Chapter 13, the chapter about getting help, it is very important that you trust and like your therapist, much less important what degrees she has.

Counseling Helps

Hi, Dr. Patti,

My name is Jackie. I'm fourteen years old, and I live in a small rural town in Texas. When I was thirteen, my brother's best friend molested me. I told my parents, and they talked to him and then told me to keep quiet about the whole situation. After that I never went to my parents for anything ever again. But recently I started to get counseling, and I'm trying to change things around in my life. Because now I know that other girls have told their secrets, and they found safe people to tell even when their parents wouldn't help them. I really like my counselor, and she also has a copy of *Invisible Girls*. We talk about the different chapters in our counseling sessions. It has helped me to open up.

I read your book every night. It makes me feel safe just knowing that I'm not the only girl in the world who feels like me. If it wasn't for your book, I probably would not be here today. I just wanted to say thank you for writing such a beautiful book. I will never forget the wonderful things it showed me, how to heal and recover. I open it up and read it whenever I want to feel that someone is listening. It helps me to go on. God bless you.

With love and hope,
Jackie

One thing that stands out in so many of the e-mails I receive is how girls are really tuning in to each other. Girls can be wonderful friends to each other. It's really heartening and important. I constantly hear from girls who are worried about a friend, girls who are protecting their friends and supporting them, listening to them, helping them find more support. It is also really vital to support yourself, take care of yourself, protect yourself.

Protecting Myself

Dear Dr. Patti,

I am writing you from a small town in New Mexico. I have been confused about my rape, and *Invisible Girls* has helped me see that I am not alone. I also feel ready to change some of my behaviors now! When reading the date rape section, I started recognizing some of my behaviors, and it gave some insight into why I do them.

When I go out with friends, I am either the girl who gets so drunk she can hardly remember the night out, or else the completely sober one who makes sure her drunk girlfriends get home safely. I won't leave them until I know they are safely tucked away for the night and no one can hurt them. I just seem to become super-protective. After reading your book, I'm thinking I will keep being protective of my friends, but now I will also be more protective of myself.

I also learned that it is normal not to feel. I have only ever gotten close to one guy and tried to be intimate with him. I liked him, but I couldn't connect with him. This was the first time I had done anything sexual with a guy other than kissing, and even though I did like him, while he was doing it, all those memories I had stored away came back to me, and I pretty much froze. I couldn't differentiate between what was done to me during the abuse from what this guy who I knew wouldn't hurt me was doing now. So I just lay there and let him do it. This was what I was used to doing during the abuse. I would just lie there while he did what he had to do, and then when he was done he would just get up and leave.

During the abuse I would often get aroused, even though I wasn't enjoying it and didn't want to. This time I actually did want to feel something, but the abuse held me back. I just lay there and let him do his thing, expecting that when he was done he would just leave, like I was used to. But he didn't leave.

Eventually, I rolled over and put my pants back on. He asked if I was alright, and I just nodded and left the room. I felt so freaked out and confused and had to have some time to myself. When I came back I just acted like nothing had happened and everything was fine! It was the act that I was so good at putting on coming through again. After reading *Invisible Girls* I know that shame is a normal part of sex abuse and sexual violation. Now I just have to work out how to get past it. Every day I get stronger!

Thank you and thanks to all the great girls in your book.

Love,

Tate

When a girl is rescued from being abducted and finds solace, strength, and confidence in our book, it reinforces the urgency of the writing of *Invisible Girls*. This letter brings us full circle from the beginning of the book, talking about how it is so important not to let the years of keeping the sexual abuse secret prevent you from facing your truths and starting your healing journey. But this story has a happy ending, with a mother beginning to break the cycle of abuse by rescuing her daughter and supporting her with love.

Sexually Trafficked—Rescued by My Mom

Dear Dr. Patti,

Thank you for writing *Invisible Girls*. It has broken open so many truths in my family that could not come out before. I am an incest survivor at the hands of my stepfather. I never told about the abuse and was suicidal and hospitalized when I was seventeen years old, still never telling. Shortly after getting out of the hospital on my eighteenth birthday, I was lured into the sex trade by being sexually trafficked. What started out in Texas, where I am from, ended up near Colorado. They drugged me every day, and I could barely remember my name. They sent in man after man to motel after motel. I had no idea where I was. I would open my eyes from time to time and see highway signs.

Before I was lured into being trafficked, I was so depressed, and I felt like no one cared enough. And yet being trafficked I was terrified day after day, and I realized I needed to escape. But I did not have my cell phone, and, every time I was sort of awake, they drugged me again. But it turns out that during this time my mother went on all social media, called police, detectives, judges, went to hotel after hotel with my picture, and contacted an underground network to rescue girls who had been trafficked. The traffickers saw my picture on the Internet, on the newscasts, and heard my mother, and they realized that I had support, and they got so scared they would get caught, they let me go. Within eight days I was rescued by my mother. I returned home a total mess. I was happy that my mother rescued me, but I was defeated and scared and totally traumatized. About a week after I was rescued, my mother's friend told her about a book that she read that really helped her heal from the incest she suffered at the hands of her uncle. The book was *Invisible Girls*.

When my mom gave me the book, I was feeling so alone and depressed. But when I read that there are other survivors out there and how other girls overcame their nightmares, I knew I could too. My mom and I read the book together, and I told my mom about the incest. Although my parents were divorced for two years by now and I never saw my stepfather, my mom went to the police to get an order of protection out against him. As she read the book, my mom started crying and hugging me, and for the first time she admitted to me that she also suffered incest, but her mother never protected her. *Invisible Girls* has given us both so much hope and insights. We are closer because of this book, and I no longer feel I am a victim. I have faith, and I am joining the survivors in this book. If you are still in touch with the girls in the book, please tell them I say thank you for giving me back my life—and my mom's.

Love,
Maria

Girls never cease to amaze me—their strength, grit, and courage, their ability to be resilient and get past abuse and then turn it into something powerful and positive in their lives. Many girls have found strength by speaking out about their experiences and helping other girls. When you speak out, if you reach just one girl, you are helping to change the world.

Speaking Out to Other Girls

Dear Dr. Patti,

I read some of your book at the bookstore the other day, then bought it and read it in one night. You challenged me and reminded me to see past this pain. Thank you.

I had been away at college for a few months by the time December 2007 rolled around and was looking forward to going home and hugging my family. During my time away I had really tried to forget having been sexually abused as a child. I wanted a fresh start, I was getting my life together and doing well in school.

As I took my seat on a train for a three-hour trip, a man sat next to me and ordered drinks. He started a conversation about our families, our goals, and dreams. He offered me a drink, and because I am a nervous traveler I took him up on it.

He was obviously flirting, and all of a sudden the flirting became much more aggressive and I tried to change the subject. I turned my head and stared out the window, feeling familiar feelings of panic rising in my chest. Suddenly, his hands were on my thighs and I was frozen there, desperately trying to remain "there." I tried to push him away. I said no and attempted to move from my seat, but he put his leg between mine to block my exit. He kept saying I was as "beautiful as a model" and how much he "wanted a wife like me." I was frozen in the same way as I was as a sexually abused child.

I felt like the smallest human being, a piece of filth, because I was letting this happen again. I asked him to stop repeatedly, and he told me I was just "too pretty."

The rest of the trip, it was evening and his hands were literally all over me, he actually put his fingers inside of me—I was frozen. Then he left, saying, "Goodbye, beautiful."

Although I froze during this—I knew it was sexual assault. He left me his business card, and I didn't take it out of my wallet for a few months. I spent two days at home for Christmas break. My mother told me it was my fault. A police officer told me it was a "case of he said, she said" and to keep my legs crossed next time. When I returned to school my partner told me just to forget about it and that it didn't matter. Needless to say, that relationship didn't last.

That shame haunted me for a year and a half. But now I'm finally standing up for myself. I just studied abroad for a few months. I needed to take a night train from Italy to Paris, and I was very nervous. I made sure I was sitting next to families. When I went to the bathroom, a man followed me—and I was almost assaulted, but this time I fought back. It was the most freeing moment I've had in the last year and a half. I fought back, and I will fight back as long as I live. I won't ever be invisible again!

I have been in counseling and now go to schools and speak about my experience. My experience with rape is usually one of the first things I tell my close friends about, and the burden lessens a bit every time. I speak about date rape at high schools and counsel young women on ways to protect themselves. I wanted to share my story with you so I don't feel quite so alone right now. Thank you for being willing to love young women like me even though I feel very unlovable sometimes. And most of all thank you and all the amazing girls in *Invisible Girls*.

Love,
Enid

I knew that sexual abuse was universal, but I guess I was not prepared to receive e-mails from Iran, Mexico, Saudi Arabia, Iceland, Columbia, and Ecuador. I not only receive e-mails from urban centers like Paris and London, where I would expect girls to have internet access and find the Girlthrive website, but from girls literally all over the world who are finding help and healing from our book and then seeking out organizations in their cities and towns to help them heal and thrive.

No Longer Alone

Dear Dr. Patti,

I live in Sweden, and your book not only made me realize the extent of my own abuse, it has also made me stop downplaying to myself what happened to me. Thanks to you, I have also taken the step of getting some support from a Swedish organization that helps adult survivors of sexual abuse. When I first applied for psychotherapy from them and got my appointment, I was still of two minds as to whether I wanted to open up all the hurt again. After reading your book, I decided that I should go.

I'm also seeing a psychologist at my local hospital who is helping me come off the antidepressants that I have been on for the past five years and is providing me with extra support with my body's physical responses to my abuse!

I was abused by my stepfather from the time I was nine until I was fifteen, at which point I started a relationship with a twenty-three-year-old guy. On the two occasions that I confronted my mother about the abuse, her responses were, "You know he wouldn't do something like that" and "Stop lying, he wouldn't do that." I now have no contact with my mother.

When I got the courage to tell my biological father and stepmother, they were initially really supportive but wanted me to contact the police, which I couldn't face. Now we don't talk about it, and I am finding my father's response harder than my own. He only ever mentions it with regards to wanting to murder my stepfather. I dare say that I will uncover more painful memories or, rather, just admit and accept them for what they are on my road to recovery, but be sure that you have helped me realize that this needn't taint the rest of my life and that recovery is possible.

I wouldn't be seeking the help and support that I am now if it wasn't for your book; I would still be hiding. It's a shame there isn't someone like you to come into schools here in Sweden. I'm sure it would save many young women like me. I'm now twenty-one, and it has taken six years after my abuse stopped for me to finally accept that I suffered abuse and to seek help; it needn't have taken that long.

Invisible Girls is truly inspirational, and I want to thank you from the bottom of my heart for writing this book and for helping all of my damaged sisters across the pond and all of the other damaged angels like me who have read your book.

I am giving this book to my partner and my father to read. I believe everyone should read it.

> My love and thanks to you always,
> Elsa

When I designed my website, I was very aware that it had to look like a site that could be about anything so girls would feel comfortable being seen reading it. I knew it couldn't scream "sex abuse"!

I also worked very hard with Seal Press to make sure that our book cover was thoughtful and beautiful and again did not scream out "sex abuse." I love the cover of our book, and our subsequent cover. Our first covers have a girl looking pensive, and this edition has three strong girls of different ethnic backgrounds exuding agency and confidence. I am so pleased that others feel able to read *Invisible Girls* on the subway, in the park, wherever they choose, without any self-consciousness and without anyone knowing they are reading about abuse.

Reading in Privacy

Dear Dr. Patti,

I am a survivor. I live in Atlanta, Georgia. I was raped by my father for many years, and until one month ago thought I had successfully put the past behind me. I found out I was very wrong, for which I am very happy. When I went to a bookstore to try to learn about what I was going though, I found about ten different books on incest that seemed to fit my situation and I promptly bought them ALL. As I read and reflected on them, I found all but one of the books extremely limiting!

For starters your book is the only one with a somewhat discreet cover. All the others screamed SEX/VICTIM/INCEST. You get the picture. Now, I am open to the idea of telling people what has happened to me, but the idea of letting every passerby know what I'm reading—perhaps it's me being paranoid, but it seems a bit much. Thank you for your discreet cover, and if you could pass the message along to some of the other book people whose book I likely bought but am now confined to reading only in the secrecy of my home, a change would be nice.

By the way I am only several chapters into the book and so far love it and am shocked to see how close the stories are to mine. Thank you!

Olivia

I learn from girls every day. I learn the ways they cope and the amazing visual archetypes they discover. I have always thought of wolves as dangerous and frightening, but the girl who sent the following letter taught me that wolves also help each other, and that a mother wolf will do anything to protect her children. This girl is able to find comfort and protection from her stuffed animal that her own family could never provide her with.

Protected by Wolves

Dear Dr. Patti,

I am eighteen years old. I live in upstate New York and I am an incest survivor. I reported my father, and he is on this sort of probation thing. I mean, at the moment and for the past couple of months, my dad hasn't come close to me (we also very rarely talk). When the abuse started up again, I went to the police and called up the social worker again, and she's getting him to go to alcohol recovery classes and anger management classes. She told me that if he touches me the slightest bit again, all I have to do is call her and the case will go straight to court, and I can get a restraining order if needed. I know that I have options now, and I'm not going to tolerate anything of that sort again. I'm spending next week in Vermont, and this weekend at a close friend's house. I have tried to cope in many ways, drinking, self-injury, and just closing off. The weird thing about my self-injury is that I don't regret it. People always say, "Look at your scars! Don't you hate having to see those all the time?" but I don't. I'm not sure why cuz they're really ugly, but I don't mind seeing them. I don't really feel ashamed of them.

I still have a fear of the dark, from those years that my father came to my dark room. For my fear of the dark, I know it sounds childish, but I sleep with one of my stuffed animals. It's a wolf, because when I was younger I thought wolves were so cute, and I did a project on them. I found out that they follow leadership and work together, and the mother will do anything to protect her cubs. I began to wish that my family worked like a wolf pack, and, ever since, they've been my favorite animal. The stuffed toy wolf that I sleep with really helps. Without it I feel alone and insecure. It's like I need that wolf to hug in order for me to fall asleep. Another way I cope with things is writing poetry and lyrics. I also play electric guitar.

I should get some sleep now. It really means a lot to me that you take the time to write.

Thank you so much!
Love,
Clara

I often hear from women who are now in their forties, fifties, and sixties, who found and read *Invisible Girls*. Although their abuse usually happened when they were teens, they are able to go back to that teenage girl and hold her, hug her, love her, and forgive her.

Twenty-Five Years Later

Dear Dr. Patti,

I am a forty-one-year-old sexual-abuse survivor. I was raped by my host father in Switzerland when I was fifteen years old. The mother worked fifty kilometers away, and I was home with him and the three children six days a week. He raised cattle and racehorses on this idyllic farm.

I can only remember two instances of the abuse—a rape—where I remember just leaving my body...floating out the window and going toward the voices of the children playing soccer in the backyard. I remember worrying about leaving them alone. He also molested me inside a building in a remote cemetery during the commemoration of a family member's death. I felt alone, trapped, with no true mastery of the language. I had no money, no car. It was rural. Yet I pushed these memories far below... always in control of myself after that....

A severe eating disorder began immediately during my seven weeks in France. I threw myself into my studies. I entered Columbia University in 1985 after graduating top in my prep school class. I was a strong athlete and perfect in the eyes of all. Just terrified of any relationship with a male. I startle whenever I am touched—if I don't see it coming. Even my own children. I am mother to four incredible children.

Yet, what is most difficult in my journey is finding the compassion in my heart to forgive that fifteen-year-old girl who never fought back... who never told... or asked for help. Your book has been incredible. So many situations and feelings of shame, guilt, and fear resonate. I am so thrilled that these girls will receive the help they need now, when they're young, before it cripples their lives. After reading *Invisible Girls* I am finally ready to begin to forgive the fifteen-year-old who could not fight back twenty-five years ago. Thank you for listening.

Sylvia

Never Too Old

Hi, Dr. Patti,

I just finished *Invisible Girls,* and I just wanted to say thank you. I'll be fifty next month and am still dealing with the aftereffects of a verbally abusive childhood and a sexualized relationship with my father as well as an absent, depressed mother. One of the more disruptive symptoms of my pain I now recognize is a desire to be invisible. The second major area the book helped me with is in identifying—clearly—the incredible pressure on women of all ages to, as I describe it, be sexual the way men are—the pressure to talk about sex and my sexual preferences on first and second dates—and with grown men!—the assumption that I'm supposed to want to go down on some guy I barely know. Or risk being considered somehow screwed up sexually and therefore damaged. So although I am fifty years old, *Invisible Girls* resonated for me deeply.

Thank You,
Natasha

When a girl sends me an e-mail asking whether I think it's all right if she takes her time with the book and skips around, I always tell her yes, any way she wants to read the book is perfect! I want girls to have the freedom to be in charge. I want survivors to be empowered by our book.

Facing the Truth

Dear Dr. Patti,
I was in Borders about a month ago skimming titles in the astrology section (my #1 personal hobby), and misplaced with the cover facing me was your book *Invisible Girls*. As I read the cover, I got totally freaked, and I wanted to pick it up and see what it was about, but I didn't. But I went home and ordered the book through Amazon that same night. It's a great book—it's just so hard to read. It makes me think of things I have tried forcing myself to forget. I have lived my entire life never telling a single soul; it is something I have repressed for almost all my twenty-

three years on earth. I hide the book in my car, and honestly, as stupid as it sounds, I have to build up courage to read it.

Many of the excerpts I can relate to. At twenty-three, I want to change and "be normal" and start whatever process to heal. Buying your book was scary, but it was the first time for me telling, thinking, or admitting to myself what happened. I am coming more and more to terms with it. I know it is a long road ahead, but at least I am finally on that road, thanks to your book. As I am reading, layers of fear are lifting—I even feel myself standing up straighter, looking people in the eye.

Love,
Bernadette

The most common e-mails I receive are from girls who are just beginning to talk about their abuse. The biggest message in *Invisible Girls* is that you are not alone and that when you start to talk about your abuse you start to get better. I know I sound like a broken record! But it is the truth—the truth about sexual abuse.

Turning Point

Hey, Dr. Patti,

I'm sitting here on a log in the middle of the forest in Utah. This has been a time of reflection for me and given me lots of time to think about my past and my future. I wanted to write you and all the girls in your book a thank you letter. *Invisible Girls* and your website Girlthrive have changed and quite possibly saved my life. Discovering Girlthrive and you sending me a copy of your book was a turning point in my life. Since then, I have started to talk about my abuse.

I am about to start counseling to help me deal with the abuse and move forward in my life (which I know won't be easy but will definitely be worth it), and I have told my second person ever face to face about my past and the abuse, and it feels so good. I'm still not ready to tell everyone about my abuse, but telling that one person was a huge relief, and he was really understanding. The copy of *Invisible Girls* that you sent me has been put to good use. When I am feeling angry or down, etc., I go back to it and read parts of it again. It's my survival guide. Fully understand the impact this book has had on me. Now that I am talking about my abuse, it is coming out of me—*Invisible Girls* has made me visible.

Love,
Nahama

Often girls who are date-raped get stuck in a date-rape mentality. They continue to blame themselves, they do not change their behavior right away, and they put themselves in danger over and over again, mostly because they are still blaming themselves for their rape. But I also hear from girls who realize they were date-raped and change their path. They're beginning to protect themselves and process what happened to them. They're finding solace in the women's centers at their universities; they're joining Take Back the Night; they're reading books. Women's support for each other is growing on campuses across the country. And young men are also joining forces.

When a girl gets herself to this place, she is changed for the rest of her life. Something just clicks, and she understands that she has agency. She decides not to get drunk, not to be the one to pass out, not to go home with the guy. She waits, she sees, she gets to know him. She tells her friends where she is. She begins to protect herself, and that also helps her have radar for good guys!

Fighting Back

Dear Dr. Patti,

I was raped on New Year's Eve night, four years ago. He was a friend.

It was my first time. It haunted me for a long time that I didn't say no. It haunted me past a little after it was over, when, shocked, he uttered that he had raped me, past the next day when he begged me to tell him I hate him and told me I could take him to the police if I wanted, past the bruises I saw as I examined my body alone back in my own dorm the next night.

It haunted me that I didn't say no. It haunted me so much that I had panic attacks. I froze, escaped my body, went numb over and over again at random times. When I confided in my friend about what happened, she told me I was immature for having been in his room in the first place when she had already judged him as an unsafe guy from the first time she met him. She said I deserved it and shouldn't complain.

I was fine with it at first. I accepted it and decided it was my choice. Then when it started feeling wrong, I listened to my best friend, who said that "technically, if you went to court, they wouldn't find anything against the guy since you didn't REALLY say no."

I lived with it for years. The shame, the guilt, the recurring panic attacks. Crying when getting intimate with the boyfriend I dated right after this happened, who I thought loved me. But in truth, he didn't, not well. He cheated on me with my best friend and manipulated my mind for a year and a half.

When I started college, I knew nothing about guys. The first time my first boyfriend fingered me on his bed, it hurt, and I cried secretly when he went to the bathroom. I wasn't ready, and I would tell him, but he wanted stuff, and he would say, "If you loved me, you'd do it." So I fell for it, because I didn't know what love was.

My mom hit me when I was young, and my dad was away at work most of the time. I knew she loved me but knew it in my head. I never felt it in my heart. How could I have known love, when she convinced me she loved me but she abused me so much, both physically and verbally? I didn't know it, and that's why I think I fell for a guy like this. It felt so dirty to do what he wanted, and yet I thought I had to, to be a good girlfriend, to earn his love.

When we broke up, he spread lies to his friends that we had sex, but we didn't. My first time was the rape, less than a year later. It must have hurt, but I didn't know it then. I didn't feel anything. I lay in his bed, arms tied as he sat on my legs, and didn't even feel him hitting me. The harder he slapped my breasts, the less I felt.

I remember hearing the belt buckle clinking. And then nothing. I didn't feel him having sex with me. I waited, until something broke inside me, and I cried and tugged on my tied wrists and tried to turn to my side. That's when he let me go.

It was soon after the rape that I started dating the guy who ended up cheating on me with my best friend. I was really vulnerable then, and I think he must have used that fact since I confided in him about a week after it happened.

Months later, after we broke up because he cheated, I was devastated. Of course, the panic attacks and nightmares continued. I was hurting, not just because of the rape but from the cheating, too, because I considered this guy my first love, my true love. So I started drinking a lot and sleeping with guys I didn't really care about. I decided I didn't want to care about sex anymore, because I thought that if I made it not be important to me, then it wouldn't matter anymore. The rape wouldn't hurt anymore. But it still hurt. The more I slept with guys, the sluttier I felt. Often, I thought it was disgusting when we were in bed. I would just lie there and wait till it was over, though they probably didn't even know it.

In my last year of college, my best friend (same friend who told me that legally I was at fault for not saying no two years before) took advantage of me when I was drunk one night. Though he denied it then, he admitted it to me a year later. He said he couldn't help himself, that I was drunk and I was the one who put myself in his apartment and looked like I wanted it to happen. That he was a guy and I was a girl, and he couldn't help himself.

After I moved to San Francisco, I met a guy. He seemed different from the others, you know, kind of a brainiac nerd. He wanted me to spend the night at his place, because we had been out late, and he said I'd be safer staying there than taking the train home alone. I decided to tell him about the rape. Surely if he knew that I'd been raped before, he wouldn't try anything. He promised not to, said he was so sorry about what had happened to me, said that his ex-girlfriend had also been raped and he remembered how that had affected her. He promised nothing would happen if I went back.

So I did. And, once we were in his room, my secret didn't matter anymore. We were just going to sleep he said, and, when we lay down, he got on top of me and pinned me down to his bed. He forced his mouth onto mine so hard that I couldn't turn my head or push him away. I was wearing a strapless top under my jacket that night, so he grabbed it and pulled it down as he still held my hands over my head. I was half naked in front of what now seemed like a stranger. I was so ashamed, and I kept struggling and couldn't get away.

I was so scared. I started to cry and begged him to stop, said please, asked over and over again why he was doing this to me. He didn't respond. He just kept going. Touching me, licking me. I went numb because I remember how I stopped fighting as he pulled my skirt up and my pantyhose and underwear down. I kept whimpering, and he didn't stop. And then he pulled his pants down and tried to force himself in, without a condom. I backed up a bit and kept crying, but he came forth and tried again. Then something in me snapped, and suddenly I thought, "I am NOT going to be raped again. Not unprotected." And with a surge of superwoman strength, I kicked him and pushed him off. He sat there and pretended that nothing had happened, that he didn't know what he had been doing. And asked, "What? What's wrong?"

I was able to get away and walk to the train in the middle of the night after all, but, to this day, I think that was the most inhumane thing I've ever experienced, worse than the first time because at least then I didn't even say no, so I was never sure what would have happened if I had. But this was proof that even if I had said no, it might not have saved me.

It's been over a year now since this happened. Soon after, I couldn't take it anymore. I broke down really bad one night, and that's when I started doing these talking sessions with a girlfriend of mine that I trusted. We went back to the beginning, and I opened up about all of it, and it helped me so much that if it wasn't for that, I don't think I would be writing this now. Once we talked about the rape, I realized that it wasn't my fault. That even though I didn't say no, I never said yes, and the guy knew that I didn't want it. He knew it, because he knew me well. But I was vulnerable, and he took advantage of me.

It's amazing how much strength I've found in me in the past year, and how much love I've felt again for myself after I let go of the guilt. I've made so much progress. In fact, I thought I was pretty much healed. But then, on Sunday, I watched a Holocaust movie. I used to have these concentration camp nightmares, but they had stopped by then. But after the movie I was in shock. I went to my friend's place, the person that I have opened up to, and I started crying. I didn't know why I was crying, but I let it all out. I cried and cried, and then something very strange happened: My body experienced the same exact sensations of the night of the rape. I relived it, everything that was underneath the numbness that night. This had happened before, twice, back when I first started opening up. Back then I would not be able to move. I couldn't move my legs, especially my right one. It must be because he had been sitting on them. I couldn't move them, even after the sensations slowly returned to the rest of my body.

This time, it was different. I went through the feelings, one by one: through the anxiety, through random pains spreading throughout my body, through the physical pain I must have felt in my vagina that night of my first time having sex, then through the quieting of senses, the letting go…and then as it ended I breathed hard. And suddenly, I cried and blurted out that I felt so bad that I let this happen to me, that I just wanted to hug the little girl, protect her, and then I yelled louder that I wanted to forgive myself.

I was SO surprised to hear that. I didn't even know that I wanted to "forgive myself." I thought I had. But I think that's why I felt it again: because I still hadn't let go of all the shame and guilt. I still blamed myself for being there in the first place, for being unable to say no.

The next day (Monday), I found your book on my lunch hour. I read it in two days. Thank you. A lot of things you said in there really rang true for me. I feel that I'm ready to heal, in a different way now. Ready to accept that it happened to me, affected me in terrible ways, and that it wasn't my fault. I had no support system then. I didn't know any better.

I think that the rape led to all the rest of the situations I found myself in with guys later, repeated itself over and over again, because I believed that I deserved to be treated like that, that it was just my destiny and I couldn't question it.

I think if you don't feel loved when you are young, you don't understand what love is supposed to be like, so you don't know to filter out the bad people from the good. You don't understand the differences, you make excuses for the clues. And you end up with a lot of bad people trying to bring you down every second they can, especially when they know you're in your most vulnerable times. You're prey then, and that's what I was.

I'm happy these days. I've never felt as calm and happy and balanced as I do now that it's all over. As you said in your book, we may not get to choose where we are and who protects us when we're kids, but, as adults, we do get to choose. I agree. I choose to offer me the love I never got as a child or as a teen-ager. I choose to wait and be with people who really love me.

The strength of the girls who shared their stories with us in your book is incredible. Inspiring and empowering to read that you, we, are not alone in this. The resilience of the female spirit is brilliant. Thank you for sharing that with the world.

Melody

Occasionally I get a letter from a boyfriend or girlfriend of an abuse survivor. They write because they have found out about the abuse or are struggling to help their partner or want to get through intimacy issues in their relationship that seem related to the trauma of the past. These partners are trying to understand. It's always heartening when I hear that *Invisible Girls* has saved a relationship or brought insight to a partner's trauma.

A Boy from Barcelona

Dear Dr. Patti,

I have a girlfriend that I love very much. She was getting very distant and I did not know why. We live in Barcelona and we are both twenty-two years old. She left her diary open on the table, and I read that she was raped when she was sixteen. I panicked. I did not know how to help her. I found your site and your book. Actually, I found it in Spanish, El Abuso. It has been two months now since I read her opened diary. We have both read your book. I want to thank you. From a boyfriend's perspective, it helped me to help her. She now is talking about her abuse to some of her friends and she is beginning to understand she can move on. Thank God for that book!

Gracias,
A Thankful Boyfriend

A Boyfriend's Perspective

Dear Dr. Patti,

A few months ago, I started dating a very successful, attractive, and intelligent girl who revealed very early on in our relationship that she was the victim of sexual abuse. Although she didn't provide details and I didn't pressure her, I had no idea the impact this could have on someone. For example, the better I got to know her, the further apart we got emotionally. This really confused and upset me because I was in love with her and I really wanted to be close to her. The more she distanced herself, the more I pushed her to be closer to me emotionally. Within a few weeks, she broke up with me; I think now it's because of the pressure I put on her, among many other factors that only now make so much sense. We remain, however, today as friends.

After we broke up, I came across *Invisible Girls* and read it cover to cover twice. As I did, so many things that happened in our relationship, and some of my friend's characteristics, became so understandable.

I wish I had read this book as soon as she told me her story. I could have been so much more understanding and supportive. I realize from reading your book that such people don't really want to push people away, it's just what they have done for years to protect themselves and shouldn't be taken personally.

This is a great book, and I highly recommend it for anyone who wants to understand the effects that sexual abuse has on people, and to hear what steps individuals can take to recover, overcome, and move forward confidently in their lives. It has given me the perspective and understanding to be unconditionally supportive, kind, loving, gentle, and understanding toward my friend, which is the very least that my awesome friend should expect from anyone in her life.

Gracias,
Manuel

I have a very specific philosophy about mothers and incest. I strongly believe that incest rarely takes place in a home with a strong, healthy, aware mother. In the vast majority of cases, the mothers in homes where abuse takes place were themselves survivors of abuse. These mothers never processed their own abuse and were blind to their daughter's abuse. In my own clinical experience and research, and in the studies of experts like Dr. Judith Herman, we have found that when a woman has been abused—sexually, emotionally, or both—she may go into denial and keep herself unaware that her daughter is being abused (as we heard in Maria's e-mail). I'm not suggesting that she is necessarily a bad mother—sometimes she is a deeply loving mother—only that she is damaged herself and cannot see her daughter's pain.

I have also never met a girl who has told her mother the truth about her abuse if she thought her mother would reject her. Girls hold their secrets so deeply inside because they are terrified of their mother blaming them or not protecting them. Over the years I have gotten a few e-mails from mothers who were horrified to discover that their daughter had been sexually abused by an uncle, a coach, or a stepfather and were concerned and confused about why their daughter hadn't told them. But after a closer look it usually turns out that, even in a loving family, at the time of the abuse there was some sort of upheaval going on at home, for example, a divorce, a parent losing a job, the death of a grandparent—some sort of chaos leaving the girl feeling that she couldn't have her mother's undivided attention and focus. This is all the more reason that during family crises mothers need to really stay connected with their daughters, especially high-functioning, "perfect" girls who seem to need so little that they easily slip through the cracks.

This mother was totally loving and committed to her daughter and admitted that early in her marriage she was not strong and she was not able to see what was going on. You'll remember my client who actually went to shoot her ex-husband when she found out about the incest (see Chapter 14). There are always exceptions, as the mothers of these next letters want you to know, but girls are always very wise and intuitive and will know they are able to go to their mothers, because their mothers will protect them.

When She Was Seven Years Old

Dear Dr. Patti,

I am a mother of a beautiful fifteen-year-old daughter who just dropped a bomb on me... telling me that about seven years ago an old boyfriend of mine sexually molested her.

First of all, I am thankful for the close relationship that she and I have had all these years (I have been a single mother for the past eleven years) and that she was brave enough to finally share this information with me.

To say the least, it has devastated me! But, beginning this week, she is now in counseling. It was recommended, for homework, that she find a book to read on the subject of sexual abuse, and this evening I ran to Barnes & Noble and found your *Invisible Girls*. I have read nearly half of the book (my daughter is with her father this evening) and have only put it down so that I could drop you a note and thank you for this wonderful piece of material!!!! I am sure that it will be a great tool for her in understanding and dealing with her feelings. It also has helped me in trying to forgive myself. You are right...young girls are very resilient, and parents have a difficult time in dealing with this situation.... I mean, HOW could I not have protected her from THIS!!!??? My heart hurts so much. But I wanted her to talk this out now and work it out in her head so that it doesn't affect her relationships in the future (she has not yet started dating).

Well, back to the book. I am sure that I will be up to the wee hours finishing it—so that I can give it to her tomorrow. I now know we will get through this.

Thank you, again!
Daphney

While I Was Sleeping

Dear Dr. Patti,
I read your book and I want you to know that a loving, caring, strong mom can't always know about incest unless her daughter decides to tell. Since the moment my daughter told me what my husband did to her, I have completely supported her and have been trying to help her (including encouraging counseling and buying her your book), but I never knew what was happening. Some offenders are extremely good at hiding it.

I never even dreamed that incest was a possibility in our house. My husband was a loving father, involved with his kids, and nothing about his behavior gave me any idea of the horror that was occurring. I don't understand why my daughter didn't come to me right away—I think she wanted to protect me. To make matters even more difficult, when she did tell someone at school, they reported to the police, who went to arrest my husband, and he killed himself before they could take him into custody.

I love my children more than anything in this world, and I would have killed him myself if I knew what he was doing, but I didn't. Even in hindsight, it is hard to find clues that could/would have alerted me to what was going on.

We are still working on healing—I'm sure it will take years. Our trust was completely violated, and no one more so than my amazing daughter. I am angry at myself for not seeing it and for not protecting her. Dr. Patti, mothers can be victims, too. I can't speak for all moms, but I know I was trying to be the best mom I could be, and yet I still failed to see it and help her. But once she did tell me I was completely there for her. If you ever write another book about this, please consider adding a mother's perspective.

I struggled with so many issues, especially trying to grieve (how could I grieve the horrible monster who did this to my daughter, yet how could I not grieve my husband of twenty-three years who I thought was the love of my life). I went to counseling and did a ton of journaling, worked on learning as much as I could about abuse and abusers (that's where your book came in) and then the messy work of rebuilding our lives.

My daughter never has opted for formal counseling. She tried but it just wasn't a good fit. I think she may still choose to and need to at some point, but that will be when she is ready. I have learned to let her steer her own course in that area. She did find a special mentor to talk with, and she and I did a lot of growing together. She also had amazing support from church.

My younger daughter Eden, who was not a victim of abuse but who was no less a victim of this tragedy, is in counseling. She really struggled, almost more than Tate and I did in some ways. She lost a father, whom she adored, and found out that he hurt her sister, whom she idolized. She was afraid to openly grieve the loss of her dad for fear of seeming disloyal to her sister, and she was concerned it might upset me. It was a mess. She actually started self-harming as a way to cope, but luckily we got help for her and she is doing much better now.

We all used music as a healing tool; we used humor—lots of it, especially gallows humor—and we clung to each other to ride through the stormy seas that we faced. There were plenty of angry fights, but we knew that we could fight with each other because we were safe with each other, and we unconditionally loved each other. The healing is a lot like peeling an onion; there are so many layers—the abuse, the guilt, the suicide, the loss, the shame. It is pretty overwhelming.

My husband's suicide really complicated things, and I felt like it kept me angry for a long time. I am finally letting much of that anger go. My daughter still hasn't dealt with many of her old demons; for example, when she visits me she doesn't stay in her old room, but she is doing amazingly well in college and she is trying to move on with her life. I guess I can say it is so hard, but there is hope.

I hope my story will help someone. I know when I found out, and then my husband committed suicide (all within a period of six hours), I started desperately seeking information and looking to see if anyone else knew what I was feeling. If my story can help even one person or one family, it would be wonderful.

Thanks for listening,
Susanna

My description of incest families is blunt, and Coral's story is blunt. We need to tell the full truth so that, when another girl reads our book, she relates, she feels less isolated. Countless girls write to me thanking me for the chapter on troubled families. They tell me that reading about how dysfunctional families hurt their daughters has been lifesaving. It has given some girls the courage to walk away from families that continue to hurt them. In some cases, therapists make the survivor feel guilty for her feelings. And sometimes our book will get a girl to leave an unhelpful therapist and get on the right path with her therapy and her healing. She begins to know what she deserves.

Her Story Is My Story

Dear Dr. Patti,

I have never believed in things like signs and fate, but I'm starting to think that there must be some truth in them, because your book found me today.

I was at the Union Square Barnes & Noble, enjoying the free air conditioning, when my mother called me to lecture me about a book I needed to look for—something about spirituality and dieting that she heard about on Oprah. Honestly, there is nothing I want to read less than a diet book, but my mother wouldn't let me off the phone, so I had to go up to the self-help section to look. She was yammering on about this book when another title caught my eye: *Invisible Girls*.

I found the diet book, too, and I got my mother to hang up by saying I would read it right then, but really I could barely hear what either of us was saying. I was just staring at your book, not really sure why I was finally ready to read about sexual abuse. I have been telling myself my whole life that what happened to me wasn't really abuse. In fact, I almost put your book back on the shelf. But I just couldn't make my hands cooperate with my doubt, so I went over to the café area, found a table (more proof of fate—finding a table on a summer afternoon at that Barnes & Noble is a miracle), and I read the entire book. Cover to cover. I couldn't feel my toes when I was done, after hours of sitting in the freezing AC, but that might have been shock.

I had never read stories that were so much like mine. I had never heard anyone stand up for me the way you defend and advocate for the women in your book. I didn't think I could ever be anything besides ashamed, that I would ever be able to stop trying to hide this horrible secret. It seemed like every few pages I was struck by something that felt like it had been written just for me, but when I read the beginning of the chapter "The Deepest Wound," where you described Coral's experience of being raped, then going around the corner to sit down to family dinner with her abuser right there at the table, it was like I was looking into my own memories. That had been my life for . . . basically my whole life. I wanted to swoop into Coral's house, kick over that dining room table, and pull her away to safety. But I realized that I had never thought of protecting myself that way, or of doing anything but pretending everything was normal and that the horrible incest hadn't happened (even when it had just happened moments before), and I was finally finding out that other people knew what that was like.

I can't thank you enough for this book. I have been seeing a therapist for about a year, but she is not well versed in sexual abuse, and I often leave our sessions feeling guilty and confused and anxious. Reading *Invisible Girls*, I see that I deserve better help and care, and that there are people and resources out there. This book is more than a collection of powerful stories or a self-help guide or a priceless bundle of knowledge. It's a beacon of hope, and it is exactly what I needed.

With Love and Thanks,
Apatha

Updating this book for a revised edition has been my honor. It is such an honor to know all the girls and women who have survived sexual abuse and then have gone on to thrive and love and have beautiful lives. These are lives with pathways and journeys filled with light. I can't say it enough—invisible girls speaking the truth about sexual abuse saves girls over and over and over again.

AFTERWORD: LETTER FROM AN INCEST SURVIVOR

How I Found Love

When I have the opportunity to see the work of *Invisible Girls* and my nonprofit Girlthrive reach a girl so deeply, I get to experience the full circle of deep-rooted healing. And now I want you to experience that full circle too.

Summer is someone I have known for the past ten years. I met her when she was nineteen years old and had just disclosed her abuse and found our book. She has been through hell. Much like Coral, she found herself in a new country without any support when at sixteen years old she moved into a home with a father she met for the first time and his second wife. A few days after the move, her father came into her bedroom and began sexually abusing her. What Summer wants to share with you is how deeply she loves now, how deeply she feels the beauty and hope all around her. What Summer wants to share with you is how an incest survivor gets past her abuse and embraces life, beauty, and love to its fullest.

HOW I FOUND LOVE

Where exactly do I begin? Let's start with a story; it's not all fun. But I assure you it gets better. When I was younger I'd always hear adults say, "What a pretty little black girl!" (I'm a fantastic shade of brown chocolate.) My sister would get "What a pretty little redskin girl." Even as children we both had enough intelligence to realize that the specification of our colors were on the outside, not what was inside of us. Yes, growing up on the island of Jamaica had its quirks, but I knew I was full of life and love.

Skip forward to puberty. My breasts grew before my hips, and I was an insecure fourteen-year-old. The bright, dark beauty of a little girl became self-conscious.

My mother was not the kind of mom who was ever really there—she was working two jobs, she had three kids with different fathers, not really a relationship role model. She sent me to a school that scared the shit out of me with a pedagogy so strict that corporal punishment was acceptable. And, one dark night when I called my granddad crying, he came and got me. He took me in and took care of me. My first experience of unconditional love.

Skip to sixteen years old.

My mother put me on a plane to the U.S.A. to come and live in New York City with the biological father whom I never met. My mother felt I could get a better education in America. Three nights after my arrival, down the hall from his three sons and his second wife, he came into my bedroom.

I woke up with my father's fingers inside me. He moved the fingering to rapes and continued to rape me for the next three years. Sometimes he was angry and violent with me when I tried to stop him. After, his apologies included something about me being beautiful and understanding him. His narcissistic abuser manipulation rhetoric included brushing my hair at times and telling me I was beautiful. Here began my obsession with makeup. Makeup was my attempt at changing how I looked—maybe if I looked different, he'd leave me alone. Maybe if I kept my room messy, kept my books on my bed. Maybe if I wore multiple layers of clothes, I'd not look so pretty. Maybe if I slept with multiple layers, he wouldn't rape me. That changed nothing, the abuse continued, and I attempted suicide. I woke up from the overdose of sleeping pills, I started covering mirrors, I could not look at myself. In spite of it all, I graduated vice president of the National Honor Society, member of the academic decathlon. I mean, come on, beauty and brains, what can I say? (This is my healed self having a proud moment, stick with me. It took me years to heal so as I write this I'm giving my eighteen-year-old self a round of applause for being so strong.)

Sounds like a horror story, but I promise you it gets better. I started at a local college, and I began to crave freedom more. I got out of my father's house, I moved to the dorms. I finally snapped and told my stepmother about the abuse. I went to the police, but they talked and talked and talked until I signed a paper saying I wouldn't press charges, and then I received a ten-year order of protection. I found the book *Invisible Girls* and Dr. Patti, and six months later a boyfriend.

Here began the purging of my wounds. I was inwardly emotionally detached, depressed, insecure, and outwardly I was driven, humble, confident! Yes, I was outwardly surviving, but inside I was slowly wishing to just die. My boyfriend would sit with me in the corner when I had a panic attack, hug me when I woke from nightmares screaming, then he'd openly flirt with other women and ask me, "You think you're talking to your father?" Yup, classic toxic relationship, but all the while I had therapy twice a week for two-hour sessions! Seriously! She helped me put in work! Thank you, Dr. Patti. I became the face of Girlthrive and I grew stronger! So I decided to reclaim myself. My second experience of unconditional love, Dr. Patti and Girlthrive.

Here begins the part where I reclaim my sexuality and my body and mind! Here is where I truly begin! I sought ways of overcoming fears. I lit candles in the bathroom and soaked in the tub, I shaved my head as a sign that I control every part of me! I changed my name! My name precedes me, and only I will decide what name I am known by. That sperm donor does not get an opportunity for me to carry his name. I choose the name they will use when they record my history. I hung mirrors in my home! I threw away my makeup! I upgraded my wardrobe! I spoke out loud and proud! I practiced walking with my head held high! I grew closer to my siblings! I slowly let people into my life! I got a tattoo! The boyfriend dumped me, I refused to take him back! I graduated college! I got my nursing license! I worked way too much! I fell in love! I traveled! I had my heart broken. I cried myself to sleep. I spent a birthday crying on my bed with four of my closest girlfriends huddled around me. I inspired countless women to live their truth! I ate, I gained weight! The extra bra size wasn't what I thought it would be, so I lost weight! I healed and I fell in love with ME.

So what is beauty to me? Beauty is my life. I've loved and I've lost. I've been used and abused, but now I love. I get excited when my partner holds my hands. Beauty is my ability to push past my fears and live in the moment. Beauty to me is the delight in children's eyes when they see their parent witness them getting it right after ten tries. Beauty is my best friend gathering the courage to propose to his boyfriend. Beauty is watching my friend have her heart broken as we are going on vacation but she pushes through to come out victorious on the other end. Beauty is my sister losing her fiancé mid-pregnancy but finding inner strength to wake up daily and raise her little girl. Beauty is my mother admitting she was a bad parent and not knowing how to comfort me, so she cooks and cleans and sits in silence by my bed. Beauty is my brother going to college and doing poetry slams, trying new things and falling in love with himself as well.

Beauty is the way my grandfather loves me unconditionally. The way he worried more about me than himself when he was diagnosed with cancer. His love for me outweighed the threat of possible death. Beauty is the way he forgets his birthday but remembers mine; it's the same day, but he'd rather celebrate me instead. Beauty is the sound of the birds when I wake, it's the soft snore by my side. The twinkle in my nieces' eyes. The glee in my siblings' voices. Beauty is the sunset on the beach, with family by your side, a fall day when the leaves are changing, hot cocoa, your lover, and a long drive. Beauty is me when I walk by a mirror at 3 A.M., no makeup, messy hair, raw vulnerability, fear of heartbreak, faith in love, faith in God, trust in me.

Ultimately that's it! Beauty is my ability to trust that, no matter what I look like, where I go, who I am with, where I came from, I can always count on me. Beauty is sitting in an empty room, nothing but a chair, the wind, me, my inner strength, and a great awareness of divine peace. Beauty is the thing within me that anchors me in the midst of all my storms. Beauty is my refusal to live between my hat and my heels. Beauty is the way I turn my famine into fortune. Beauty is when that little chocolate-skinned girl gets herself back, hugs herself, hugs the sixteen-year-old who was abused and feels the self-love.

Love is having this opportunity to share my journey with you all. *Invisible Girls* started my healing, because other girls told their stories. And I know that when you read *Invisible Girls*, there is someone whom you will tell your story to. You too can find the beauty in your lives and fall in love with yourselves. I love you all already!

Love,
Summer

Thank you so much for taking this journey with us. I told you sexually abused girls are the most eloquent and resilient girls I know. You are all precious and beautiful flowers ready to blossom!

With love and admiration,
Dr. Patti

RESOURCE CENTER

There are a lot of organizations that help teens and their families. In this Resource Center I give you my vetted resources, starting with hotlines in case you ever feel you need help right away, followed with a mix of novels, films, websites, blogs, and podcasts for you to explore. The books, blogs, podcasts, and websites are feminist leaning. Feminists continue to lead the way in making the voices of girls and women heard in all areas of life. Although some of these books are written quite a while ago, they are the classics and I believe the best. I want you to reach out and get the help you need. Often girls are ready to take serious steps to change after reading our book. Invisible girls are becoming visible every day!

Hotlines and Websites

If you feel you need to talk with someone right away, here are some hotline listings that are available 24/7. These organizations can give you guidance and advice, direct you to counseling and resources in your area, and in many cases provide you with concrete services.

National Hopeline Network
(800) SUICIDE (800-784-2433)
www.hopeline.com

National Office of Victim Assistance
(800) TRY-NOVA (800-879-6682)
www.trynova.org

National Runaway Switchboard
(800) 621-4000
www.1800runaway.org

National STD/HIV Hotline
hab.hrsa.gov/get-care/state-hivaids-hotlines

National Sexual Assault Hotline
(800) 656-4673

Rape, Abuse, and Incest National Network (RAINN)
(800) 656-HOPE (800-656-4673)
www.rainn.org

Professional Advocacy Organizations

End the Backlog
www.endthebacklog.org
An organization dedicated to ending the backlog of processing rape kits.

Generation Five
www.generationfive.org
A nonprofit organization that brings together diverse community leaders working to end child sexual abuse within five generations.

ECPAT USA

www.ecpatusa.org

ECPAT USA is an organization driven to end sexual violence against children and women. It is the leading anti-trafficking policy organization in the United States.

Legal Support

You may be ready to take legal action against your abuser. These listings are run by feminists.

Jane Doe Advocacy

janedoeadvocacy.wordpress.com

Wonderful young feminist lawyers founded this nonprofit legal service located in St. Louis, Missouri, to help girls and women who are survivors of sexual abuse.

Legal Momentum

www.legalmomentum.org

Legal Momentum advocates legally for girls and women, and it has a clearing house of resources.

Ultraviolet

www.weareultraviolet.org

An organization fighting against violence against women—they can help you to find legal representation.

Finding a Therapist

Healthgrades

www.healthgrades.com

Healthgrades is a nationwide clearinghouse of therapists. Therapists do not pay to be listed; thus, it is not advertising but patient reviews.

Women's Health

Planned Parenthood

www.plannedparenthood.org

Planned Parenthood is the largest single provider of reproductive and health services. There are approximately 650 Planned Parenthood clinics in the United States. Teen girls and young women are provided with reproductive health services across the board.

Websites and Magazines

Girlthrive

www.invisiblegirlsthrive.com

This is the website I designed as a companion to *Invisible Girls,* for teen girls and young women. It includes the sex-abuse experiences of more than fifty girls, my responses, basic information, and excerpts from the book. I respond to girls through the website. Girlthrive is also the name of my nonprofit providing "thriverships" for female incest survivors.

Advocates for Youth

www.advocatesforyouth.org

Partners with organizations that serve youth with online resources for teens, parents, and professionals on adolescent sexual and reproductive health

Scarleteen

www.scarleteen.com

A comprehensive sex-education site for teens covering everything from STDs to sexual abuse. Scarleteen is owned by Scarlet Letters, an adult women's sexuality journal, and is a companion to the book *S.E.X.* authored by Heather Corinna.

Sex, Etc.
www.sexetc.org
Launched in 1994, and still going strong with the help of two health educators and a professional journalist, Sex, Etc. is a sexuality and health newsletter written by teens for teens, covering issues from dating to STDs.

Bitch
www.bitchmedia.org
A feminist response to pop culture, *Bitch* is a print magazine and website that critiques TV, movies, magazines, and ads from a feminist perspective.

Teen Voices
www.womensenews.org/teen-voices
The only online magazine written by teen girls and young women focusing on all areas of being female, going strong for more than twenty years.

Bust
www.bust.com
A website and print magazine, *Bust* offers an "uncensored view on the female experience." Links to the girl wide web, shopping, discussions, chats, and more.

Feminist.com

www.feminist.com

Feminism 101, with loads of resources for girls, including sections on activism and anti-violence resources. This website covers the world.

Feminist Majority Foundation

www.feminist.org

This website gives information on feminist news and events, opportunities for activism, a feminist career center, and great links and products.

Hardy Girls Healthy Women

www.hardygirlshealthywomen.org

Started by Lyn Mikel Brown and her partners to help young girls begin to find positive ways to grow and learn in "hardiness zones" located in Maine.

Ms.

www.msmagazine.com

Ms. magazine was "the first national magazine to make feminist voices audible, feminist journalism tenable, and a feminist worldview available to the public." Visit the website for a wealth of resources, stories, and links.

National Organization for Women (NOW)

www.now.org

NOW is the largest organization of feminist activists in the United States.

For Teens
https://www.plannedparenthood.org/learn/teens
An award-winning website sponsored by Planned Parenthood, providing information on sexual health, self-esteem, body image, drugs and alcohol, communication, and relationship advice. Also available in Spanish through the en Español section of the site.

Youth Connections/Youth Communication
youthcomm.org
YCteen, formerly *New Youth Connections* (or *NYC*), is a general-interest teen magazine written by and for New York City youth, covering topics from sex abuse and rape to adoption and family issues.

Rookie
www.rookiemag.com
A fun online magazine for teen girls created by fashion blogger Tavi Geyinson when she was a teen. There are stories and art about every topic in pop culture.

Clover
www.cloverletter.com
This is another fun teen girl website with stories about many topics, such as growing up gay, going on your first date, and how to say no.

Books
Strong Books on Teen Girl Image
Here are a few books on girls' health and sexuality as well as teen girls talking about a variety of issues.

Our Bodies, Ourselves, new edition, by the Boston Women's Health Book Collective. New York: Simon & Schuster, 2005. Probably the most complete book on teen sexuality. The teen version of the revolutionary feminist classic, including invaluable information on bodies and sexuality with plenty of diagrams.

Body Outlaws: Rewriting the Rules of Beauty and Body Image, edited by Ophira Edut. Emeryville, CA: Seal Press, 2003. Vignettes from young women writing about body image, some from a feminist perspective. This book gives girls an alternative to the standard measurements of beauty.

The Girl's Guide to Taking Over the World: Writings from the Girl Zine Revolution, edited by Karen Green and Tristan Taormino. New York: St. Martin's Griffin, 1997. This collection, like the zines themselves, gives voice to real opinions from young women.

Ophelia Speaks: Adolescent Girls Write About Their Search for Self, edited by Sara Shandler. New York: HarperPerennial, 1999. Sara Shandler edited this when she was eighteen years old. It includes short vignettes written by teen girls on topics like sexuality, eating disorders, depression, and sexual abuse.

Books on Teen Dating Violence

Here are some books that I encourage parents to read along with their daughters.

Dating Violence: Young Women in Danger, by Barrie Levy. Seattle: Seal Press, 1991. Features twenty brief but powerful first-person accounts from abused teens and their mothers.

In Love and Danger: A Teen's Guide to Breaking Free of Abusive Relationships, by Barrie Levy. Seattle: Seal Press, 1997. This book, directed to teenagers, includes teens' stories and advice from Levy. Helpful topics include sexual abuse and relationship abuse.

Saving Beauty from the Beast: How to Protect Your Daughter from an Unhealthy Relationship, by Vicki Crompton and Ellen Zelda Kessner. Boston: Little, Brown, 2003. This is aimed at parents of teenage daughters.

A Girl's Life Online, by Katherine Tarbox. New York: Plume, 2004. Terrifying true story of a girl assaulted by a man she met in an Internet chat room. A warning for girls and parents.

Novels and Memoirs of Survivors

There are many novels and memoirs that can help to heal. Here are a few to consider reading. Although these authors are adult women, they are writing in the voice of a teen girl who has survived sex abuse.

Bastard Out of Carolina, by Dorothy Allison. New York: Plume, 1993. Beautifully told story of Bone, a young girl growing up in the rural South amid violence and sexual abuse with a heartbreaking mother-daughter relationship.

Fifth Born, by Zelda Lockhart. New York: Atria Books, 2003. Novel about a young African American girl dealing with family violence and abuse in 1970s Missouri and Mississippi.

I Know Why the Caged Bird Sings, by Maya Angelou. New York: Random House, 2002. A classic. This is a beautiful novel about growing up, and part of its focus is on incest with the heroine's uncle.

Feminism

Against Our Will: Men, Women and Rape, by Susan Brownmiller. New York: Fawcett Columbian, 1993. This is one of the most important books on rape and injustice to women.

The Feminist Mystique, by Betty Friedan. New York: Norton, 1963. This is the groundbreaking book that awakened the world to feminism. Totally relevant today.

Breaking Down the Wall of Silence: The Liberating Experience of Facing Painful Truth, by Alice Miller. New York: Meridian, 1997. Alice Miller, a German psychoanalyst and child advocate, tries to bring out the truth about the abuse of and injustice to all children.

My Life on the Road, by Gloria Steinem. New York: Random House, 2015. Gloria Steinem's life, legacy, travels, philosophy, history of fighting for gender equality, and her glorious feminism.

Feminist Fight Club: A Survival Manual for the Sexist Workplace, by Jessica Bennett. New York: Harper Wave, 2017. Excellent book with strength and a sense of humor for young women entering the workplace.

Full Frontal Feminism: A Young Woman's Guide to Why Feminism Matters, by Jessica Valenti. Berkeley, CA: Seal Press, 2007. Brings back feminism as forward looking, young, and kick ass.

Many of these books also have websites.

Podcasts

Teen Life from a Real Teen Girl
Teens talk about real-life struggles and pressures.

Feminist Current
Canada's leading feminist podcast, run by Meghan Murphy, dealing with sexuality, violence against women, and current events.

Beyond Surviving with Rachel Grant
A young woman covers many topics, including conversations about trauma, healing, and reclaiming your voice. There are guests talking with Rachel about many topics.

The Rookie Podcast
This podcast is quite upbeat and covers a lot of pop culture when you want a break from the heavier stuff!

For Teen Boys and Men

Men Can Stop Rape, Inc. (MCSR)
www.mencanstoprape.org

Founded in 1997 and still the cutting-edge organization dedicated to ending men's violence against women with the goal to mobilize men through training programs to create cultures free of violence against girls and women.

Men Stopping Violence
www.menstoppingviolence.org
Men Stopping Violence works locally, nationally, and internationally to dismantle belief systems, social structures, and institutional practices that oppress women and children. They conduct training and social justice work in the areas of race, class, gender, age, and sexual orientation, because are all critical to ending violence against women.

White Ribbon
www.whiteribbon.ca
Founded in 1991, their motto is, "Our future has no violence against women and girls." White Ribbon reaches out internationally through media, education, and brands to stop violence against women and girls.

Films

There are few films that portray sexual abuse of teen girls in a clear way with a hopeful outcome. So many films portray pedophiles in a sympathetic way. You won't find those here! Here are a few films that deal with the subject in a respectful way. Some are classic oldies but goodies.

Bastard Out of Carolina (1996). Based on the autobiographical novel written by Dorothy Allison, this is a heart-wrenching film in which a mother rejects her daughter for her abusive husband. Directed by a woman.

Loyalties (1999). A Canadian film made by a woman film-maker. Very supportive to women, with extraordinary scenes of a mother and her fifteen-year-old daughter. Directed by a woman.

Monsoon Wedding (2001). An all-around beautiful film that includes one of the most wonderful examples of family support around incest. Directed by a woman.

Nuts (1987). Barbra Streisand stars in this amazing film about incest. Although the story is told from the point of view of an adult, it is about her girlhood and contains insights into the incest mother and father.

Hard Candy (2005). A very powerful revenge film against pedophiles. A driven teenage girl exposes a man she suspects is a pedophile.

All About Nina (2018). A powerful depiction of an incest survivor who becomes a brash stand-up comic—a great portrait of a thirty-year-old woman who did not disclose her abuse and her struggles as a result (explicit language and sex, not recommended for under 18).

ENDNOTES

Chapter 7: The Deepest Wound: Father-Daughter Incest

1. From a January 2000 interview with Kay Jackson, a psychologist who specializes in treating pedophiles.

Chapter 11: Rape Always Hurts: Stranger Rape/Date Rape/Gang Rape

1. According to the Bureau of Justice Statistics, National Criminal Victimization Survey, 2016.
2. Allen J. Ottens and Kathy Hotelling, *Sexual Violence on Campus: Policies, Programs, and Perspectives,* Springer Series on Family Violence (New York: Springer, 2001); Our Bodies Ourselves, www.ourbodiesourselves.org, "Preventing Sexual Assault on Campus," 2018.
3. S. Humphrey and A. Kahn, "Fraternities, Athletic Teams and Rape: Importance of Identification with a Risky Group," *Journal of Interpersonal Violence* (2000), as cited in Rana Simpson, *Acquaintance Rape of College Students,* Problem-Oriented Guides for Police, Problem-Specific Guides Series no. 17 (US Department of Justice Office of Community-Oriented Policing Services, 2000) 2016.
4. Three percent as cited by the Justice Department's National Institute of Justice and Bureau of Justice Statistics, *Report on the Sexual Victimization of College Women* (2001); 25 percent as reported by B. Fisher and J. Sloan III, *Campus Crime: Legal, Social and Policy Perspectives* (Springfield, IL:

Charles C. Thomas, 1995). According to National Sexual Violence Resource Center (NSVRC), www.nsvrc.org, 2018.

5. According to *Ms.* magazine online, Summer 2004: "India, Malaysia, Tonga, Ethiopia, Lebanon, Guatemala, and Uruguay exempt men from penalty for rape—if they subsequently marry their victims." Once they are married, there is, from a legal standpoint, no such thing as rape.

6. According to Robin Warshaw, *I Never Called It Rape* (New York: Harper Perennial, 1994), 75 percent of the men, and 55 percent of the women involved in date rape had been drinking or taking drugs before the attack occurred.

7. According to Fisher and Sloan, *Campus Crime,* fewer than 5 percent of college women who are victims of rape or attempted rape report it to police. According to the Bureau of Justice Statistics, National Crime Victimization Survey, only 39 percent of rapes and sexual assaults are reported to law-enforcement officials—about one in every three. This strikes me as a very high estimate. According to RAINN Rape and Incest National Network, Criminal Justice System: Statistics, out of 1,000 rapes 994 perpetrators walk free (2018).

8. According to the National Center for Policy Analysis, probability statistics compiled from US Department of Justice Statistics suggest that only one out of sixteen rapists will ever spend a day in jail.

9. From http://www.nd.edu/~ucc/ucc_sexualvictimhospital .html.

10. Equality Now, Sex Trafficking Fact Sheet, https://www .equalitynow.org/sex-trafficking-fact-sheet.

11. Melissa Farley, *Prostitution, Trafficking, and Traumatic Stress* (New York: Haworth Maltreatment and Trauma Press, 2003).

ACKNOWLEDGMENTS

Of course, the first ones to thank are my beautiful clients, the hundreds of teen girls and young women whom I continue to be blessed to work with. I never stop being inspired by them. I also thank the girls and young women I have met at my workshops. Special thanks to all the survivors that have added their voices to *Invisible Girls*.

Then I need to thank Caroline Pincus, a wonderful collaborator for being the extraordinary midwife for our first and second editions. She helped to bring my words to life. I thank her family, Esther and Ruby, for their support in giving up precious time with Caroline! I thank my agents, Loretta Barrett and Nick Mullendore, who has taken the helm for Loretta, for his handholding. Thanks to them both for their unwavering support and faith. I thank my circle of women friends for their deep sisterhood and for always being there: Candy Talbert, Mary Krause, Connie Grappo, Mary Walker, Susie Stevens, Pam Wheaton, Diana Stevens, Tracy Gilman, Selima Salun, Eva Vives, Bridget Malloy, Elizabeth Hasse, Leigh Kamioner, Serena Schrier, and Jeri Cohen.

Thanks to Lyn Mikel Brown for her openness and early read and great collegial networking on our first edition. Also thanks to Kay Jackson for deep insights, her early read of the first edition, and her steady support. A special thanks to all the

women of Seal Press who supported this project with understanding and excitement: first, Laura Mazer, executive editor
for her encouragement, patience, time, energy and personal
editing to help bring our third edition to life; second, the Seal
team, including Kerry Rubenstein, designer for a cover that I
love, and Sharon Kunz, publicist for her social media savvy. I
thank my kick-ass copyeditor, Carrie Watterson, as well as my
senior project editor, Amber Morris, for her patience and encouragement. All the designers, formatters, and editors on the
Seal team were wonderful.

I thank Krista Lyons for extraordinary sensitivity and understanding for the first and second editions. Also a special
thanks to Brooke Warner, who envisioned this third edition
even before I did and helped me to articulate my vision. I
thank all the wonderful students and staff at Edward R. Mur-
row High School for their participation in this project. A special acknowledgment to Ms. Sandy Pindar, Abdul-Wali, for
being so open to the thoughts and feelings of teenagers and
sexual abuse. Special thanks to GEMS for opening their doors
to me.

Heart-filled thanks and gratitude to Ludwig Shepherd,
Ms. Doris Rowley, Ms. Lindsay Shea, Olivia Shea, Julia Shea,
Bobye List, Louisa Farr, and B. J. and Bob Adler for their generous and unwavering support of Girlthrive, Inc. I thank all
the donors who have kept Girlthrive alive and thriving.

Special thanks to Nicky, Raven, Victoria, Priscilla, Erika
and all "my girls" for being such righteous girls who have made
those fields of daises for themselves.

I thank my little doggie, Posey, for sitting with me constantly during the writing of this edition. I thank my husband,

Mark, for being who he is, so solid, focused, strong, and loving, and the best man I know. I thank my daughter, Aviva, for finding the perfect cover photo and for being such an amazing daughter who is a deep source of love and pride. Being a mom to Aviva is my most precious honor.

INDEX

ABOUT THE AUTHOR

Patti Feuereisen, PhD, a feminist psychologist in private practice in Brooklyn, New York, is a pioneer in the treatment of sexual abuse for adolescent girls and young women. She has worked for three decades helping girls find their voices and their healing. She continues to develop training programs for staffs, run workshops, and speak widely on this topic. "Dr. Patti" is the founder of Girlthrive, Inc. She holds a doctorate in psychology and lives in Brooklyn, New York, with her husband and her dog, Posey, and is the proud mother of a fabulous millennial daughter.

A portion of the proceeds from the sale of this book will benefit Girlthrive, Inc. (Girl Teens Healing Rape and Incest Victoriously Emerge), a 501(c)3 nonprofit charity established by Dr. Patti in 2004. Girlthrive, Inc., provides thriverships funding creative endeavors for incest survivors. Girlthrive also donates copies of *Invisible Girls* around the world to the girls who need it. At www.invisiblegirlsthrive.com you will find more stories, great links, a blog, and more support and resources as well as a link where you can write to Dr. Patti directly.